Experimental Americans

Experimental Americans

Celo and Utopian Community in the Twentieth Century

GEORGE L. HICKS

University of Illinois Press

URBANA AND CHICAGO

Library of Congress Cataloging-in-Publication Data
Hicks, George L.
Experimental Americans : Celo and Utopian community in the
twentieth century / George L. Hicks.
p.   cm.
Includes bibliographical references and index.
ISBN 0-252-02661-6 (cloth : alk. paper)
1. Celo Community—History. 2. Collective settlements—
North Carolina—History. 3. Utopias—United States—History—
20th century. I. Title.
HX656.C45H53   2001
335'.9756873—dc21   00-012454

To the memory of
Linné Hall Hicks
December 9, 1935–November 26, 2000
who in her small community of family and friends
kept harmony and autonomy in perfect balance

Contents

PART 4: VARIATIONS OF UTOPIAN AMERICA

Foreword

Experimental Americans originated in ethnographic and historical research conducted by George Hicks in Celo Community during 1966–68, research first presented in his 1969 dissertation "Ideology and Change in an American Utopian Community." Over the following thirty years, George remained engaged with the issues—local and ethnographic, national and cultural, and methodological and theoretical—raised by his encounter with utopia. He carried out fieldwork with and wrote about Appalachians and Azoreans but never put aside his study of utopia. In his teaching, in dialogue with colleagues, and in papers and published articles he worked and reworked his understandings of Celo and other intentional communities.

A first draft of the present work was completed in November 1996 and accepted, pending revisions, by the University of Illinois Press. In December 1997, while completing those revisions, George was hospitalized with the heart disease to which he would succumb the following May. During those months of severe illness he continued to edit the text and completed the rewriting of all chapters, save "three paragraphs" he intended for the conclusion.

As a participant in that thirty-year dialogue on the making of community and a reader of drafts of *Experimental Americans,* I assumed the task of preparing the manuscript for publication. Much of this consisted of reconciling versions of the text—the floppy disk invites proliferation—and interpreting somewhat cryptic notes for changes.

The ideas, arguments, analysis, and expression are entirely George's. I made decisions regarding inclusion and ordering of material: removing unnecessary duplication and in some cases rearranging the presentation for clarity.

George did not write a note of acknowledgement for *Experimental Americans*. Here is what he said in 1969:

> Without the interest and cooperation of the residents and former members of Celo Community, my field research certainly would not have been nearly as pleasant and stimulating. I am especially grateful for their willingness first, to become subjects of my research and second, to give me complete access to their Community files.
>
> Wives and families are customarily left until last in acknowledgments, and I see no reason to violate this tradition. More than the usual patience and forbearance, however, my wife, Linné H. Hicks, and my daughter, Beth, displayed a keen interest in the research and were partners in what rapidly became a family enterprise.

For the present work, he would have acknowledged the undergraduate and graduate students and colleagues with whom he learned. Special mention would have been made of Norris Lang, whose sustaining friendship spanned the years from graduate school to George's final days, and his student Dan Odess, who brought such good humor to hospital rooms and practical assistance to George's efforts to complete this book. For thirty years the research remained a "family enterprise," and George's final word would have been for his son and daughter, Les and Beth, and his wife, Linné.

—Mark Handler

Acknowledgments

On May 5, 1998, George L. Hicks Jr. passed away. I have been honored by his wife, Linné Hall Hicks, who asked that I write a note of acknowledgment and gratitude. On behalf of my close friend George, I wish to express gratitude to two of his students from Brown University, Daniel Odess and Mark Handler, for the care they gave him during his final days. Dan assisted George in the revising and editing of this volume. I am deeply grateful. No words can adequately sum up Mark's contribution not only to bringing this manuscript to publication, but also to the close, spiritual relationship between teacher and student that lasted for three decades. Thanks also to the members of George's family, his students, his colleagues, and his many, many friends. And finally a note of appreciation to the friends and people in the two communities in North Carolina that he came to know, study, and respect.

—Norris Lang

Note on Sources and Style

Actual names are used for the founders of Celo Community, and geographical locations. Members of the community are referred to with pseudonyms. Although kinsmen of the founder, Arthur E. Morgan, are mentioned, they are identified only by their relationship to him, not by name. For the most part, this follows customary usage in ethnography. (For more detailed justification, see Hicks 1978.)

Participants usually referred to their project as "CCI" (Celo Community, Incorporated), particularly when they meant to indicate some aspect of its legal apparatus. Hence minutes of Community meetings are cited as CCI (abbreviated form of CCI Minutes), with dates. The functioning Community itself is spelled with a capital initial, to avoid confusion with the community of local people.

Sources for the information vary, and include manuscript documents from the Community's files, a manuscript history of the group written by the physician in 1957, a manuscript copy of recollections by the founder in 1957, letters between the two initial supporters, A. E. Morgan and W. H. Regnery, and between them and various Community members.

A primary source of data is records of my more than two years of fieldwork in the area, and an effort has been made to place that information more precisely with some indication of the year it occurred and/or was recorded.

Introduction: Utopian America

CLOSELY FOLLOWING President Nixon's threatened impeachment, his resignation, and the peaceful transfer of office in 1974, there arose from social commentators of all persuasions the surprised and gratified cry: "the system worked!" Only two years shy of its two hundredth birthday at the time, the American system had long ago anticipated and provided procedures for such an event. There were no grounds for doubt that the system would "work." In the circumstances, it seemed a strange reaction.

Strangeness evaporates, however, if we consider that behind the comment lurked an unspoken fear that the system might *not* have worked; that, two centuries after its formation, the American system is still experimental and tentative, still subject to crucial tests of its viability. Since the departure of President Nixon, the phrase has taken on life as a cliché: sure to be invoked upon the release of an innocent after years on death row, the successful pursuit and punishment of almost-forgotten political crimes, or the joyful presentation of medals or awards long overdue and won only by dogged persistence and effort.

The resilience of this sentiment of impermanence and seasonality reflects what always constituted much of the European fascination with America. It was a testing ground for new ideas, a haven for experiment, a place to pursue dreams not possible in a homeland of fixed social position, refractory traditions, and centralized religious institutions. Added to the idea of America as experimental terrain was the notion that once the experiment appeared successful, the dream close to fulfillment, news of it must spread and adoption elsewhere be advocated.

Long before the American Revolution, a variety of goals drew settlers to the new continent. Although the reason for settlement might often be cast in materialistic and individual terms, there has been a consistent theme in public declarations, presumably with some resonance among much of the population, of exceptionalism, of high moral purpose, of showing a benighted Europe how life might be lived on a higher plane. America, it has been declared in one form or another since the initial incursions to Jamestown, Plymouth, and Massachusetts Bay, had a mission. The settlers in New England, at least as reflected in statements by their literate leaders, came not for glory, nor gold, nor individual freedom, but to set a beacon for mankind, to build a "city on a hill" which would guide humanity to an earthly condition in tune with divine commandment.[1]

Even when the early cohesiveness of purpose, as viewed and enforced by religious leaders in New England's theocratic social order, fragmented in the late seventeenth century, the notion of a special and experimental mission persisted. Through the next hundred years, challenges to religious authority increased until, following the American Revolution, evangelical churches displaced older established Congregationalists, Anglicans, and Presbyterians. "Just as the people were taking over their governments, so, it was said, they should take over their churches. . . . The people were their own theologians and had no need to rely on others to tell them what to believe" (Wood 1992, 332).[2]

European-derived characteristics of colonial American social life—the unquestioned moral authority of church leaders, the sumptuary rules, the laws of primogeniture, but most significantly the sharp distinction of gentle folk and commoners—fell aside in the decades following the Revolution. The linked ideas of individualism and equality assumed prominence. Society was now conceived as an agglomeration of volunteers. "Patrons, dependencies, indeed government itself, no longer mattered in holding society together. All that was needed to tie people together was what was now called the 'voluntary principle'" (Wood 1992, 364). Societies, and all social groups except the family, were seen to rest on, and were made possible by, the propositions of individualism and equality. All members of social groups were equal, and each could belong or not, as he or she saw fit.

Society was seen as contingent, its formation and maintenance dependent upon the will of individual participants. From a national society with its encompassing political institutions to the smallest village of cooperating neighbors, social order must be constructed. And this construction could be established on new principles of association and could purpose new designs. Deliberate, self-conscious attempts to create new towns and settlements are abundant in the history of America and are particularly visible in accounts of the westward movement of the Euro-Americans.

But the sense of mission, a sense of vast opportunities in territorial settlement, has been extended to even greater possibilities in social arrangements within the continuous line of American utopian experimentation. From the onset of European migration, hundreds of utopian experimental communities have been founded in an unbroken historical stream that stretches from Plockhoy's communal Mennonite settlement of 1683 (Miller 1993) to the present, when communities are still being created.[3] One historian's survey found that "there was not a single decade in the history of the United States in which no new commune had been founded." Furthermore, "the extent and continuity of the communal phenomenon had no equal outside the United States" (Oved 1988, xiii).

Most attention has been given to the florescence of utopian community-building in the early nineteenth century, and widely known examples of these communities run from the religiously based Shakers and Oneida to the secular efforts of Robert Owen at New Harmony and the intellectuals gathered at Brook Farm and Fruitlands. Within the past several decades, however, more recent experiments in utopia have come under scholarly scrutiny by sociologists and anthropologists as well as in numerous works by historians. With this increased attention, analyses of utopian communities expanded to include consideration of the linkage of one community to another and to the historical ties of contemporary communities with those of earlier periods (e.g., Garrett 1987; Cooper 1987; Johnson and Wilentz 1994; Fogarty 1990). Still, what is often missing from these reports is an extended effort to provide the context, utopian and conventional, in which communities appear and within which they change.

Hewing rather closely to a line of ethnographic and local historical detail, I hope to provide a different perspective, if not new answers, for some persistent questions about utopian experimental communities in America. This effort includes a consideration of how communities are established, how conflict among members is controlled and decisions made, and the kinds of relationships maintained with groups and institutions outside their gates. The vehicle for this task is a detailed examination of a single American utopian experiment in the mountains of North Carolina, with briefer mention of other communities of the same era and with close attention to the community's relationships with outsiders. On one level, then, this is a historical report of an American utopian experiment, Celo Community Incorporated, a project previously known only in sketchy detail and mostly among those with special interests in American communal history. Although my account is based on extensive ethnographic fieldwork as well as documentary records, at this level, it essentially fills a gap in the historical record of these enterprises.

How can we explain the large number of utopian experiments, extending over the entire history of the United States? I argue that it is not only the availability of open land, or the lack of rigid social limitations, or the peculiarities of one or another historical era that need consideration. Certainly these are significant factors in any attempt to answer the question. More, however, seems to be involved in accounting for the substantial numbers of utopian experiments. While utopian communitarians might hope to secede from American society in varying degrees, and to institute new and improved cultural models, nonetheless they express in many ways the conjunction of three intertwined postulates of American culture: individualism, egalitarianism, and exceptionalism. The examination of American culture is critical in any attempt to account for the persistence of utopian community-building in America.

This is not a brief for American utopias as microcosms or small-scale replicas of the nation. The wide variation among these experiments is enough to forestall such an argument. It can be suggested, however, that one kind of sorting of utopian communities might set them along a range of greater or lesser emphasis on individualism and equality. In such a classification, the Society of Brothers, Stephen Gaskin's The Farm, and the Children of God, for example, could be seen as placing heavy stress upon the loss of individuality and the achievement of harmonious unity through egalitarianism. At the other end of the range, we might use Lou Gottlieb's Morning Star Ranch as a celebrated case of the do-your-own-thing philosophy of the 1960s and 1970s communal movement. At Morning Star, individualism rode very high in the saddle (Selth 1984).

Unlike Morning Star's radical individualism or the Society of Brothers' struggle to surrender individuality for group harmony, Celo Community tried to preserve both individualism and equality among its members. There has never been an ideological or religious test for membership in Celo (pronounced See-lo), and diversity among its residents has consistently been prized. While it offers us neither a microcosm of America nor a laboratory for the investigation of the application of extremes, Celo provides instead an apt setting for an inquiry into the attempt—characteristic of the nation itself—to balance the often contradictory demands of individualism and egalitarianism. Its lengthy duration, and the preservation of many of its historical documents, strengthens its usefulness for an investigation reaching beyond the immediate present. The Community began long before the eruption of communes in the 1960s and 1970s, as part of the relatively unnoticed wave of utopian community-building of the decades of the Great Depression and post–World War II and, in modified form, it still survives.

Method and Evidence

Most of the ethnographic information in this book comes from my fieldwork and documentary research in Celo Community. Started as an attempt to build an alternative way of life, to establish a more satisfying social and cultural milieu, Celo was one of a number of efforts to revitalize and reform America in the 1930s and 1940s.[4] An interpretation of the community must take into consideration this cultural and historical period. Thus, my account also draws on material about the subsistence homestead communities sponsored by the federal government in the 1930s and on a number of other contemporaneous utopian projects.

Although the Community still exists, this account stops at about 1980, when it became clear that Community members had redefined their project from utopian experiment to stewardship of their land holdings. The shift from utopia to land management involved significant change in the conception of Celo, by its members and by its allies outside. Redefining the Community required new visions of its history and its purpose; this change is thus an important part of this study

For the two years 1965–67 and for a period of ten weeks in 1979 (with briefer visits in the intervening years), I lived with my family in the western North Carolina valley where Celo is located, doing ethnographic fieldwork in the Community and among its local neighbors (see Hicks 1992). My intention to incorporate in my research the relations of Celo members with those immediately outside the Community demanded that ethnographic fieldwork be carried out simultaneously among people who at times harbored suspicion and antagonism toward each other. This, of course, called for patience (and frequent but muted exasperation) on my part, and for a good deal of forbearance by both local and utopian informants. From my point of view, the effort was well rewarded.[5]

Locating ex-members of Celo and interviewing them led me on long excursions from upstate New York to Florida: recollections of those formerly part of the Community added historical information that did not appear in Celo's uneven documentary record. Moreover, my discussions with former members provided different assessments of a number of controversies in the Community's past.

Celo Community was chosen as a research site for two main reasons: (1)

at the beginning of research, it had existed for over twenty-five years (1937–65) and therefore met the then customary measure of "successful"; and (2) it lacked any requirement for its membership to accept a single religious or ideological creed, hence its longevity seemed problematic.

Scholars in both the nineteenth and twentieth centuries have seen religious ideology as a binding force in utopian ventures. Oneida Community's founder, John Humphrey Noyes, for example, held in 1870 that "earnest men of one religious faith are more likely to be respectful to organized authority and to one another" than those of disparate beliefs (1961, 656). Charles Nordhoff, five years later, expanded this to include nonreligious ideology, provided that the belief was "so important as to take the place of a religion, if it is not essentially religious" (1961, 387). Similarly, Melford Spiro characterized the belief system of a Marxist kibbutz as secular in name only, since "in the absence of traditional religion, ideology becomes religion" (1963, 194). And Kanter's examination of what makes for success arrives, at least implicitly, at the same stress on religion: all those communities she lists as "successful" were sectarian (1968, 503n).[6]

Quite early in my field research, it became apparent that the members of Celo Community—and the ex-members I later visited throughout the eastern United States—not only did not share a single religious belief, they did not agree on a consistent set of ideological principles. To understand Celo's endurance for several decades, one had to consider the involvement of its membership with groups and persons outside Celo (Hicks 1971). In other words, analysis of this single community required some attention to its context, both historically, in an attempt to explain changes in the community, and spatially, to try to assess the significance of its relations with sympathetic allies and potential enemies.

Utopians and Cultists

Although I do not deal specifically with groups often labeled "cults," they are for the most part meant to be included in my broad use of the word "utopian." What distinction can be made between utopians and cultists hinges on the positive or negative perception of the observer. This became quite evident in many popular books of the 1960s, which, in an apparent effort to take advantage of the fearful curiosity aroused by a new wave of communes, offered an odd mixture of American utopians indiscriminately flung together with lurid description and trite phrases. So, for example, John Humphrey Noyes is designated a "Communist of Love" and Oneida reduced to a "love cult" (Orrmont 1961). Father Divine and his followers, the evangelist Aimee Semple McPherson, Mexican-American Penitentes of the Southwest, Jehovah's Witnesses—all are grist for the entrepreneurial millers of American cultism (Bach 1961; Beam 1964). Similar treatment can be found for the Shakers and the Mormons, and, in the recent past, the Jonestown colony with its mass suicide, and the Branch Davidians raided by federal officers in Waco, Texas. Yet all can be considered utopian groups and, in their mixture of tactic and purpose, demonstrate both the intensity and the variety of alternatives to American social life.[7]

Plan of the Work

In part 1, I discuss major postulates of American culture (chapter 1); I consider some problems involved in creating communities and in the scholarly attempts to account for them (chapter 2). Part 2 takes up the historical background of Celo's initial founding and settlement in the years of the Great Depression (chapter 3) and includes an extended description of its founder, Arthur E. Morgan, and his social and philosophical ideas (chapter 4). Chapters 5 and 6 sketch the history of Celo. In the third section of the book, I turn to the operation of the Community and give special emphasis to consensus as a method of reaching decisions (chapters 7 and 8). These two chapters, like subsequent ones, break the chronological pattern of Celo's history to allow for the inclusion of suitable instances of long-standing patterns of Community activity. Just as important to the Community's continuation and change were its relations with the world outside Celo, including both nonutopian neighbors and allies and sympathizers. These relations are examined in chapter 9.

Part 4 considers variations in the paths taken by utopian communities. To further highlight those aspects of Celo which figured powerfully in its historical journey, chapter 10 offers a comparative analysis of Celo and its close cousin in Appalachia, Macedonia Community. The comparison sets the stage for a consideration of the merits, and lapses, of the most recent campaign to revise the methods and objectives of research on utopian experiments, set forth by Donald Pitzer and his colleagues (1997c). The Conclusion is an extended commentary on utopian communities in general.

Notes

1. The purposive nature of their enterprise, as felicitously captured (in their own words) by the historian Perry Miller's title, *Errand into the Wilderness* (1956), was the conscious application of morality to social relations.

2. By the early nineteenth century, calls for the recognition of Christianity as the basis for social and moral order had paradoxically led to greater emphasis upon the individual as the ultimate arbiter of moral and religious truth.

3. A good argument can be made for the beginning of communal organization with the settlement of Jamestown, and certainly with the colony at Plymouth in its early years.

4. Miller (1992) provides bibliographic material for more than twenty communities founded in these two decades. As happened in the 1960s and 1970s, there were probably many communities which left no trace in the historical records.

5. An outstanding precedent for this demanding and potentially disastrous technique of doing fieldwork across an established and unambiguous boundary is reported in the classic monograph *Deep South,* by Allison Davis and Burleigh and Mary Gardner. Davis, an African-American sociologist, carried out research among African Americans in Old City and Old County (Mississippi), while his coauthors, the Gardners, worked among white residents. Their collaboration was kept secret from their informants, and meetings to discuss research plans and results took place at some distance from the research site (1965, orig. 1941).

6. Kanter does suggest that, although religion provides the most effective mechanism of solidarity, other kinds of "commitment mechanism" can ensure utopian success (1972, 136–37).

7. In a careful and serious study of Jonestown, David Chidester places the group firmly in the utopian tradition: "Jonestown was designed as a utopian heaven on earth, a socialist paradise in the jungle where racism, sexism, ageism, and classism would be eliminated, and people who had been deprived, discriminated against, and persecuted in America could live in peace and freedom" (1988, 10).

Though he objects to "accounts of utopian communities [that] suggest that extreme groups . . . are somehow 'typical,'" Robert Fogarty, a major historian of American communitarians, holds that "no single type of commune dominates or has prevailed in our history, because utopian communities, like our country, have been both varied and 'in process'" (1993a, 428; see also Fogarty 1993b).

PART 1

American Contexts,
Utopian Visions

1. Culture and Utopian Americans

In AMERICAN CULTURE, the symbols that express and reflect equality and individualism are fundamental and pervasive (Schneider 1976; Varenne 1986). These are matters of value and belief. But, more, they encompass propositions Americans see as self-evident truths. The idea that all human beings have rights deriving from their existence as individuals is part of a taken-for-granted reality that is not ordinarily subject to challenge.

Symbolic references to American individualism and equality can and do have multiple interpretations or meanings. In Anthony Cohen's useful formulation: "Culture requires us to think, gives us forms—metaphors, dogmas, names, 'facts'—to think with, but does not tell us *what* to think: that is the self's work" (1994, 154). From the perspective taken here, it is not necessary that all people called Americans agree on exactly what constitutes their taken-for-granted reality. Indeed what is undeniable truth for some is doubted by others.

For Varenne, "America" refers not to a particular people "in their psychological plurality. . . . It is not an object, nor is it a population" (1986a, 25). What is intended is, as he puts it, "the pattern in terms of which human beings must construct their lives when they interact in the United States. American culture is whatever one cannot escape in the United States" (1986c, 6).

Here I deal only with certain postulates that seem to be quite pervasive in that larger patterning. Whether or not agreement on the postulates is found among a large or small proportion of the population of the United States is not at issue. What is most important is that most of those residents—and Varenne suggests a far broader range that appears to include the entire world—must somehow deal with these American cultural terms.

Consistent with the position of public symbols/private meanings is Joseph Gusfield's suggestion that "American society" is constructed as a "public event," largely by "mass education and the mass media . . . , [which] develop and transmit a sense of what is public rather than private; what is typical, shared, and socially organized" (Gusfield 1979, 42). Any social order is supported by "the belief that it exists; that violations of legal, moral, or cognitive precepts will lead to sanctions. Whatever one's own doubts about the legitimacy of institutions and authorities, their continuance is enhanced when doubters see their own internal dissent as unique and unshared" (46). In societies as socially diverse as the United States, an additional and especially important factor is what Gusfield terms "pluralistic ignorance." He explains, "Each member of the group imputes to the others meanings and criteria that he himself does not share. Each, ignorant of the others, believes in a wider consensus than exists" (ibid.). What is crucial here is that there are some cultural postulates which can be labeled "American" (but which might also exist under other labels), and that they figure in the lives of utopian communitarians as they do in the lives of other Americans.

The Mission of America

The intention of making a better social order as a way of leading others to progress, even earthly perfection in some of its versions, is more than just a dream for utopian dissenters in America; it is part of the national history of the United States. As a self-conscious experiment, America was different, a new and extraordinary effort to improve the lot of all people. The moral tone of American relations with other countries, based on the idea that the United States has a special national mission, has been the subject of commentary from the early years of the Republic to the present. The notion of our "manifest destiny" to spread across the continent from ocean to ocean is well known from its repetitive declaration in our early history. Perhaps the most profound statements of the idea of America as a beacon to the world came from Abraham Lincoln. The founders of the nation, he declared in 1860, "meant to set up a standard maxim for free society, which would be familiar to all, and revered by all; constantly looked to, constantly labored for, and even though never perfectly attained, constantly approximated, and thereby constantly spreading and deepening its influence and augmenting the happiness and value of life to all people of all colors everywhere" (quoted, Wills 1978, xviii).

The declarations—by foreign-policy designers, scholars, and journalists—continue. Two examples should suffice. Apparently oblivious to the raw arrogance of her remarks, the Secretary of State–nominee told the Senate confirmation hearings in 1996 that in the post–Cold War era, Americans "must be more than audience, more even than actors; we must be the authors of the history of our age." And a recent British commentary noted the influence of Americans' "conviction that America has a particular obligation, almost a moral mandate, to set the world straight" (*Economist*, October 30, 1993, 21).

A reexamination of the idea of American exceptionalism by Lipset, based on extensive statistical and survey data, claims that the sense of exceptionalism (and superiority) persisted well into the 1990s: "Regardless of evidence of corruption in high places and higher violent crime rates, Americans continue to be proud of their nation, to exhibit a greater sense of patriotism and of belief that their system is superior to all others" (1996, 51).[1]

The conception of America as a moral experiment, with an "extraordinary birth, outside the processes of time . . . a nation apart, with a special destiny [as] the hope of all those outside America's shores" (Wills 1978, xix), might have suggested it as a favorite site for utopian experiment. For the decades preceding the Civil War, utopian community-builders were part of a much broader search for the appropriate embodiment of American democracy. In this vein, Fellman contends, their exertions were

> not different in kind from the moralistic, deductive manner with which many more Americans sought to achieve their agreed-upon task of perfecting their world. Utopian thinking, in other words, though especially clearly exemplified by utopian communitarians, was by no means limited to them in all respects. The correction of evil, the reshaping of the formless through the discovery and the implementation of some key truth enacted in a cleansed small locale characterizes the process of much of nineteenth-century reform. (Fellman 1973, xvi)

If America itself is conceived as a utopian endeavor—and public rhetoric from the Puritan intention of setting an example for a benighted humanity down to the latest rhetorical political claim that American military expeditions are solely humanitarian surely points to that conception—then the fit of utopian community experiments with the nation is much closer than merely the provision of ample social and geographical space and tolerant or fretful indifference. As I try to demonstrate, utopian communitarians are dedicated participants in American culture, regardless of their apparent desire to secede from it.

Individualism and Equality

When Alexis de Tocqueville coined the term *individualism* in 1840, he meant to indicate a peculiar new notion of how people in America perceived their relation to society. Distinguishing it from selfishness ("a passionate and exaggerated love of self"), Tocqueville defined individualism as "a mature and calm feeling, which disposes each member of the community to sever himself from the mass of his fellows and to draw apart with his family and his friends, so that after he has thus formed a little circle of his own, he willingly leaves society at large to itself" (1945, 2:105).

Individualism results from the "equality of condition" Tocqueville saw as pervasive in America and inclines the citizens of democratic polities to comprehend themselves as neither owing nor expecting anything from others, "considering themselves as standing alone," imagining "their whole destiny . . . in their own hands" (Tocqueville 1945, 2:105). In a much-quoted passage, he noted the poignant situation of one living in democracy, where the inevitable individualism it spawns "throws him back forever upon himself alone and threatens in the end to confine him entirely within the solitude of his own heart" (2:106). Unconstrained by allegiance to past and future generations, or to any group larger than the family, the individual confronts the necessity of choice, of making independent decisions. As rights inhere in individuals, so too do responsibilities: one has the right of choice and the obligation to accept the consequences of choice. When ascent in status and prosperity is highly prized, as it is in America, where "the goal of monetary success . . . has been firmly entrenched," there occurs the "subsidiary theme that success or failure are results wholly of personal qualities; that he who fails has only himself to blame, for the corollary to the concept of the self-made man is the self-unmade man. To the extent that this cultural definition is assimilated by those who have not made their mark, failure represents a double defeat: the manifest defeat of remaining far behind in the race for success and the implicit defeat of not having the capacities and moral stamina needed for success" (Merton 1968, 221, 222).

Enshrined in the founding documents of the nation, the ideas of human equality and individualism are related to the conception of the individual as a source, perhaps the ultimate source, of morality and moral decisions. All humans are created equal and, as individuals, have "unalienable Rights" which include but are not limited to the examples given in the Declaration of Independence: "life, liberty, and the pursuit of happiness." Much of the Constitution, most notably the first ten amendments, enumerates the rights of individuals.

Even if we seek divine reassurance, and place our faith in the Creator for guidance in choosing, we have individually made the initial decision to rely on the supernatural. It first requires a leap of faith, a leap predicated on the necessity of individual decision. In this respect, Robert Bellah remarks that "one cannot defend one's [religious] views by saying that they are simply those of one's parents or of the church in which one was raised. On the contrary they must be particularly and peculiarly one's own" (1987, 370).

Tocqueville discerned a tension between equality and individualism and noted the strain in his prediction of contradictory "tendencies" of the "principle of equality." One tendency leads "the mind of every man to untried thoughts [individualism], the other prohibits him from thinking at all [equality]." Under certain conditions, he went on, "democracy would extinguish that liberty of the mind to which a democratic social condition is favorable; so that, after having broken all the bondage once imposed on it by ranks or by men, the human mind would be closely fettered to the general will of the greatest number" (Tocqueville 1945, 2:12–13). This, of course, acknowledges the democratic threat of the tyranny of the majority, which extends further than political contests into a general intellectual conformity. In a democratic society, the "readiness to believe the multitude increases, and [public] opinion is more than ever mistress of the world" (2:11; see also Wood 1992, 364).

Not only in America, but throughout the modern Western world, "a transition develops, at least in popular mentality," according to Louis Dumont, "from the moral principle of equality to the belief in the basic identity of all men, because they are no longer taken as samples of a culture, a society or a social group, but as *individuals* existing in and for themselves" (1961, 39).

An important implication of individualism and equality is that society or any social group beyond the family must be constructed. Any such constructed group rests on the voluntary will of its constituent members, and the agreement of any member may be withdrawn. Hence, groups formed on this basis are always contingent and their continuation uncertain.

This conception of how society is formed and maintained is reported in a number of recent ethnographies (for example, Greenhouse 1985, 1986, 1992; Varenne 1977, 1986; Schneider 1968, 1976, 1977, 1980; Moffatt 1989). In these reports there is a marked distinction between the interpretation provided by participants and that proposed by the anthropological analyst. Even so, the idea of society as existing only by the continued affirmation of its members is surely only part of the participants' construction of reality. That is, it constitutes a justification for potential action, for withdrawal of assent and participation, in much the way that the notion of democratic government rest-ing on the "consent of the governed" carries the potential for remedial action when it is perceived to rest elsewhere. Consent can be (and is) differently construed by the governed; warrants of consent, given in elections, are subject to renewal and cancellation. Yet to acknowledge that, at any given time, some participants are displeased with decisions made by their elected leaders—that, for example, the "system" or the "establishment" has lost touch with the electorate and should be changed—is not at all to deny the power of the idea of society as contingent.

To his surprise, Varenne discovered the vitality of this aspect of individualism among the people of Appleton, a farm town in the Midwest, who "perceived that individualism generates community. For them, individualism is natural, community problematical. *Society has to be built.* This is a statement that must be understood both as a model *for* behavior ('Let's join together to make this a better world') and as a model *of* behavior ('This is the way the United States began'). . . . Society was created by a joining of individuals for the greater good of each of them. And the institutions of society . . . were created in the same manner for the same purpose" (1977, 70). To Varenne, this idea of a social group as "*not* necessarily greater than the sum of its parts" stood the ethnographer's worldview on its head. It was "radically opposed to what I as a social scientist consider to be the true reality of the human condition and what I take to be the central message of the social sciences in general" (ibid.). This "central message" of anthropology and social science in general is that individuals are linked by reciprocal rights and obligations, that a group is more than its constituent members. The emphasis is upon relationships rather than upon individuals.

Drawing upon her ethnography of Hopewell, an affluent suburb of a metropolitan center in the Southeast, Greenhouse considers further implications of individualism that amplify Varenne's analysis. To her informants, "one's role is an aspect of one's identity, developed over the life's course." Roles are not conceived as relationships, in the manner of social scientists, but "as clusters of [personal] traits." Relationships among individuals, from this view then, are nourished and improved by individual growth and maturity. "Interpersonal problems are not relational problems, but individual problems stemming from immaturity" (Greenhouse 1985, 262). Thus, families are comprised of individuals who "strive to attain" particular characteristics through maturity; fathers and mothers, husbands and wives "are not created by families; rather, in the local concept, families are made up of these roles" (ibid.). Motherhood, for example, is seen as a natural step in the progression from female child to adult woman to wife and mother.

Writing in 1944, the Swedish scholar Gunnar Myrdal saw individualism and equality holding a crucial place in the "American Creed." Beginning his classic work on the position of African Americans, Myrdal charted some features of American culture. Compared to all the Western nations, he wrote, the United States "has the *most explicitly expressed* system of general ideas in reference to human interrelations" (1962, 3). Every American, he insisted, is aware of the "American Creed" and to varying degrees accepts it. Its premises are pervasive and inescapable: "The schools teach them; the churches preach them. The courts pronounce their judicial decisions in their terms. They permeate editorials with a pattern of idealism so ingrained that the writers could scarcely free themselves from it even if they tried. They have fixed a custom of indulging in high-sounding generalities in all written or spoken addresses to the American public, otherwise so splendidly gifted for the matter-of-fact approach to things and problems" (4). Myrdal notes an "anarchistic tendency" reflected in the American citizen's inclination to judge for himself whether a law or judicial decision is just or unjust "and has *the dangerous attitude that, if it is unjust, he may feel free to disobey it*" (16). Together with his observation that Americans have "acquired a comparatively low degree of personal identification with the state and the legal machinery" (18), this addresses other aspects of American notions of individualism and equality (see also Lipset 1996).

Of course Myrdal's research was geared to trying to explain the discrepancy of American culture with the behavior he and others observed in the treatment of African Americans. The gap between the idea of equality and empirical observations of inequality, a disparity still widely observed and discussed, should not lead us to dismiss the idea as having little influence. Americans might hedge their claim that equality reigns with qualifications and exceptions, but it remains a dominant cultural postulate for them.

In his analysis of equality in America, Tocqueville was plainly concerned with perception and belief, with cultural postulates. As Sennett notes, "Tocqueville's analysis of equality of condition relies not so much on proving that equality is in fact being established as on the belief of a people that such equality is established. *People behave as if they were equal in condition.* If in fact they do not move roughly within the same band of action, in order to feel that they belong to a common social order, they change their tastes, habits, and outlook to appear as if they did" (1979, 123, emphasis added). That is to say, postulates of equality and of individualism, as well, form part of a taken-for-granted reality.

Put another way, we should expect no one-to-one correspondence between the cultural system and observed social life. Indeed it is one of anthropology's basic assumptions that a discrepancy between culture and practical action is inevitable. Exploring this discrepancy, trying to discover how people justify and explain their perception of the distinction between what should be and what is, leads to some of anthropology's most stimulating analytical efforts.

Opposition of Individual and Group

In much of American life, public and private, constant reference is made to the inherent conflict between the demands of individual and group. American political discussion at every level is replete with concern to balance the necessity of individual choice, liberty, and freedom with the requirements of group activity.

National politics in the latter part of the twentieth century provide ample illustration of the urgency of decisions that seek this balance. Welfare reform is couched in terms that call for adequate care for defenseless children while expecting needy parents to take up their individual responsibility to furnish life's necessities through their own effort. Abortion arguments are phrased as an opposition between the individual's right of privacy (as in the *Roe v. Wade* decision of 1973) or individual choice, and a higher claim of society, often rooted in religious tenets, to foster birth by forbidding most or all abortions. Debates on proposals for national health care pivot on the extent of individual choice of treatment, hospital, or physician that must be incorporated. Discrimination is widely banned on a growing number of bases, including gender, age, ethnicity, religion, and physical disability in the attempt to achieve "a level playing field" by offering equality of opportunity to all. Yet programs of "affirmative action" are attacked as placing group rights above individual rights, as inexorably leading to quotas of groups (i.e., categories) rather than selection by individual merit. Claims that private citizens have an unlimited right to own firearms are challenged with accounts of the increasing violence in the nation and a call for tighter control of guns in the common interest. Arguably all political issues might be reviewed through the lens of this basic tension of individual and group.

But if Americans consider the individual as the source of virtue, as the building block of community and society, as indicated in the ethnographically specific studies of Varenne, Greenhouse, and others, then "group" is probably not very useful as an oppositional term. If individuals are the raw material from which groups are constructed, and groups are no more than their parts, then groups (or communities) are, from the perspective of the participants, simply aggregates of individuals. Groups are, from this point of view, categories of presumptively similar individuals. Within such collections of individuals, the relationships are not conceived as the unavoidable ties of obligation, of reciprocal rights and duties. The adhesive that binds a group is similarity, usually and implicitly shared values and beliefs. Greenhouse notes that this view of social life, based on individualism, "does not lend itself readily to diversity." The American "melting pot is more a demand or a wish than a description, since, in the absence of affinity or familiarity, only two possible relationships remain: a stranger can be either an adversary or an alien" (1985, 263).[2]

A corresponding argument for the nation as a whole is developed by Garry Wills. He takes the modern conception of America, dating to the nineteenth century and most eloquently expressed by Lincoln, to be above all an "American *idea*." The consequences are very much like those calculated by Greenhouse. Wills writes, "To be fully American, one must adopt this idea wholeheartedly, proclaim it, prove one's devotion to it. Unless we know what our fellows *think*, we do not know whether they are American at all, much less whether they are *truly* American. Indeed, since the idea is so pure and abstract, we must all be constantly striving toward it, trying to become *more* American" (1978, xxii).

There is, however, one natural social unit for American culture, the family," in the sense that human nature preordains it" (Greenhouse 1985, 262). That is, the family is the single social group where cohesion does not rest solely on common belief and common consent. It is not seen as a contingently organized group. Family bonds are those of what Schneider terms "diffuse, enduring solidarity" (1968).[3]

Families are made up of individual persons, communities are aggregates of families, and society as a whole is composed of communities. Families are seen as protective bastions against the demands of social units (community, government) outside them. An ideal society, in this view, is simply the family writ large. This outlook has significant consequences: "the image of society as family is not only a call for loyalty, trust, and feelings of mutual identity and commitment, but a claim that these traits already prevail and are articulated by the law" (Greenhouse 1985, 263). The centrality of the family is demonstrated in, for example, Westbrook's consideration of appeals to patriotic endeavor in World War II, when "no obligation ranked higher in American war propaganda than the obligation to protect the family" (Westbrook 1993, 207). He suggests that not only were Americans called upon to fight for their families, but overall, "the felt obligations of Americans suggests" that the most effective appeals "both as individuals and as families to join the war effort" were those phrased as the defense of "*private* interests and [to] discharge *private* moral obligations" (198; see also Perin 1988, 25–62).[4]

An Instrumental View of Society

Individualism strongly endorses an instrumental view of social order. Social groups and institutions are constructed, from this perspective, so that individuals can better satisfy private needs and desires. The strain between the demands of individual freedom and the necessity of cooperative activity, constantly played out in political rhetoric, also forms a decisive issue in scholarly debate about America.

Expressed in economic terms, it has provoked historians of early America to search for the period when an entrepreneurial spirit became prominent in the nation. When did significant numbers of Americans accept self-interest and profit-seeking as an unavoidable part of life? Studies of early American communities, particularly in New England, have found social life in colonial America much like that of traditional peasants (Demos 1970; Greven 1970; Lockridge 1970). Villages tended to be stable, homogeneous in belief and outlook, self-sufficient, and very religious. Dedham, Massachusetts, for example, was labeled by Lockridge "a Christian Utopian Closed Corporate Community," its "utopian theory . . . summarized in the words autonomy, exclusiveness, and unity" (1970, 16, 30). Public good far outweighed any individualistic tendencies toward private profit-making; more than personal gain, villagers of the eighteenth century wanted stability and order in their lives.

Recent scholarship has pushed the "take-off point" of American individualism, expressed in the market terms of entrepreneurship and the profit motive, back to about the time of the Revolution (Rothenberg 1993). Gordon Wood's landmark study of the American Revolution shows it to have been far more radical than previously supposed, a defining moment in ushering in modern individualism (Wood 1992).

But more than disinterested scholarship is involved. Some historians, says Wood, go well beyond description and interpretation of the communal America of the eighteenth century to champion that era as a "noncapitalist vision of what still might be" (1994, 46).

Among scholars of other disciplines, too, the tone of partisanship is marked. Frequently the argument is phrased as undesirable change in the American character. David Riesman's *The Lonely Crowd* (1950) claimed that American character had changed from the "inner-directed" type of the nineteenth century to the "other-directed" type that was conspicuous in the post–World War II period. Inner-directed Americans had "incorporated a psychic gyroscope" from the teachings of their parents which "could receive signals later on from other authorities" resembling the parents (Riesman 1950, 41).

Yet Americans of this character type were far less independent and individualistic than they appeared. Although they craved the esteem of their fellows as the reward for upholding shared values, they did not need constant social reinforcement. By contrast, other-directed Americans of the mid-twentieth century lacked the internalized values learned from their families and, wanting to be liked by everyone, were "at home everywhere and nowhere, capable of a rapid if sometimes superficial intimacy with and response to everyone" (ibid.).

The publication and success of *The Lonely Crowd* is a good starting point from which one could trace through the following decades a growing distress with what was variously described as a loss of a sense of community, a weakening of public life as Americans turned toward the privacy of family life or indulgent self-fulfillment, or a prevalence of inauthenticity in social relationships. Charges that Americans had become more lethargic, more selfish, more manipulated, and more insincere were conveyed in prose that was by turns impassioned (Slater 1970), romantic (Reich 1970), doleful (Henry 1963, 1971), and didactic (Lasch 1977, 1979). Whatever the specifics of the argument, something was clearly wrong with America and Americans. Contained within most of these arguments was condemnation of the psychological "false consciousness" or, in Henry's terms, the "pseudo self" brought to the fore in modern America (see also Fromm 1947). The authenticity of American selves had been displaced or destroyed, and a situation approaching Tocqueville's fears had appeared. Turning inward toward the private affairs of their families, Americans had become fearful, self-centered, narcissistic. In the process, community life, formerly a source of strength and fulfillment both individually and socially, had withered to insignificance.

The morality of an individualistic vision that seems to defy the very possibility of cooperative effort has come under recent attack by a loose coalition of intellectuals calling themselves "communitarians."[5] Prominent among these are the authors of *Habits of the Heart,* who deplore the "sense of relative isolation and powerlessness that results from the insecurity of life in an increasingly commercial society" (Bellah et al. 1985, 38). They urge Americans to work toward "a new conception of public authority built upon a new sense of public participation" (Fox 1988, 243). Bellah and his coauthors see the debasement of public life as "utilitarian" where "expressive" individualism has obscured an older sense of the "public good [as] . . . that which benefits society as a whole and leads to what the founders of the American republic called *public happiness* . . . [which] includes everything from adequate public facilities to the trust and civic friendship that makes public life something to be enjoyed rather than feared" (1985, 335). The dispute is often framed in moral and philosophical terms as a battle between liberalism and communitarianism. Liberal philosophers concentrate on the rights of individuals and the "limits on what can be done to individuals for the sake of the general or common good" (Phillips 1993, 185). In many ways, liberalism expresses the view discussed here as individualism, with an emphasis on rights that are inherent for all human beings. "Communitarians," like Bellah and a number of others (Etzioni 1993; Sandel 1982; Walzer 1983, 1990), take a Durkheimian position that the most important features of human social life are those derived from group or community membership.

In considering the critique of liberalism over the past two decades, Lasch contends that the liberal view "is at its best when it condemns invasions of privacy; but this best is still not good enough." Liberals and conservatives alike place too high a value on what is an "empty ideal of freedom and privacy; they disagree only about what is truly private" (Lasch 1988, 184). For political conservatives, it is economic freedom that should remain for the most part beyond the reach of communal restriction. Political liberals stress individual freedom of religion, speech, and association. Both are shortsighted and narrow, in Lasch's opinion. He suggests that "a wide variety of familiar issues—including the separation of church and state, say, or the regulation of big-time athletics—can be recast in a new and much richer form once we set aside the distinction between private and public life and talk instead about practices and institutions" (ibid.).

Doubting the historical accuracy of the communitarian proposition that a former sense of community and the common good ever existed, Derek Phillips mounts a full-scale assault by examining the three periods of Western history his opponents suggest as exemplars of strong community life: eighteenth-century America, the European Middle Ages, and classical Athens. He concludes that in all three periods "the historical prevalence of the kind of [homogeneous] community they describe is a fiction. It rests on a myth that looks to the past for reassurance and guidance" (1993, 150). His stress on diversity, conflict, and oppression leads Phillips to repudiate the communitarian notion that, in a more humane past, economic competition was tempered by civic responsibility. Not only is the communitarian view based on faulty history, says Phillips, but from his liberal point of view, the quest for community entails grave dangers. The "pursuit of community often has very negative consequences for those who are to be excluded from membership," as true, he says, for modern efforts as for the short-lived closed communities of early Boston and classical Athens (1993, 163–64). Phillips summarizes his negative opinion of communitarianism this way:

It is in the nature of the communitarian ideal that membership is restricted to those having certain things in common: place of habitation, ancestors, language, tradition, religion, cultural patterns, and the like. The salience of these attributes rests not only on difference but also on an assumption of hierarchy. That is to say, evaluation of difference commonly has an explicitly normative basis. A genuine community is marked off from other groups and individuals by what its members see as their distinctive characteristics. (1993, 164)[6]

But Bellah, his collaborators, and allies make their brief on *cultural* grounds (Bellah 1988; Peacock 1988). Particularly for Bellah, the trouble for Americans is that all rights are translated into the terms of liberalism, that we lack a vocabulary for discussing rights and obligations in terms that are not anchored in individualism and philosophical liberalism. That is to say, Bellah's position is an explication of the cultural postulates of the participants, while Phillips and other critics take the point of view of the analyst, for whom the obvious critique is that, regardless of how rights and obligations were formulated, regardless of the discourse of early America, the European Middle Ages, classical Athens, a reasonable analyst knows that the "reality" was of power held by a minority, exploitation of one class or category by another, in short, of inequity that favored the few.

Utopian Communities and American Culture

The profound dissatisfaction with existing social and cultural arrangements, and the associated deficiencies in the character of modern Americans, also nourishes utopian efforts at building improved models of community. In addition to shared belief, wrote Nordhoff in 1875, success for utopian communitarians depends "upon a feeling of the unbearableness of the circumstances in which they find themselves. The general feeling of modern society is blindly right at bottom: communism [communalism] is a mutiny against society" (1961, 408).

Similar conclusions are found in the twentieth century, both from observers and participants. Generalizing from his study of Japanese utopians, David Plath, for example, struck the same note as Nordhoff. "A utopian community's claim to a better way of life is at the very least a tacit rejection of the great society's way, and usually the rejection is overt and emphatic." The very existence of such ventures "is a challenge and a criticism against the ambient culture" (1966, 1155). From the point of view of participants, the denunciation of existing culture and society is sharp and decisive. In his report on the activities of Macedonia Community in 1948, one member wrote that, apart from their pacifism, "what may be the strongest binding force in the group is an attitude of disillusionment with modern industrial society." They rejected the "sterility of urban living" and had "little faith in the usual kind of political activity or the wistful thinking of liberals" (Newton 1948, 29). A participant in a Californian utopian community in the 1970s defined herself and her colleagues as "refugees escaping a society which had no place for us and to which we no longer cared to belong" (Anderson 1990, 3).

But the "challenge and . . . criticism," the rejection of urban sterility, and the "mutiny" posed by American utopians has rarely been a wholesale dismissal of individualism, equality, or the sense of special mission that forms a substantial portion of the taken-for-granted reality of the "ambient culture," to adopt Plath's phrase. Rather, utopians aim to reinterpret that reality, to enhance the freedom of choice of the individual, to institute a more perfect equality, and to set before the world a model of improved society and culture.

The confession of the Californian about the 1970s echoes the ideas of most utopians that "our nation was on an irrevocable course of decline, headed for disaster, and . . . there was nothing we could do about it but take ourselves as far out of harm's way as we could get" (Anderson 1990, 1; see also Anders 1990). Like most of those who attempt the creation of utopia, she and her comrades were certain about what they renounced and hopeful in their belief that an alternative could be constructed. "We didn't like greed, hypocrisy, intolerance and oppression. . . . we believed in voluntary simplicity . . . in individual liberty and tolerance of individual differences . . . [and in] nonviolence, the transforming power of love and our duty to preserve the environment for our descendants" (Anderson 1990, 5–6).

In the next chapter, I examine some of the problems involved in creating communities and in the scholarly attempts to account for them. Subsequent chapters take up specific materials from the years of the Great Depression before a focus on the history of my major example, Celo Community.

Notes

1. Different views of the persistence of older ideas about America and Americans can easily be found. Hence, it is not unexpected to hear another view from Daniel Bell, astute sociological observer of modern America, who declared *The End of Ideology* in a book of that title in 1960. By 1975, in a well-argued essay—"The End of American Exceptionalism"—Bell announced that the American "sense of destiny has been shattered" and called on American leaders for "the re-creation of a moral credibility whose essential condition is simple honesty and openness" (Bell 1980, 270–71). But one presidential scandal, in this

instance President Nixon and Watergate, is not sufficient, in my view, to so thoroughly undermine American notions of righteous exceptionalism.

2. The confusion of category and group is so widespread among Americans that it afflicts even some of the best scholarly stylists. In a recent essay, Garry Wills, for example, nods to the distinction with "Critics say it is unAmerican to treat citizens as members of categories." But for the rest of his article, he relies on "groups," as in the conspicuous: "For most of our history, people were treated as a group when it came to filling all the important jobs in government, business, the professions, or the academy. The group was white males" (Wills 1996, 14). Rarely does one encounter "category" in, for example, a television or radio newscast; "group" is the preferred and ubiquitous term. Perhaps this accepted usage is related to the kind of notion of the relationships of individuals to one another discussed by Greenhouse.

3. On a very general level, Schneider suggests that such bonds of what might be called "love" characterize for Americans one side of an opposition; on the other are sentiments of rational means-to-ends, instrumental ties that connect people in work groups (see also Gray and Wolfe 1982). But as we shall see, instrumental links are seen to be a feature of all groups outside the family, with perhaps exceptional extensions to ethnic group as a kind of extended family (see Bentley 1981).

4. Even more broadly, Louis Dumont tracks the historical development of Western individualism and equality and contrasts it with traditional societies based on hierarchical relationships. His examples for demonstrating this contrast are traditional India and the United States. Just as equality and individualism are pervasive in modern America, the idea of hierarchy forms the taken-for-granted reality of traditional India. Hierarchy, as applied to group formation and maintenance, refers to groups as unequally bound together in a manner that does not depend upon the individual agreement of members. Groups are seen as preexistent to individuals, individual human beings are difficult to conceive outside the bonds of group membership. Rights accrue to persons because of their membership in groups, quite unlike the American conception of the rights of individuals that take precedence over whatever privileges or rights they might have as group members (Dumont 1970; also see Dumont 1986).

5. The distinction between the "intellectual communitarians" and the usual use of the term "communitarian" to refer to members of utopian communities is an important one. The "intellectual communitarians" appear to have little or no interest in utopian communities, either living in them or establishing them. Their crusade is to change the individualistic temper of the entire United States by means other than building a model for emulation.

6. The opposed cultural postulates of hierarchy and equality, seen in Dumont's work as guiding principles of traditional India and modern America, respectively, appear in this controversy as positions of adversaries on either side. Dumont's dispassionate effort to pursue the development of modern individualistic society from its roots in traditional Europe (with India as an instance where hierarchical principles were more recently found) has no place in this version of the contest (Dumont 1977, 1986). At least, this seems to be the case in the way Phillips casts the argument.

2. Utopian Problems and Explanations

IF A CLOSE RELATIONSHIP exists between the efforts at construction of utopian communities and central features of American culture, particularly the emphasis on individualism and equality, then one should find a persistence of utopianism in American history. Granted, changes in style and organization would occur, as the historical context changed, but there should appear a recognizable tradition of utopian attempts. Until the mid-1970s, however, commentators presented American utopian community-building as locked into the first half of the nineteenth century, claiming that unique opportunities for widespread social experimentation on a small scale had come and gone in that period. Model communities, "patent-office models of the good society," might then have had immense effect in shaping the future of the country. After about 1850, however, utopian experimentation rapidly declined, according to Arthur Bestor, the historian most influential in arguing this view (1953, 1957, 1970). The few communities founded after the Civil War, Bestor calculated, had a negligible influence on American life. Rapid growth in industrial size and centralization, and "social patterns [that] had become so well defined over the whole area of the United States" doomed small-scale efforts at change; pilot plants and models of new societies lost their relevance. Ideals of remaking society by establishing a model community shrank "into mere escapism," and reform efforts turned toward "legislation, or collective bargaining, or organized effort for particular goals, or even revolutionary seizure of power" (Bestor 1953, 525–26).

Variously expressed, this conjecture rapidly grew into an "unchallenged historical truism" (Fogarty 1990, 1). Rather than a reduction to escapism, utopian communitarianism underwent, in John Thomas's view, a "collapse" in the 1850s (1965, 679). If not escapist, then perhaps postwar communities were simply superfluous, a position taken by LeWarne in characterizing the Puget Sound utopias of the 1890s as "futile . . . an anachronism from an earlier and presumably simpler time" (1975, 235). Granting the presence of a few recent efforts, Lockwood declared that "today, the utopian community is an anomaly, a curious revival of a dead tradition" (1965, 410; see also Holloway 1966).

New Facts, New Questions

Although earlier compilations and descriptive summaries of post–Civil War communities were not lacking (e.g., Skinner 1901; Bushee 1905; Albertson 1936), Bestor's thesis came under serious attack only in the 1970s, when Robert Fogarty unleashed a critical challenge (Fogarty 1975). Subsequent research demonstrated that the sheer number of communities founded was greater *after* the Civil War than *before:* between 1787 and 1860, 137 communities were established, while 142 were set up from 1861 to 1919 (Fogarty 1980, xxiv). Communal and utopian "ventures continued largely unabated in the post–Civil War period," but they were largely ignored, since they offered no easy solutions to the problems of "urbanization, industrial depression, and religious change" (Fogarty 1981, 132; 1975, 146). Mindful of Fogarty's argument, Howard Segal nevertheless insists that "serious utopians" turned their energy in the late nineteenth century to "other means of articulating their ideals and of trying to realize them. Utopian writings then became their principal form" (Segal 1985, 99).

The new historical truism concedes that utopian communities have continually existed in America since the seventeenth century. Older explanations for the cessation of utopian community-building have been scrapped for other questions: How did the purposes of utopian communitarians differ, if they did, from one historical period to another? Why were more communities founded in some periods than in others? What influence, if any, did utopian communities have on American life? Addressing the first question of differing ideals of communal reformers, Fogarty concludes his study of communities from 1860 to 1914 by proposing that late nineteenth-century communities tended to combine the strategies of "mission" and "retreat" (the terms are Rosabeth Kanter's). Founders of these communities sought "to establish . . . a place that would be both safe haven and an example for others to follow" (Fogarty 1990, 224) and tacitly agreed that large-scale problems in modern America might yield to a change in individual attitudes. As William Demarest Lloyd admonished: "A thorough, stalwart resimplification of life governed by simple needs and loves is the imperative want of the world" (quoted, Fogarty 1990, 224). Similar statements of goals, as we shall see, appeared in the utopian communities of the mid-twentieth century.

The periodicity of utopian experiments, and the possibility of these experiments increasing or decreasing in number in some sort of cyclical fashion, has led to efforts to connect the rise and fall of community founding with economic cycles. Breaking down the stream of utopian activity into shorter periods, Barkun finds four decades of unusual concentration: the 1840s, the 1890s, the 1930s, and most recently, the 1960s. It is immediately apparent that an unrefined economic explanation for these differing rates in community-building fails; economic prosperity in the 1960s contrasts vividly with the economic disaster of the 1930s. Although his thesis that these surges of activity can be correlated with the economic troughs of "the long or Kondratieff [sic] wave" of forty to sixty years is tepidly argued and quite unconvincing (but see Berry 1992 for an extended and more powerful argument along the same lines of economic determinism), Barkun does show an affinity between communalism and "substantial millennialism movements in the society at large." These, he says, are "responses to perceived disturbances in the moral order" and "byproducts of high levels of collective stress," both far more unsettling in earlier periods than at the present time. Even as we gain proficiency in predicting economic cycles, the rise and fall of utopias will "likely remain enigmatic," since the "locus of disruptive events will . . . shift to less well-understood and less tangible phenomena, such as perceptions of the quality and purpose of life" (1984, 46–48).

No easy duty to align highpoints in utopian communalism with economic downturns or panics, but Barkun makes another point: "although there are clearly discernible waves in the founding of communities, there are no comparable waves of dissolutions, at least for the period 1787–1919, where ample data is available." Utopian communities are "better designed for survival" than centralized, national movements since they are separated experimental settings, hence "no single community's demise determines the failure of others" (1984, 46).

Utopian Success and Failure

Another issue that has intrigued scholars of utopian experiments has to do with the measurement of success and failure. In her examination of nineteenth-century utopias, Kanter followed a long tradition in measuring success "by length of time in existence." Unlike earlier writers, who tended to equate success and longevity in an off-hand manner, Kanter was more precise. By her scale, "a system had to exist as a utopian community for at least twenty-five years, the sociological definition of a generation, in order to be considered successful" (1972, 245). Others have questioned the usefulness of her yardstick of longevity on a number of grounds (e.g., Fogarty 1981, 134–46; Wunderlich 1992, 174; Pitzer 1989, 1997a; but compare Shenker 1986).

Acknowledging the changes undergone by some communities in her sample, Kanter only provokes additional questions when she elaborates on her measure of success: "A case was regarded as a utopian community if all relevant relations among members were centrally controlled by a single organization" (Kanter 1972, 245). This assumes that the change from one kind of organization to another—say, from utopian community to industrial corporation, as happened for Oneida and Amana—can be dated with confident precision. But in the reorganization of Oneida, for example, the end of its unusual social system began several years before utopia gave way to corporation.

To take another famous case, the Shakers: at what point can we no longer classify them as utopian? Is it when they change from a band of perfectionist visionaries to mere "places of refuge for members of broken families," as seems to have happened in the 1850s (Bainbridge 1984, 34)? Or at some necessarily vague point in the twentieth century, when membership dwindled to a mere handful of aged women? Given that, as Kanter clearly recognizes, the zeal of the founders rarely stirs the children born in utopian communities, one can propose that utopian communities can continue in existence—that is, not undergoing change of organizational form or demise—for some years while the original utopian elements fade. One mechanism for this kind of development is a turnover in population so that very few people reared in the community remain for their adult years. Conversely, and perhaps more likely, a change in membership can bring about a revitalization of the original community goals and utopian fervor. For the Shakers, this is precisely what happened. Fifty years after the Shakers began, as those personally acquainted with the founder Ann Lee died, doubt and dissension arose in the Shaker settlements. Beginning in 1837, renewed spiritual excitement, exhibited in trance, ecstatic dance, and glossolalia, swept through Shaker communities. The disruptive potential of these outbursts was averted with the departure of the most radical members, a few of whom had gone so far as to demand the end of celibacy, and the leadership's proclamation of "the Millenial Laws of 1845, the strictest and most rigid in Shaker history" (Foster 1991, 38).

The latest framework for inquiry into utopian communities, initiated by Donald Pitzer, is "developmental communalism" or "the developmental approach" (Pitzer 1989, 1984, 1997b). This requires a change of emphasis from "internal factors that produce or inhibit longevity" of single communities to "a consideration of the entire history and influence of the movements of which communalism is a single facet" (Pitzer 1989, 70). An added advantage is the elimination of the "unfortunate 'success-failure' pattern of earlier studies," in which longevity of communal structure formed the key criterion of success (Pitzer 1997a, 13). Pitzer's analytical outline avoids the limitations of Kanter's Procrustean twenty-five-year gauge, allows for the inclusion of short-lived but obviously influential experiments like Brook Farm, and calls attention to the various social and political reforms inspired by such famous efforts as Robert Owen's New Harmony.[1]

There are conspicuous shortcomings in Pitzer's approach, to which I return in chapter 10. Among them are the diffuseness of indicators of success, the uncertainty about whether the process of "development" is calculated from the viewpoint of participant or analyst, the extent to which "development" is historically contingent or a consequence of the original utopian design, and the occasional abrupt change of focus from particular communities to broader tides of social reform. Even so, the developmental approach, exhibited in the historical studies edited by Pitzer in *America's Communal Utopias* (Pitzer 1997b), represents a substantial turn in the study of experimental utopias. His innovative analytical frame dislodges utopian from its status as wistful fantasy to a position as active possibility: "Anything but static, as the term utopian immediately implied to earlier writers, the communes of the most vital historic and current movements are creatively engaged in a developmental process that both precedes and may extend well after their communal phase" (Pitzer 1997a, 12).

Defining Utopia

To speak of utopian elements and development or change from utopia to non-utopia necessarily involves the definition of utopia. Modern communities like Celo have been classified under different names, including communitarian societies, intentional communities, experimental communities, utopian societies or colonies or communities. They are, for some, best labeled communitarian societies, and Bennett (1975, 65) declares that communalism is the diagnostic feature: they arrange their lives in a communal fashion, sharing a great deal of property and activity. Hence, Oneida, Robert Owen's secular New Harmony, and the Hutterites are, in Bennett's estimate, all the same kind of social group. For Pitzer, extensive communalism is usually secondary to other goals: "communal living may be a labor of love, but it is also a means to an end, not an end in itself" (Pitzer 1989, 72). Others suggest that more weight should be given to the goals of the community (Fogarty 1981), and some distinguish between communes and utopian communities. Abrams and McCulloch, for example, point to "the sense of mission to establish a new social dispensation" (1976, 36) as a marker that applies to utopian communities but is ordinarily not found among communes. Put another way, utopian communities seek, by their example, to convince the world of the superiority of the new social institutions they have built. In communes, particularly those of the late twentieth century, "the cultivation of relationships *within* the commune tends to be the most important thing in the lives of the members" (Abrams and McCulloch 1976, 37). Very often one finds that in communities founded since the 1890s, as Fogarty remarks, the two goals are combined. One or the other is frequently given precedence, and as was true in Celo, participants are at some pains to demonstrate that mission is more important than retreat. Sustaining a balance of the two goals has been a matter of grave concern and constant adjustment for almost all utopian groups (Oved 1983; 1996, 241–305).

Since at least the 1950s, participants in these communities tend to prefer the term "intentional community," defined by one alliance of communities as "an effort to create a social order which may in time become more universally accepted and so help to create the inclusive human community" (Fellowship of Intentional Communities 1959, 2; see also Shenker 1986). With the added element of withdrawal, Hine selects much the same definitional tack for "utopian colony," which

> consists of a group of people who are attempting to establish a new social pattern based upon a vision of the ideal society and who have withdrawn themselves from the community at large to embody that vision in experimental form. The purpose is usually to create a model which other colonies and eventually mankind in general will follow. The concept of withdrawal, an important element in the definition, eliminates those organizations which through cooperative effort seek to transform society by working from within: consumers' and self-co-operatives, factory profit-sharing leagues, or even labor unions. (Hine 1953, 5)

With the understanding that the purpose of withdrawal is usually some mixture of mission and retreat, it is Hine's definition that seems most useful in classifying Celo and those similar to it.[2]

Linked Communities

Discrete as they appear in many treatments, subjected to counting of cases and statistical manipulation or used to establish generalizations about social cohesion (e.g., Kanter 1968, 1972; Deets 1939), utopian communities in America have long been involved in a variety of relationships among themselves. Even a cursory glance discloses considerable interconnections among the groups in Okugawa's annotated list of 270 communities founded from 1787 to 1919 (Okugawa 1980). When he turned his hand to closer analysis of these relationships, Okugawa managed to classify 230 of them into a small number of "categories of interrelatedness" (1983). He includes relations maintained among communities existing contemporaneously, and sequential linkages extending over time. In a set of elaborate charts and tables, keyed to his annotated list (1980), he arrives at a conclusion undermining the notion that accounts of mere death or continuity of single cases are adequate. Communities branch off from one another (e.g., Shakers, Hutterites); communities split as schisms develop (e.g., some Icarian and Mormon colonies); and communities are associated as what Okugawa calls "ideological confederates" (e.g., some Fourierist phalanxes, single-tax settlements). Along historical lines, connections occurred among communities founded by those who had belonged to previous groups, by "repeated attempts on the part of individual leaders" to establish new settlements, through efforts to imitate existing communities, and by independent communities issuing from a "parent" group (Okugawa 1983, 69–70).

A vivid sample of the variety and scope of these intercommunity linkages is provided in Conkin's description of the ties of one single community, the socialist utopia of Llano del Rio (1914–38), which was founded in California and then moved to Louisiana. Relying primarily upon accounts in the community's weekly newspaper, the *Llano Colonist,* Conkin writes:

> In one way or another Llano was related to practically every communal colony or adventure in the twentieth century, with the Hutterites almost alone excepted. The pacifistic Doukhobors of British Columbia sent regular letters to the *Colonist,* and received sympathetic support. A son of one colonist attended the organic school in the single-tax colony at Fairhope, Alabama. Gerald Geraldson, of the Brotherhood House in New York City, supplied Llano with badly needed shipments of old clothes. Several English garden city exponents inquired about Llano, and one leading colonist left Sir Ebenezer Howard's Welwyn Garden City to join what he hoped would be the true heaven on earth. Some of the older colonists had been at Ruskin or at the early cooperative com-

monwealths in the State of Washington. Long articles described the Amana Colony in Iowa, while Sherwood Eddy contributed detailed articles on his Delta Co-operative Plantation in Mississippi. The depression-motivated but unsuccessful Jewish colony at Sunrise, Michigan, rendered periodical reports to Llano, which it adopted as a model. . . . Ernest Wooster, the former manager of Llano, wrote one of the most comprehensive descriptions of utopian communities in his *Communities of the Past and Present,* which was published at Llano. (Conkin 1964, 123)

Similar portraits might be limned for many other communities.

With such connections, applicable to communes of the 1960s and 1970s as well as to earlier cases (Hine 1981, 73–76), simple survival of single communities becomes a less engaging issue, since "even when a group did not 'survive' it often went on to live again in another commune—usually a related one" (Okugawa 1983, 82). Plainly only a very limited understanding of utopian communities emerges from the disparate chronicles of separate groups. A different unit of analysis is required. Okugawa's nomination of "examination of the communal movement as a whole" (1983, 68) asks perhaps too much of a single study, but his insistence that relations with those outside experimental communities be taken into account is certainly on target. It is a version of this perspective that frames the historical accounts of Pitzer and the other contributors to *America's Communal Utopias* (1997).

If one extends the sense of context, as does Laurence Veysey, constructing utopian communities is only one segment of American radicalism. Veysey distinguishes "political radicalism" where participants join "directly in the immediate struggle for power" from "cultural radicalism, [which] is usually related to a communitarian impulse." Utopian experimental communities are the projects of cultural radicals, whose "primary aim" is the "self-directed living of life rather than the contest for power. . . . their main intention has been to go off, sometimes as individuals but more commonly in groups, to practice a pattern of existence which is their own creation" (Veysey 1973, 52). Cultural radicalism, "for instance, the founding of intentional communities—has had a long tradition in the United States," but from another angle, "it is its continuing promise of novelty which seems so very striking." The combination of new and old is a key feature for Veysey: "Secession from society may be a perennial tendency, and various forms of the desire for it may jell into historical traditions, linking the early nineteenth century to our own times. But each social movement or would-be culture, as it comes into being, is 'new' in the sense that it aspires to differ sharply from the existing culture of the moment" (62). Stretching the frame even

further, utopian communities can be examined (and have been by, for example, Fitzgerald 1986) as instances of Wallace's "revitalization movements,"
which include different kinds of efforts to establish a more satisfying culture
(Wallace 1956).[3]

It might be that characteristic forms of revitalization arise in particular
situations, and that utopian communities are, or were at least until a century ago, a form of revitalization peculiar to Europe and Euro-America.[4]

In the more limited scope of this study, aside from brief comparisons with
other American experimental communities, I concentrate primarily on Celo
Community. A main part of the analysis of the community's change and
persistence requires consideration of the relationships of Celo with other
similar efforts.

Changing Utopians

The chain of experimental utopian communities extends far back into colonial American history and, as with any historical succession, changes have
occurred. New interests excited the utopians after about 1870, when communities usually sought to combine goals of mission and retreat. At the same
time, the interchange of members, both serially and among groups existing
simultaneously, demanded constant if subtle tilts in practice and creed.
Changes in the definition of social problems led to alliances with different
reform movements. For example, the influence of socialism in the early twentieth century was instrumental in the founding and maintenance of Llano
del Rio.

Yet another facet of the analysis of utopian communities is their relationship with nonmembers, both potential recruits and the nervously hostile. The
indifference, tolerance of eccentricity, or dislike of immediate neighbors must
also be taken into account as influences on communities' growth, migration,
or decline. Oneida again provides an illustration of the importance of events
outside the group of experimentalists. Started in Putney, Vermont, the Perfectionists, who later built their impressive settlement in upstate New York,
were persuaded to leave Vermont by the threats of local authorities (Robertson 1977, 1–26; Noyes 1961, 614–16). Several decades later, the Oneidans quickly
declined with the loss of their leader, John Humphrey Noyes, who fled to
Canada in 1879 to evade arrest (Carden 1969; Kern 1981; Klaw 1993). In another case, the migrations of the Mormons were often motivated by the frequently violent hostility of nonmembers. Withdrawal further to the western

territories generated more fury as the Mormons met attack with counterat-tack (Anderson 1942; O'Dea 1957; Flanders 1965; Arrington and Britton 1979).

The adaptation of utopians more often did not involve imminent assault or local animosity. Sometimes vital events played out on a stage larger than the immediate locality. In dealing with ex-members, for instance, a number of court cases solved the problem of whether a disgruntled defector was due a portion of the community's property. Even when members were required to contribute their entire worldly goods upon joining, said the courts, they were not entitled to reclaim them upon leaving (Weisbord 1980; Oved 1988, 411–46).

Including details of utopians' relations to their neighbors is often difficult or impossible. When records exist for communities of the past, they tend to treat internal matters rather than how the utopians got along with nonmem-bers in the immediate vicinity. Too frequently this aspect of community con-text is masked by references to the "larger society," if not ignored altogeth-er.[5] Local events, however, often have significant consequences for the communities involved. This was certainly the situation for Celo Communi-ty and will be given extended consideration in later chapters.

From One Generation to Another

Utopian communities' problems in retaining the second generation have been observed by commentators and participants. A second-generation member of the modern Society of Brothers explained the difference between first and succeeding generations in this way:

> The founding generation of the utopia is actually the only generation of the utopia. You cannot inherit an ideal through birth; you cannot be educated for idealism. . . . As the first generation is educating the second, there is an implied criticism of the second generation at the same time, mainly that they're not as vital, that they're not as determined, as committed, as energetic, as intellectu-ally sharp, as the founding generation, and community kids labour under in-credible guilt that this is so. Against it they can do nothing, because at the same time they have been educated to profoundly admire the founding generation. The founding generation are heroes. They're human giants in many cases. (Hazelton 1970, 15)

Similar expressions about the "founding generation" can be heard from members of kibbutzim. Other testimony of this sort comes from a son of Oneida's leader. After recalling that his childhood in the community had been "healthy and happy," Pierrepont Noyes described the end of Oneida's communal phase: "And then . . . came the shock. My father had grown old. A generation of young men and women who lacked the religious enthusiasm of the early Perfectionists had arrived at maturity; internal dissention was rife, and external pressure increasing. During 1879 the Community decided to abandon their radical social system, hoping thereby to salvage Bible communism and their religion, Perfectionism" (1958, 6). The transformation to a joint stock corporation soon followed (Foster 1991, 115).

Community founders often confront physical adversity, but the beginning years are those "when the spirit of community, the sense of purpose and dedication is also high" (Fogarty 1981, 80). Those reared in the idealistic setting of a community's initial period lack the fervor and perseverance of their parents. For the Mormons, this led to a retreat to more conventional practices and standards. The generation of Mormon leaders who succeeded Brigham Young "gave up polygamy . . . and other distinctive features of their background and attempted in many respects to become more American than the most American" (Foster 1991, 211).[6] The same problem plagued the celibate Shakers. Offering a haven for orphans, the Shakers raised many children, but few remained after reaching maturity.

Obviously the problem of the second generation is a serious one for utopian communities. Kat Kinkade, a charter member of Twin Oaks (see Kinkade 1973 and Komar 1989 for details on Twin Oaks), a community originally formed in 1967 to enact B. F. Skinner's principles of behaviorism (Skinner 1948), faces the issue squarely:

> It is important for the [Twin Oaks] Community to keep the flow of young people coming in to the Community. We have only fifteen children with an adult population of eighty-five, so are not a natural village. Those children we do raise are typically unwilling to spend their teen years here and unlikely to settle down in the place where they grew up. This means that our member replacements come entirely from the outside, and so our ultimate survival depends on attracting people in their twenties. (1994, 295)

With the usual decline in commitment to the original purposes on the part of their offspring, utopian communities frequently experience crises, and the result differs from one group to another. It has meant dissolution for some groups, internal dissension and renewal of purpose for others, and a changeover from utopian experimentation to conventionality for many. The interchange of members facilitated by the linkage of communities with one another and with groups of similar ideals is crucial for their very existence. In these circumstances, one should not expect a utopian community to remain static and, indeed, the evidence points to change as a regular feature of even the most conservative (see Pitzer 1997).

Utopians in the Great Depression

The Great Depression of the 1930s was a time of intense activity in utopian communities. Celo and Macedonia were established in 1937, and a number of community projects were sponsored by government and private groups. Whether the Depression era was one of the three grand cycles of American experimental utopian community-building (the others being the period 1800–1840 and the decades of the 1960s and 1970s), as Barkun contends (1984; Oved 1988 takes an opposing view), the developments of that period proved to be significant for community-building over the next several decades. In the next chapter, I examine some of these developments.

Notes

1. Besides New Harmony, Indiana, with which Owen was directly (if somewhat periph-erally) involved, and which endured only three years, other notable Owenite settlements included: "Frances Wright's Nashoba near Memphis, Tennessee; Adin Ballou's Hopedale in Massachusetts; Josiah Warren's Utopia in Ohio and Modern Times on Long Island; John Collin's Skaneateles in New York" (Pitzer 1989, 69).

2. A similar definition is proposed by Wagner. For his purposes, utopia is "any com-prehensive vision of an ideal society or any community that attempts to model itself on such a vision" (1982, 4). Communes, he writes, "are deliberative alternatives to the exist-ing social order; they attempt consciously to implement social innovations, not through the direct reform of the larger society, but through withdrawal into a small community composed of those who choose to live by the alternative structures" (ibid). The main difference from Hine, and an important one in my view, is that Wagner does not explic-itly include the utopians' goal, and usually expectation as well, of making a model that will be emulated by others.

3. Wallace's definition certainly applies to many American utopian efforts: "A revital-ization movement is defined as a deliberate, organized, conscious effort by members of a society to construct a more satisfying culture. Revitalization is thus, from a cultural stand-point, a special kind of culture change phenomenon: the persons involved in the process of revitalization must perceive their culture, or some major areas of it, as a system (whether accurately or not); they must feel that this cultural system is unsatisfactory; and they must innovate not merely discrete items but a new cultural system, specifying new relation-ships as well as, in some cases, new traits" (1956, 265).

4. Plath's Japanese groups (1966) and Barrett's African utopia (1977) appear to result from the influence of Western ideas. See Kumar 1989 and 1991, for the position that uto-pianism is restricted to the Western tradition.

5. Foster (1981) provides an example of how events and activities in the world outside

these communities can be relegated to a "larger society"—an unexpected lapse by a careful historian in an otherwise detailed and accurate account. Quite different is Fogarty's analysis of the House of David group, where the noncommunity neighbors and institutions are given extended treatment (Fogarty 1981).

6. "Whereas Mormonism grew up as a unique species of religious communitarianism, in time it developed into one of the staunchest defenders of the capitalist system that it had once so vehemently rejected. This social transformation provided the impetus for the emergence of various sectarian groups within modern Mormonism" (Baer 1988, xii). Baer counts more than one hundred splinter sects which emerged from Mormonism. See also Leone 1979.

PART 2

Creating Utopia

3. Utopia in the Great Depression

THE GREAT DEPRESSION of the 1930s called forth a multitude of schemes for social and economic salvation. Share-the-Wealth crusades, for example, assumed diverse forms, including the versions commended by Huey Long and the Townshend old-age pension plan. Socialist and Communist parties gathered new recruits and their programs assumed a public importance lacking in the previous or subsequent decades. Communist groups, adopting a "popular front" strategy, proclaimed their patriotism and loyalty to democratic principles. Earl Browder, general secretary of the Communist Party in the United States, declared that "communism is twentieth-century Americanism."

Quite a few reformist proposals "were crackpot illusions," in the words of one government report, but "many were the product of disciplined thought. Every idea of the reform or change of society that in good times lay hidden and unheard of came bounding to the surface when hard times grew harder" (Lord and Johnstone 1942, 11). With unemployment, hunger, and destitution so widespread, the demand for change and innovation could hardly have been clearer. It was a time of fear and desperation that is difficult for later generations to appreciate. Circumstances so dire called for urgent and exceptional measures.

Not just hunger, but the threat of revolution seemed to require immediate attention. In Congress, compassionate pleas for help were mixed with ominous predictions of social disorder. Addressing a House of Representatives committee in 1932, Bernarr MacFadden, a prominent physical cultist and publisher, declared: "Gentlemen, I think that unless something is done to relieve the serious unemployment we have everywhere we do not know what may happen to us. Firebrands of some kind may start most anything. Idleness is always dangerous, but when idleness is associated with hunger, and children are crying for bread, we cannot blame the people for being desperate" (quoted, Lord and Johnstone 1942, 27). On the Senate floor a member asked, "Senators, why are we so conceited as to think that the social and political structure of our country is so secure that nothing can destroy it? I should hate to voice in this public place the fears that I have as to what may happen. Hungry men are not going to stop because of the restrictions of laws imposed by orderly government . . . we cannot afford to disregard the menace of the situation" (quoted, Lord and Johnstone 1942, 28).

Even before Franklin Roosevelt's New Deal took the election of 1932, a number of private agencies had devised schemes to provide employment and relieve hunger and homelessness. Organizations as different as the Veterans of Foreign Wars, the pacifist Fellowship of Reconciliation, and the American Red Cross, among many others, shared in operating soup kitchens and organizing distribution networks for food that might otherwise have been wasted. Government-owned wheat was disbursed to cooperating bakers, who passed on the bread they baked to the hungry. Barter systems sprang up all over the country, to facilitate exchange in the absence of cash. Working hours were shortened in many areas so that available employment could be more widely shared.

The major ills of the country, as diagnosed by religious groups and government leaders of the New Deal, including President Roosevelt, were rooted in selfish individualism that had gone too far in the pursuit of profit. Glaring and unacceptable inequality resulted. Roosevelt's acceptance speech at the 1932 Democratic convention called for a new era of cooperation and a return to the virtues of the past. We must admit, he said, that "the profits of speculation, the easy road without toil, have lured us from the old barricades" (quoted, Shi 1985, 233). Cut-throat competition had to be replaced with cooperation and mutual aid. The cooperative motif was repeated in Roosevelt's inaugural address—the "moral stimulation of work no longer must be forgotten in the mad chase of evanescent profits"—and by his associates. Henry Wallace, Roosevelt's agricultural advisor, presented a somewhat different view of the past when he declared that the "keynote of the new frontier is cooperation just as that of the old frontier was individualistic competition" (quoted, Shi 1985, 233). Either recapturing former virtues or substituting cooperation for competition, a new balance of individualism and equality must be reached.

It was generally accepted that American cities were congested and that decentralization in industry and population would reinvigorate the economic as well as the moral life of the nation. The influential National Catholic Ru-

ral Life Conference pointed to "overcrowded industrial cities" as "incuba-
tors of disease, poverty and immorality unspeakable" and urged that people leave the choked cities to return to the "sane, normal mode of life" of rural
areas. Not only were there spiritual and economic benefits to be derived from
"this back-to-the-land movement," but political turmoil might also be averted: a "list of the large industrial centers will give you a list of the Communist hotbeds." The "sooner [urban] crowding is relieved the sooner . . . will
the Communist bogey vanish" (quoted, Lord and Johnstone 1942, 15).
Roosevelt seemed to agree: in a January 1933 speech, he said it was an urgent
task "to restore the balance of population" and remove the unemployed "out
of the big centers of population, so that they will not be dependent on home
relief" (quoted, Shi 1985, 234).

In addition to the primary effort to relieve the suffering of the unemployed
and revitalize the economy, Roosevelt "dreamed that he could engineer a
massive back-to-the-land movement" (Shi 1985, 234). Roosevelt and many
in his administration, as David Shi suggests, "harbored a desire to use Hamil-
tonian means (centralized planning and public financing) to encourage a
revival of Jeffersonian values" (233). The guiding principle of his New Deal,
declared Roosevelt in a Kansas City campaign speech in 1936, had been and
would continue to be a "fundamental belief that the American farmer, living on his own land, remains our ideal of self-reliance and of spiritual balance—the source from which the reservoirs of the nation's strength are constantly renewed" (quoted, Shi 1985, 234).

An early attempt to remove the unemployed from the cities and to instill
them with the superior virtues of rural life was the creation in 1933 of the
Civilian Conservation Corps. It was by far the most popular of all New Deal
programs and practically immune from criticism. Within two years, over half
a million young men were enrolled, living in austere conditions in CCC
camps, known as "Roosevelt Roosts" by many recruits, earning a dollar a day
(an additional twenty-five dollars a month was sent to their families) for
building bridges and roads, planting trees, and maintaining parks. When the
program was abolished in 1940, over two and a half million men had served
in the corps (Green 1992, 83).

Federal Sponsorship of New Communities

A less familiar part of the New Deal was the plan to establish, with federal
support, a number of new communities. Beginning in 1933, lodged in the
recently created Division of Subsistence Homesteads in the Department of

the Interior, the major goal of the plan was to settle poor families from city and country in new homestead communities. Inspired by the community planning and back-to-the land movements of the several decades before the Depression, the new communities "were to be examples of a new, organic society, with new values and institutions" (Conkin 1959, 6). Like many of the innovative steps taken by the federal government, building new communities was an ad hoc attempt to provide immediate solutions to problems of hunger, homelessness, and unemployment. Congress appears to have given little consideration to the long-term implications of such a project. It was, to be sure, a small part of the New Deal's programs of relief: ninety-nine communities were built (at a cost of 109 million dollars) before opposition in an increasingly conservative Congress ended the program in 1940.

Originated as a practical means to assist needy families, the project was "an experiment to meet a crisis rather than a measure of considered and fundamental long-term policy" (Lord and Johnstone 1942, 35). As it passed from one agency to another under a succession of administrators, it acquired different goals and justifications. One administrator remembered the project as "the beginning of a decentralization program for workers in industry" that could be widely applied. "The picture was," he went on, "of millions of workers living on small homesteads with some two or three acres of land for gardening or small farming, in some instances keeping a cow or a pig, certainly chickens, in this way having some backlog in case of unemployment" (Pickett 1953, 44). Variation in the program's goals and implementation was encouraged by the vagueness of the enabling legislation. Anxiety was voiced in congressional hearings that such an approach could lead to government-sponsored socialism, thus embracing exactly the kind of collectivism and radical egalitarianism some supporters meant to avoid. The name itself, "subsistence homestead," was significant; the intention was to reject any appearance of competition with commercial farming. To allow the homestead program to be seen as involved in farming for profit would alienate a powerful segment of the electorate that was itself in difficult economic straits. Moreover, it was not only the agricultural aspects of the program that were potential political snares. There was a general and "extreme sensitiveness on the part of government" to move in directions that might be claimed as competing with private enterprise (Pickett 1953, 44). As we shall see, the fears of government industrial competition were not misplaced.

Unclear as the objectives were, there was, in its first phase, clearly a utopian goal for the program. In an outline written just before he became head of the homesteads project in August 1933, M. L. Wilson stated that it should be regarded as "somewhat experimental and as foundation laying." Further, the "project is breaking virgin soil . . . by laying the basis for a new type of civilization in America" (quoted, Lord and Johnstone 1942, 39–40). That basis would in the main consist of widespread social and economic cooperation, which Wilson saw as "the only means of retaining democratic institutions" (Conkin 1959, 202).

Unlike most of the leaders of the back-to-the-land movement, Wilson was by background, training, and experience a farmer. Born on a farm in Iowa, he graduated from the state agricultural college, managed farms in Montana and served in various field capacities with the U.S. Department of Agriculture. Then, from a position as departmental chairman at Montana Agricultural College, he joined the New Deal in Washington. Respected by reformers and conservatives alike, his appointment as the first chief of the Division of Subsistence Homesteads was taken by conservatives "as assurance that the ideas of zealots and extremists would not dominate a movement in which he had a hand" (Lord and Johnstone 1942, 21).

Reflecting on relief programs in 1939, Wilson struck directly at the problem of welfare assistance for people so thoroughly imbued with the values and postulates of individualism. The psychological sense of inferiority felt by the involuntarily unemployed is not assuaged by welfare gifts and payments, he wrote. Furthermore, "Relief in the form of opportunity to help oneself by practice of subsistence farming would minister both to physical and psychological needs. It would redeem the spirit of independence and individual dignity along with supplying material needs. It would tend to create a sturdy rather than a servile citizenry" (Wilson 1939, 41).

Complementary and more forceful arguments for cooperative effort came from Rexford G. Tugwell, "whose desire for a collectivized, co-operative society was almost a religion," when he took over the program as chief of the new Resettlement Administration in 1935 (Conkin 1959, 202). (He retained his title as Under Secretary of Agriculture.) Tugwell later recalled that there was widespread nostalgia among New Deal intellectuals "for the simple days of the past when such terrible troubles were still unknown." Their historical picture was, he said, "largely imaginary . . . but it had reality in people's wishes" (quoted, Shi 1985, 234). While perhaps himself exempt from the desire for a return to those imaginary days of simplicity and Jeffersonian virtue, Tugwell maintained that "the most iniquitous institution was uncontrolled capitalism or, related to it, free enterprise, laissez-faire theories, competition, or, in his terms, any system that permitted the 'ganging up' of the unscrupulous few against the many, any system that invited struggle rather than cooperation, divisiveness rather than unity, bitterness rather than tolerance" (Conkin 1959, 149). Tugwell and his colleagues intended the communities to be the first stage in the creation of "a new society, with altered values and new institutions." The settlements were to serve as seedbeds of a new age of co-operation, "to demonstrate and advertise the new society to the rest of mankind. Planned by social scientists, financed by the vast resources of the government, they were to be visual signposts pointing to the future" (Conkin 1959, 186).

Among the community planners there existed a strong belief that the economic future of the United States lay in a mixture of self-sufficient homestead farming and industry. Industrial recovery, even at full employment (which many expected never to return), was clearly not foreseen as sufficient to cure economic depression. There was, as well, a sentiment that the uncurbed individualism that had marked the development of capitalism in the United States was the primary culprit in bringing on economic failure. For these visionary bureaucrats, "voluntary, democratic co-operation was to be the alternative to the economic insecurity and chaos of an individualistic, capitalistic past and to the involuntary, totalitarian collectivism of both fascism and communism" (Conkin 1959, 202–3).

From the beginning of the new-communities venture in 1933, an attitude of pragmatism prevailed. Lacking experience in the details of social planning, the designers of these new showcases of cooperation "were largely exploring new territory" (Conkin 1959, 329). The communities, particularly those established in the early years, were frankly designed as experimental. Each was in many ways a unique undertaking (Eaton 1950, 6), testimony to the trial-and-error attitude that marked many of the New Deal's projects. In its initial phase, the program took over funding for projects already started by private groups at the same time as plans were drawn for further construction by government. The intertwining of private and public sponsorship can be illustrated by the developments in two communities, one in Ohio, the other in the coal fields of West Virginia.

Experiment in Dayton

By late 1931 the full force of the Depression was felt in a number of American cities, including Dayton, Ohio, where a coalition of private welfare groups took action. Trying to maintain a philosophy of self-help, the coalition organized destitute families into "production units" that were supposed to relieve the city's welfare burden by meeting some of their own basic needs through handicraft. Lacking measurable success in their effort, the welfare coalition appointed Ralph Borsodi, a leader in the back-to-the-land movement, as consultant. Plans were drawn to settle poor families in the countryside outside Dayton, where they would occupy three-acre homesteads and support themselves with a mix of subsistence farming, wages (if possible), and handicraft production. Ownership of the land would remain vested in the homestead unit. Each family would pay an annual rent to the homestead unit for use of the land, but families would own improvements. The plan bore the unmistakable stamp of Borsodi's anti-industrial, decentralist agrarian ideas.

Borsodi, who until 1920 had been a marketing advisor in New York City, had moved to a seven-acre homestead in upstate New York and became an expert on subsistence farming. His success in achieving economic independence was described in two of his books, *This Ugly Civilization* and, later, *Flight from the City.* Borsodi abhorred the ugliness of urban industrialism, decrying this "civilization of noise, smoke, smells, and crowds—of people content to live amidst the throbbing of its machines; the smoke and smells of its factories; the crowds and discomforts of the cities of which it proudly boasts" (1929, 1). The factory rather than the machine was destructive, he thought; it was the factory system "which fills country and city with hideous factories and squalid slums, and which consumes forests, coal, iron and oil with a prodigality which will make posterity look back upon us as barbarians" (14). The savings of mass production, according to Borsodi, was not sufficient to cover the extra costs of distribution it required. Small labor-saving devices he favored, but the centralization or concentration of production he strongly condemned.

In the Dayton project, "recruits for the homesteads . . . were not chosen for their interest in homesteading as a way of life for escaping from the ugly civilization" (Issel 1967, 160). They would continue to work for wages in Dayton, and many of them complained about Borsodi's leadership. Borsodi emphasized home production, handicrafts, and self-sufficiency. He was convinced that the goal was primarily educational: "to change the homesteaders' notions of the good life and their ways of securing the necessities and satisfactions of life" (quoted, Issel 1967, 160).

After the first steps in the homesteading effort, the Dayton coalition found itself short of funds and applied for a federal government loan. M. L. Wilson, in charge of approving loans for the purchase of subsistence homesteads, solicited Borsodi's advice about how the funds could best be used. To no one's surprise, Borsodi recommended that the Dayton project receive a loan. It was an attractive request, since the project was already underway with local support and was directed by Borsodi, a recognized expert in homesteading. Also, Wilson was in sympathy with Borsodi's decentralist ideas and his view that homesteading was educational (Issel 1967, 161). Indeed, Borsodi's own account singles out Wilson as a kindred spirit: "So I went to Washington and persuaded the New Deal, through Harry Hopkins, Harold Ickes [Secretary of the Interior] and, above all, M. L. Wilson, to finance the projects. Of all the men in places of power with whom I dealt, Dr. Wilson alone understood what I meant when I said that the Dayton homestead plan was different— that it was essentially educational in nature" (Borsodi 1948, 1:vii–viii).

For a number of reasons, the project collapsed in late 1935, after only eighteen months. Property losses by fire, homesteaders' complaints about Borsodi's "arbitrary and autocratic" management, and the protests of farmers in the area that the coalition was shuttling city slum dwellers without considering local residents—all were serious problems. Most acute, however, was the bitter opposition from an association of property owners over the plan to build a homestead unit for African-Americans. The breaking point came when two Dayton newspapers declared strong opposition to Borsodi's ideas and his leadership (Issel 1967, 162).

Meanwhile, Secretary Ickes had decreed an end to the kind of local initiative and control encouraged by Wilson, and the federal program took on a centralized aspect. Shortly thereafter, in the summer of 1934, Wilson resigned his position as director. Borsodi left Dayton, where the homesteading effort had been, he wrote later, ruined by "red-tape, absentee bureaucratic dictation and politics" (Borsodi 1948, 1:viii).[1]

From Dayton, Borsodi went to found the School of Living in Suffern, New York, where he carried out a number of carefully recorded experiments in homesteading. His efforts subsequently led to the building of several homestead villages in rural New York and New Jersey, with financial assistance from the Independence Foundation, a private foundation Borsodi had formed. None of the projects survived for more than a few years, although Borsodi maintained a position well into the 1950s as a leader in homesteading and community building (Fogarty 1980, 17–18; Loomis 1965, 186–96; Issel 1967, 165–66). Several decades later, advocates of land trusts credited Borsodi's School of Living for pioneering steps toward decentralization and land reform. His venture in Dayton was heralded in the 1990s as an important benchmark in the history of land trust formation. Liberty Homesteads, the settlement established outside Dayton in 1933, is now confidently described as "chartered as a land trust with leases for individual homesteaders according to non-speculative, Georgist principles" (Questenberry 1992, 117).

Blessed by the First Lady

The creation of a model community near Reedsville, West Virginia, was an instance of a private effort in which the government stake was obvious from the start. Before Roosevelt took office and set the New Deal in motion, the American Friends Service Committee (AFSC), at the request of President Hoover's Committee on Unemployment Relief and the Federal Children's Bureau, began a series of relief programs among the families of coal miners in West Virginia, Maryland, Kentucky, Tennessee, Illinois, and Pennsylvania. Soon the AFSC programs, directed by its executive secretary, Clarence Pickett, grew from feeding and clothing children to a larger enterprise in which coal miners and their families were resettled on subsistence farms, handicraft shops were set up, and garden clubs organized (Conkin 1959, 35). Eleanor Roosevelt took special interest in the AFSC's planned community called Arthurdale located at Reedsville, West Virginia. This became one of the first federally sponsored projects and led, partly through Mrs. Roosevelt's recommendation, to the appointment of Pickett as a senior administrator in the Division of Subsistence Homesteads (Conkin 1959, 36; Pickett 1953, 41–64).

Not only were the first steps of the federal community project influenced by these and other private ventures, the public projects shared the utopian vision of the part such communities might play in a new American society. In addition, the people involved in government and private projects tended to overlap. Clarence Pickett was chosen by Borsodi as a member of the board of directors of the new Independence Foundation, established in 1935 to provide assistance to new homesteading settlements. (Later, Pickett would fill a similar slot on the board of directors of Celo Community.)

An unmistakable legacy of the earlier efforts of Pickett and the AFSC was the "fervent attempt to revive handicrafts, such as weaving, wood-working, and metalwork" in the federal communities program (Conkin 1959, 193). This seriously intended but economically minor part of the federal plans for the model communities demonstrated the strength of a nostalgic yearning to recover from a romanticized rural past those elements deemed useful for self-sufficiency in the new economic future. Reviving handicrafts was one element in the movement to provide impoverished rural folk a larger measure of autonomy and self-direction as they set about the creation of a democratically cooperative society.

Borsodi's position was forthright, as he reported on his family's progress in their withdrawal from urban life to search for economic independence and self-sufficiency on a rural homestead. A champion of the revival of domestic handicrafts wherever practical, Borsodi held neither Luddite disdain for modern machinery nor commitment to willing endurance of discomfort for the sake of principle. He explained his family's experience: "it is no exaggeration to say that we started our quest of comfort with all the discomforts possible in the country, and, because of the machines [we purchased and used] we have now achieved more comforts than the average prosperous city man enjoys" (Borsodi 1933, 7). Generalizing from his own experience, Borsodi was convinced of the benefits to be derived from widespread adoption of homesteading. His soaring declaration of belief proclaimed:

> Domestic production, if enough people turned to it, would not only annihilate the undesirable and non-essential factory by depriving it of a market for its products. It would do more. It would release men and women from their present thralldom to the factory and make them masters of machines instead of servants to them; it would end the power of exploiting them which ruthless, acquisitive, and predatory men now possess; it would free them for the conquest of comfort, beauty and understanding. (Borsodi 1933, 9)

It was a vision widely shared among government bureaucrats and utopian reformers (Whisenhunt 1983), a vision that Tugwell and Wilson aimed to realize in their planned communities. Once achieved on a small scale, in an assortment of pilot projects, the example would surely lead to widespread emulation. But obstacles to bringing the dream to fruition arose almost immediately.

Opposition to Community-Building

The expectation that private industry would build plants near the communities to provide at least part-time employment was not met. Cooperative industries seemed to many to be the obvious solution, but the homesteaders' inexperience and the need for immediate employment led to the abandonment of this option. The recourse was to government-owned factories, but opposition was swift and effective. Late in 1933 plans were underway to build a furniture factory to put the idle miners at Arthurdale to work making post-office equipment. Land had been purchased and blueprints drawn when a congressional committee got wind of the project. The opinions of congressmen were emphatic: the government, said one representative, is "embarking in a business in direct competition with private industry." The "entire policy," declaimed another, "is one of nationalization of industry" and a third declared it "just a proposition to further the socialistic program already launched by this administration." A lengthy speech by an Indiana representative summarized his colleagues' objections, branding the project a "real menace to posterity" which would "tend to lead the Government God knows where in the direction of sovietizing all industry" and "sound the death knell of individual liberty in America" (quoted, Lord and Johnstone 1942, 49–50). The plan for a furniture factory was discarded; postal fixtures continued to come from private industry.

In general, opposition to the homestead program came from two directions: from a Congress highly critical of the program and increasingly reluctant to fund it, and from the conservative recalcitrance of the inhabitants of the new settlements. Congressional opposition began within a year after the Farm Security Administration was established. A long and bitter controversy followed, during which "the communities, once so loved and cherished by their planners and creators, became, in the minds of many congressmen, disreputable, heretical, and exceedingly wasteful symbols of misguided idealism or even of ideological treason" (Conkin 1959, 214). With industrial labor enjoying many benefits in the New Deal, the Farm Security Administration, "inheritor of Tugwell's distinct class feelings," took on the coloring of a "labor union for small farmers, tenants, and laborers" (Conkin 1959, 221). Congress appropriated funds in 1938 for the "liquidation" of the settlements, but little action followed. The next year, funds for completion of communities under construction were refused, and in 1940 Congress canceled a federal loan program used for the same purpose.

Congressional charges focused on the cooperative basis of the federal communities, particularly the feature of long-term leases for community settlers, which was labeled as contrary to American traditions of individual land ownership. One congressman declared fee simple ownership of land "one of the fundamentals in the establishment of this country"; another held the issue of lease or ownership crucial "because it involves a great principle; it goes deep into the traditional land policy of this country" (quoted, Conkin 1959, 226). Finally, in 1944, in the minority report of an investigation that led to the end of the FSA and its community program, "Tugwell was falsely accused of filling his agency with 'thousands of utopian planners who were "hell bent" on remaking the United States into a Communist State.' They argued that the [investigating] committee had 'uncovered hundreds of communistic projects'" (quoted, Conkin 1959, 228).

The second source of difficulty, like congressional opposition, grew over the course of several years and, in the end, proved insurmountable. From the first, there were inconsistencies in the criteria used to recruit families into the program. To satisfy the demands of fiscal responsibility, the program had been centralized within a year of its birth, and rents for homesteads were set at rates that would reasonably meet the costs of building and maintaining the communities. This meant that the most needy families had little chance of being accepted. Most of those who did move into the new communities had little interest or experience in gardening or animal husbandry. Some homestead projects were located too far from urban centers, thus making it doubtful that residents would find jobs to provide necessities they could not raise on their three-acre plots. When a new community was judged success- ful, it was usually due to the homesteaders' prior involvement in consumer or farm cooperatives (as in Granger Homesteads, Iowa).

Between those who planned the communities and those who lived in them there was a lack of agreement about the nature of the project. This lack of fit between Tugwell and the community designers in Washington, on one hand, and, on the other, the farmers and unemployed workers who were resettled in the new communities, was expressed in various ways. At first, in the early years of the New Deal, widespread enthusiasm for reform existed in the United States. Eager applicants for life in the new settlements were easily found. As opposition to the early New Deal formed, in government and among the country's citizens, the flush of experimentalism paled. The gov- ernment's resettlement communities became objects of curiosity, subject to a steady wave of visits by academic researchers, government investigators, and news reporters. Thus put on display—some communities "aroused almost as much critical curiosity as nudist colonies or the early Oneida"—the resi- dents were understandably resentful (Conkin 1959, 212). More important than their dislike of this show window aspect of community life, and more than the frequent expressions of disagreement with the "close supervision and rigid limitations on individual initiative" (Conkin 1959, 213), the simple fact was that the new settlers overwhelmingly had the goal of economic security for themselves and their families. They were not out to show the world a new society; a home of one's own was a far more powerful incentive. As the econ- omy improved with preparations for war, jobs outside the communities at- tracted more and more residents; a high rate of turnover in the communi- ties resulted. Even before the improvement of economic conditions in the late 1930s, dissatisfaction had led to turnover rates as high as 400 percent in a single year in a few communities. As Conkin sums it up,

> At a time when public opinion was becoming more conservative, the commu- nity program was becoming more daringly experimental, and departing far- ther from traditional institutions, than ever before. The community idea, so appealing in the abstract, was much more difficult to achieve in actuality than

almost anyone believed possible in 1933. The raw material for the completed communities was both physical and human, and the latter proved very unpredictable and sometimes intractable. All too often the settlers were not anxious to participate in experimental reforms leading to a new America which they could not understand or appreciate. They simply wanted economic security. (Conkin 1959, 329)

New Deal Outcomes

Although relatively brief in its existence, the federal homestead program was in many ways part of a renewed interest in experimental communities in the United States and elsewhere (Shor 1987, 82). In some instances, social reformers who failed to achieve sufficient attention for their plans turned to community-building to demonstrate the soundness of their reform proposals (Whisenhunt 1983, 103). Other settlements continued the long tradition of utopian community-building in America, now with the emphasis on homesteading and self-sufficiency as a path to greater social and economic security. All promised alternative routes to a better life through decentralization and cooperation.

The difficulty of finding residents who shared the utopian vision of community founders often shaped the early history of nongovernment projects. The Sunrise Colony in Michigan, for example, was founded in 1933, subsequently received financial support from the federal government, but lasted for only three years as its membership responded to improving economic opportunities outside the settlement. The dreams of community leaders and assessments from intellectual allies outside Sunrise were frequently at odds with the goals of colonists. Sunrise's founder, Joseph J. Cohen, claimed: "We saw ourselves building a new world, a heaven on earth, a kingdom of justice for all who would join and do their share." The Socialist leader Norman Thomas visited the community and pronounced: "Here we have a living and inspiring example of the coming socialist order that will liberate mankind from its bondage" (quoted, Shor 1987, 85). The promise of conventional chances for economic security through employment outside Sunrise, however, proved a more potent attraction than building a new world.[2]

The consequences of economic improvement for other communities established during the Depression, and before, varied. Llano experienced a rapid increase of population as the unemployed poured in; sometimes up to a dozen arrived daily (Conkin 1964, 124). Macedonia Cooperative Community and Celo Community, both founded in the later years of the decade, survived by drawing in idealistic new members who seemed to share the vision of creating a new social order. Both communities underwent a total replacement of membership as their original residents left to take jobs in war industries.

Aside from the efforts of the various agencies involved in building resettlement communities, and the strenuous push for a new era of cooperation and decentralization, other New Deal endeavors held out utopian visions of building a new society. Of a different magnitude from the homestead communities was the federal government's application of community ideas to urban planning. While only three greenbelt towns were completed, they "remain the grandest monuments of Rexford G. Tugwell's work in the Resettlement Administration" (Conkin 1959, 305).

One of the most enduring of these New Deal efforts, the Tennessee Valley Authority, was initially directed by Arthur E. Morgan, whose credentials as a utopian planner were unassailable. Under Morgan, a "practical visionary devoted to the simple life" (Shi 1985, 235), the TVA aimed to bring enlightenment and vigor to the rural regions of the Tennessee Valley. Near the end of his tenure as chairman of the TVA, Morgan arranged for the purchase of land and the establishment of Celo Community. Although Celo occupied only part of Morgan's attention, and was only one in a lengthy series of similar utopian projects that he inspired, assisted, or developed, his relationship with Celo continued to the very end of his long life and the members of the Community attempted to put into practice many of his ideas about community life. An effort to understand Celo therefore requires, first, some attention to Morgan's biography.

Notes

1. Borsodi's *Flight from the City* includes plans for the houses and homesteads at Dayton.

2. Similar conditions prevailed in Puget Sound, as the economy rose from the depression conditions of the 1890s: utopian communities failed to attract new members, and a local demand for labor drew off those who had already joined (LeWarne 1975, 234–35).

4. A New Deal Utopian

IN RECOUNTING some details of the life of Celo's founder, Arthur E. Morgan, it is not my intention to endorse a "great man" theory of history or a psychological explanation for Celo Community's existence. The primary purpose is rather to deepen the understanding of Celo's history, to explore the assortment of factors which led to its birth and lengthy endurance. For this purpose, it is significant that, in his own view, Morgan's career as professional engineer was secondary to his role as moral tutor. He considered himself above all an educator, not just for the particular projects he directed but as a model-maker for the nation as a whole. A lack of formal education did not deter him from becoming an acclaimed college president and the first head of the Tennessee Valley Authority. His reputation as scholar and social philosopher was enhanced by his many books and articles, and by his association with intellectuals like John Dewey and H. G. Wells. With Ralph Borsodi, Rexford Tugwell, and others, he gained a national reputation for his advocacy of moral reform and he was, like Dewey, a strong advocate of the position that the basis of American civilization was the small community. And only his life history can convey his attitude of arrogant self-righteousness observed by many associates.

Perhaps most important for Celo Community, Morgan had firm associations with business and industrial leaders which paved the way for Celo's financial security. Quite different from other similar community experiments, Celo began with solid financial support. Finally, although Morgan paid only brief visits to Celo over the years, the members constantly aspired to exhibit his ideas in the Community's structure.

Morgan's Early Years

Born into a family of modest circumstances in 1878, Arthur Morgan is easily taken as an example of that American hero, the self-made man. His father was a self-taught engineer and surveyor. As Morgan's wife recalled, doubtless basing her opinion on what she had heard from her husband, the father "had considerable initiative along some lines, but his 'laziness,' from whatever cause it sprang, kept him from following his calling energetically, and prevented him all his life from being a success financially" (L. Morgan 1928, 6; see also Morgan 1957b, 7–10; Talbert 1987, 9). Morgan's mother, "a slight and rigidly puritanical schoolma'am from Massachusetts" (L. Morgan 1928, 17), molded Arthur into "a most pious young man" (Talbert 1987, 9).[1] Nevertheless, his father's scientific interests won out over the mother's religious convictions and, from early in his high school years, Morgan maintained a liberal religious outlook and a strong interest in science.

At the age of sixteen Morgan had a vision of an ideal community. It was an experience so impressive that, even at age ninety, he could give a detailed account of it. Obviously the extent to which his memory was embellished by a lifetime of utopian experimentation is unknown, but his vision provides an unusual glimpse of concrete details otherwise lacking in his many prescriptions for utopia. As he described it,

> There was a group of houses, unpainted and in the natural wood color, with perhaps four to eight rooms. There were also a blacksmith shop, barns, farm lands, and some little industries. Living standards were very simple indeed. The teachers or leaders lived in modest homes with or near the boys and girls. They all learned practical things by the processes of living, and a philosophy of life by reading and group discussions and by thinking things out by themselves. There was complete freedom to think, to inquire and to doubt, but also a strong spirit of aspiration, of commitment, and of self-discipline. The product of the school would be young men and women who had achieved a way of life, and who had learned how to make a living without compromising their convictions, who had learned to love nature, and who had an appetite for mental and spiritual growth.
>
> I had come to the conclusion that the way to build a new world was to build it on a small scale, where a desirable life might be lived in all respects, as a unity. At that time my ideas had not found expression in such formal language but all the elements were there.
>
> This picture gradually took definiteness and I began to dream of making it my major life interest. At first this was more or less a dream of what would be desirable. I might have grown up and have written a Utopia about it. But grad-

ually I began to think—perhaps I can do it. (quoted from tape recorded interview, Leuba 1971, 55–56)

Living with kinsmen in Denver for a few years, Morgan dropped out of college after two attempts, took various jobs at casual labor, then returned to Minnesota in 1900 to work with his father as an engineer. Within a few years, he had achieved a reputation as a specialist in drainage and flood control engineering and held offices in Minnesota's state engineers society. His stature as an engineer grew as he took on more projects in the design of flood control dams.

It was his work in the aftermath of the devastating flood of 1913 in Dayton, Ohio, however, that brought him national prominence. Called in to design a series of dams to prevent a recurrence of a flood that had left three hundred dead and huge property damage, Morgan systematically collected data on floods in this country and Europe. Based on this research, Morgan designed and built five earthen dry dams, which "represented a new concept in this country. . . . Morgan was the first to put the principle into operation" (Talbert 1987, 37).

In his ideas about social reform, Morgan was a Progressive. Underlying the moral authoritarianism of Progressivism, certainly for Morgan and the young engineers of his acquaintance, was a "propensity to assume a moral and scientific advantage over other people" (Talbert 1987, 33). Moral elitism formed a consistent theme of Morgan's writings and plans for reform: as he declared in 1930, "in ethics, as in every field, genius sets standards which become authority to those who recognize excellence, even where they cannot create" (quoted, Talbert 1987, 57). There is no doubt that Morgan included himself among those who set authoritative standards.

Morgan found support for his plans for reform in his personal life as well. His first marriage, in 1904, ended with the death of his wife within a year, leaving him with an infant son. His second wife, Lucy, whom he married in 1911, became his lifelong companion and partner in a number of efforts at social improvement. A teacher of chemistry and home economics at Wellesley College, Lucy was a Quaker with ardent reformist tendencies: "as a nutrition expert she could be righteous in her assertion of the necessity of a proper diet and efficient, moral living" (Talbert 1987, 28). She seems to have revived the visions of Morgan's youth, and she shared his dream of creating a model community and school.

As important as preventing floods through innovative dam construction, in Morgan's view, was the opportunity offered by the Ohio project for wholesome improvement. He built new model communities for workers, with day schools for children, and set up night classes where immigrants could learn English, along with technical skills and ethical codes. He provided health and accident insurance for workers, with newspapers, recreational programs, and town meetings at each work site. As his biographer, Roy Talbert Jr., notes, "reform, both technical and social, was the order of the day, and no other major construction project could boast such enlightened leadership" (1987, 37; see also McCraw 1970, 8).

With the successful completion of the Ohio flood control project, Morgan abandoned any day-to-day involvement with the engineering profession and turned his efforts in other directions, beginning with educational reform. While still living in Ohio, he established an alternative to what he and his associates perceived as the inferior public schools of Dayton. Supported by a number of business leaders—among them were Edward Deeds, chairman of Ohio's flood control board; Charles Kettering, inventor of the electric automobile starter; and Orville Wright—Morgan founded the Moraine Park School as a coeducational program with classes from kindergarten through college preparatory. It opened in 1917 with sixty students. Although his involvement rapidly diminished, it was Morgan's educational ideas that found concrete expression in the curricular principle that the learning of values outweighed the learning of facts. The school stressed self-reliance, student self-governance, and student participation in teaching. A 1920 handbook of private schools singled out Moraine Park School as "one of the most promising educational experiments in recent years" (quoted, Talbert 1987, 43).

Association with the experimental school in Dayton led to national recognition for Morgan, and he was asked by the *Atlantic Monthly* to write about his educational ideas. He took the opportunity to issue a sharp criticism of the separation of education from practical matters (1918). Morgan was strongly influenced by the ideas of Pestalozzi and modern American educators and writers, including John Dewey, that education had to do with real life and should not be separated from it. For the next two decades, the pages of the *Atlantic Monthly* served up Morgan's ideas on civilization, education, and community in article after article (e.g., Morgan 1942a).[2]

Architect of Community

These achievements were but prologue to Morgan's greatest opportunity, this time as a college president, to influence American educational practice. In 1921 he became president of Antioch College. The college trustees, having failed to sell the financially stricken college to the YMCA, named Morgan to the board of trustees in 1919. Within six weeks he had devised a plan to rescue the school from financial ruin and to overhaul the educational program.

His wife fondly recalled traveling with him from Dayton to Yellow Springs, Ohio, just prior to Morgan's appointment: "We will never forget that trip. . . . Arthur's verdict was, 'I believe it is near enough dead to start over in the form I dream of.' We decided to give up the idea of a school at Jacob's Pillow [Massachusetts], and dedicated our lives to embodying our dreams at Antioch College" (L. Morgan 1928, 100).

Armed with a broad grant of authority from the trustees, Morgan radically restructured the college curriculum. The result was what became known as the Antioch Plan. Although it was not his invention, and he many times disclaimed credit for the plan, Morgan became identified as its initiator. As first conceived, Morgan wanted a number of small industries near the college, to "provide practical life experiences for students, an income for the college, and an opportunity to pioneer in creating a new industrial atmosphere in which the profit motive, though present and essential, would be subordinated to more significant human values" (Leuba 1971, 151).

The main feature of the Antioch Plan called for each student to spend four hours per day in class and four hours working at a job in the community. Unable to attract sufficient industry where students could shift from class to work, he was forced to modify the work/study plan by broadening the geographical area for employment and setting the alternation of work and study at periods of several months rather than by hours per day. Morgan's accomplishments at Antioch flowed directly from his conviction that school and community, life and education, should not be separated. In the assessment of his biographer, "What Morgan did that was innovative was to extend the cooperative concept to the liberal arts program. All students at Antioch would work, whether they needed the money or not. In making practical experience a core requirement, Morgan introduced the pioneering aspect of his work at Antioch and made his greatest contribution to modern American higher education" (Talbert 1987, 48).

Within a year of Morgan's inauguration, Antioch's enrollment quadrupled, from less than one hundred to four hundred students, its faculty doubled, and the revived college was the subject of numerous newspaper and magazine stories. The new curriculum received the endorsement of many nationally known writers and educators. More important for the long term, the Antioch Plan attained permanence and was adopted in some form by a number of American colleges.

Nevertheless, Morgan was disappointed; his success at Antioch fell far short of what he had envisioned. He had begun with wide powers to hire and fire.

As a condition of accepting the presidency, he had demanded, and received, the resignations of all trustees and faculty. Very few incumbents of either category were reappointed; Morgan's new twenty-member faculty included only five who had taught at Antioch before 1921. Ruling the college with a heavy hand, Morgan aimed at more than educational reform: Antioch would be the place where new standards of morality were developed. In his vision, the college should serve as a model for the moral regeneration of American society in general (Talbert 1987, 61).

If Antioch were to become no more than a respected liberal arts college, then he wanted out. As he announced to his faculty in 1931, he had hoped to build at Antioch a community with spiritual qualities and "a marked and sustained difference of purpose and of commitment from those of society at large" (quoted, Talbert 1987, 64). But his efforts reaped only disenchantment. As he said, "When I compare Antioch with what I believe to be my reasonable expectations for such an institution, and what were certainly my hopes for Antioch, I feel a very keen disappointment. . . . I am disappointed that we do not break through the current ways of life with greater creative discontent. . . . We too largely accept as a whole the mental and emotional pattern of the day and we are bent chiefly on improving and refining it in detail" (quoted, Leuba 1971, 160).

The basic problem was a contradiction in Morgan's leadership. On the one hand, he repeatedly called for students and faculty to eschew conventional morality and to seek their own standards through rigorous and independent thinking. Yet, on the other, he demanded total allegiance from faculty, staff, and students, including adherence to the moral code promulgated by Arthur E. Morgan. From the beginning of his term as Antioch's president, in Talbert's words, "To work for Morgan meant either to become his devotee or to leave. Only those who shared the vision could stay. His relationships, like his morality, were absolute, and he had a way of forcing conversion or rejection" (1987, 54). It was not a new attitude in Morgan's dealings with others, and the label of "sanctimonious Yankee moralist and mystic," given him by one historian (Shi 1985, 237), was not far off the mark. The Antioch faculty posed the problem to him in a straightforward question: "Is it possible to conduct a college with definite moral aims on democratic principles?" (quoted, Talbert 1987, 65).

Morgan discerned serious deficiencies in democratic procedures. Democracy was wasteful, for one thing, and thus contrary to his progressive principles of efficiency. "In the determination of public issues," he declared in 1936, "the ballot of the most stupid and ignorant voter counts as much as that of the wisest and most public spirited. By this arbitrary device valuable resources of public judgment are lost" (1936, 67). He had for many years made business decisions along Quaker lines, through his conception of consensus. This did not mean, he wrote, "taking formal votes on the 'one man, one vote' principle. Consensus of judgment may be arrived at by the deference of the many who do not know to the superior judgment of the few who do. The balance of competence to judge may shift endlessly as different subjects for judgment arise" (quoted, Talbert 1987, 150). There was no question that Morgan counted himself among the competent on most issues.

His relations with the faculty continued to deteriorate. Convinced of failure in his attempt to build a model for a new society, but that the failure was largely due to character faults of faculty members and students, Morgan prepared to leave Antioch. He was saved from the distress of an unpleasant separation by President Roosevelt's call to service as the first chairman of the new Tennessee Valley Authority. For Morgan, it was a summons to a moral pulpit of far grander proportions than that available to a college president. It was a chance to construct a new society to match his vision.

Visions of Community

Morgan firmly believed that the small community was the indispensable foundation of civilization. Over many years, in one book and article after another, he argued for the superiority of small communities, not as they existed but as they might become. American communities, deficient in imagination and cultural variety, were sterile and provincial, victims of "great, centralized, impersonal organizations" which had steadily erased the "intimate and refining influences of small communities" (Morgan 1942b, 280). No wonder most young people in such places left as soon as possible! An advocate of eugenics, he asserted that "one of the most dysgenic customs has been for the abler, more vigorous and more purposeful young people to leave the small communities, where people more generally have large families, for the cities where in the past the birth rate has been altogether too low to replace the parents" (Morgan 1957c, 148–49). Communities were indispensable, he wrote, for the preservation of democracy. Individual freedom must be nourished but it can only exist where there is "mutual regard and responsibility" (Morgan 1942b, 280). Blending community life and democratic government, he wrote, is

> to save and to enlarge the priceless values of [individual] freedom, while yet developing the qualities of mutual regard, mutual help, mutual responsibility, and common effort for common ends. That is the problem of democracy. Ac-

tual democracy cannot originate in large masses or by legislation. It is a way of
life which must be learned by the intimate associations of family and community. While the community is developing a sense of mutual responsibility, and
while it is working out common plans, there should be constant endeavor to
save individual freedom and initiative. (Morgan 1942b, 280–81)[3]

Efforts to create new communities, particularly the utopian experiments
of the nineteenth century, elicited his admiration. Critical of Oneida and
Amana (among others) as "lacking a mature and well-proportioned concept
of the community as a fundamental element of human culture," Morgan
nevertheless applauded them as worthy experiments (1942b, 101). "The creation of new communities . . . [is] among the more important and universal ways in which societies the world over have maintained their vitality and
have advanced in type" (Morgan 1957c, 140–41). Building intentional communities has been one of the "great creative forces in history," and the great
"proportion of failures" should not blind us to the recognition that "the rewards and fruits of those that have succeeded have extended to the furthest
reaches of mankind" (141). One way to achieve success in community-building, he suggested, was that such communities, each with "its own unique
character," might associate themselves and "each perform some service which
helps the whole to meet varied needs" (144).

Aside from his inspirational and practical advisories, Morgan tackled utopianism from a scholarly angle. As a young man he was captivated by Edward Bellamy's *Looking Backward* and took Bellamy as a model for himself
(McCraw 1970). Later, he published a well-received biography of Bellamy,
followed the next year by an explication of Bellamy's philosophy (Morgan
1944, 1945). *Nowhere Was Somewhere,* in which Morgan presented the "theory that [Sir Thomas] More's book [*Utopia*] in the main is not a fictitious
story, but a record of a trip to Peru and of what was observed there," has not
fared nearly as well (Morgan 1946, 34). Critics have taken a rather negative
view of Morgan's thesis; Bestor, for example, labels it an "extreme subjective
interpretation" (Bestor 1970, 293; see Filler 1954 for a more positive view).[4]

But *Nowhere Was Somewhere* covered far more ground than More's fantasy. Morgan's main goal was to demonstrate the reciprocal influence of utopian ideas and historical occurrences. Most of the book is skillfully argued,
especially if one accepts Morgan's definition of utopia as including "plans
of government or schemes for social improvement which present the possibilities of a good society" (Morgan 1946, 3). Thus, the Constitution of the
United States, "offspring of utopias as it was, became itself a utopia to be
taken, often blindly and uncritically, as the fundamental law of many other
nations" (Morgan 1946, 8).

Morgan's hero Bellamy comes in for special attention. Constructing an ideational genealogy, Morgan writes that *Looking Backward* "largely crystallized and gave form to liberal thinking in America. It gave birth to the 'Nationalist' movement, the principles of which in turn were fumblingly adopted by the Populist party. . . . [and] the Democratic party took over Populist doctrines and further infected America with them" (Morgan 1946, 9). Bellamy's novel is credited with significant influence on Roosevelt's New Deal. Not only are there "striking parallels" between Bellamy's book "and various important and detailed elements of New Deal public policy," but Morgan declares "with considerable force that to understand the long-range implications of the New Deal one must read *Looking Backward*" (ibid.). Morgan set out to follow a "great *pattern* of action" offered in the New Deal, a pattern based ultimately in a transmutation of Bellamy's liberal and progressive ideas. Following the pattern, Morgan the social engineer might make real the utopian "possibilities of a good society" (4, 3).

The Tennessee Valley Authority

Legislation passed by Congress in May 1933 established the Tennessee Valley Authority as an independent government agency and endowed it with broad powers for the integrated development of the Tennessee River basin, an area of forty-one thousand square miles with a population of three million. In addition to taking over an existing dam and fertilizer plant at Muscle Shoals, Alabama, the TVA, under the command of a three-man board of directors, was to construct a series of dams along the river and its tributaries. The dams would produce hydroelectric power, control flooding, and improve navigation. Along with the generation and distribution of electric power, the agency would build plants for the manufacture of low-cost fertilizer. The TVA was to conduct economic and social surveys in the region and promote the improvement of agriculture and the expansion of industry. It was acknowledged to be a public works project of unprecedented size and eventually led to the building and control of over thirty dams.

Morgan, called to Washington by President Roosevelt to discuss his appointment as chairman of the board of the new TVA, recalled many years later that he had made it clear to the president that he

> had reservations about public service, because of the usual necessity for following the dictates of political patronage, and that I did not want to be associated with that process as I thought it had long-range harmful effects on the course of government. He [Roosevelt] pounded his fist on the table and said, "There

is to be no politics in this!" I felt then that I wanted the job. When he spent most of our time together talking not about dams or electric power or fertilizer but about the quality of life of the people of the Tennessee Valley, I was quite certain of it. (Morgan 1974, 7)

As it turned out, under the direction of both Morgan and his successor as chairman, David E. Lilienthal, employment at all levels of the TVA was remarkably free of political patronage, although, as Morgan reported, there was strong pressure by congressmen and some of Roosevelt's cabinet officers to use TVA jobs as political rewards.

Acceding to Roosevelt's demands, Morgan chose an expert on southern agriculture and "a man competent in power development" as the other two directors (Morgan 1974, 7). H. A. Morgan (unrelated to A. E. Morgan), the agriculturalist, known for his research in the problems of controlling the cotton boll weevil, had been president of the University of Tennessee (McCraw 1970, 12–16). For the third director, Morgan selected David E. Lilienthal, a young lawyer who had served on the Wisconsin public utilities commission and came with the high recommendation of Supreme Court Justice Louis Brandeis (McCraw 1970, 18). In the first few months, Morgan made a number of decisions on his own, leading H. A. Morgan to complain of some of the chairman's pronouncements as decision-making by "official bull" (quoted, McCraw 1970, 31). Only in August, at the suggestion of H. A. Morgan, was a division of authority agreed upon: H. A. Morgan would plan and supervise the agricultural aspects of the project, Lilienthal would take charge of the electric power and legal aspects, and Arthur Morgan would direct the construction of dams, social and economic planning, and "integration of the parts of the program into a unified whole" (McCraw 1970, 32). Cordiality among the three directors seemed assured; only later did a vast difference emerge in their respective visions of the potentialities in the TVA.

For Arthur Morgan, the TVA "was to be nothing less than the culmination of his life work, and for that reason it was a combination of what he had done before" (Talbert 1987, 109). It was a chance to recapture and fulfill his dream of a new moral and cultural order that had been disappointed at Antioch. Near the end of his long life, he noted the similarity of the TVA and his plans for a new kind of community, centered on Antioch College:

As I discussed the TVA with President Roosevelt, it seemed to me that for twelve years in Yellow Springs I had been actively engaged in an undertaking that was almost identical in spirit to the one he outlined. The TVA seemed to offer a chance to create a new cultural environment, where almost no field would be closed to a competent, able person. I was surprised and pleased to find that

Roosevelt had much the same outlook: he wanted the country to loosen up and become conscious of a wide variety of economic and cultural interests. He wanted a new breath of life. (Morgan 1974, 54)

True to the demands of his rigorous moral standards, Morgan insisted that there be no salary differential among the three directors and, in a gesture quite unusual for government officials in that era, he made public disclosure of his financial interests. But behavior based on an ethical code for himself was not sufficient; one of his first actions as chairman, as he rode the train from Washington back to Yellow Springs in July 1933, was to sketch a list of ethical demands to apply to all TVA employees, "An Ethical Code for the Staff of the Tennessee Valley Authority" (Talbert 1968, 110). Given Morgan's conviction that good results could flow only from ethical measures, some examination of his code is important in understanding his vision of the TVA.

Defining the New Deal as "the new social and economic order we are striving for," Morgan saw the realization of this new order as fundamentally educational, requiring "conscious deliberate effort" to bring about change in "deep seated habits, social, economic, and personal." It was axiomatic for him that "poor ethical habits are the chief preventive of a better civilization," and "unless we realize that ethical attitude and conduct are the very foundation of a new order, we will resent changes in habits and attitudes, and our talk of a new social and economic order will be nothing but talk" (quoted, Talbert 1968, 121–22). Among the items in his ethical code, Morgan specified that employees should not accept gifts and favors from those who might profit from making such offers; that the general interest should take precedence over individual and particular interests; that TVA affairs were in every respect to be conducted honestly and openly; and that employees should take on their appropriate share of work in "a spirit of friendliness and good will." Further, the TVA intended to "develop a staff of men and women who are whole heartedly and enthusiastically committed to the project of helping build a new social and economic order," and those who showed "calculating, selfish ambition, or habitual cheapness of conduct," even though such behavior was not illegal, would be dismissed.

It was another display of the Morgan authoritarian temper to which students and faculty at Antioch had objected. As college president, Morgan had published "A Moral Code" in 1926 which he thought should receive "universal acceptance in principle, and will cover almost every circumstance of life." It lacked the specificity of his TVA code, and following a statement on the responsibility for maintaining good health, there was: "*Eugenics.* The best lives should be perpetuated." Aware of Morgan's paternalistic attitude, says his biographer, we should not be surprised "that he included eugenics in his moral code, and in that area he was to observe almost literally that if the best lives should be perpetuated, the worst should be terminated" (Talbert 1987, 57–58). To Morgan, most individuals were simply not capable of developing their own ethical standards. The TVA code was offered on the same grounds of universality; it would serve as "principles that most well informed, intelligent, reasonable and well intentioned men agree are desirable" (quoted, Talbert 1968, 123).

But the code went too far, in the view of Morgan's co-directors, when it required that employees lead exemplary private lives: "Tennessee Valley Authority employees should maintain wholesome and self respecting standards of personal conduct. Intemperance, lax sex morality, gambling, and the use of habit forming drugs are not in keeping with the spirit of the Tennessee Valley Authority personnel" (quoted, Talbert 1968, 126). Within a few weeks, Drew Pearson's nationally syndicated newspaper column ridiculed Morgan's TVA code, under which "every worker, from white collar executives to ditch diggers, would be subjected to a searching questionnaire about his private life and public views" (quoted, McCraw 1970, 48). Morgan was taken aback by this public exposure; he had mentioned the code only to the other two TVA directors, H. A. Morgan and David Lilienthal. The shot was just the opening volley in what became a lengthy and frustrating battle between Morgan and the other two.

For Morgan, the spirit of the TVA program involved much more than the behavior of its employees, and he spent a great deal of time and effort in traveling through the region, making speeches and suggesting reforms. Unlike H. A. Morgan, who cultivated allies among local leaders and used existing institutions to sponsor agricultural innovation, Chairman Morgan did not hesitate to throw out proposals that appeared at times strange. For example, as one element in his crusade for economic invigoration, he spoke in favor of the use of substitutes for the cash that was critically lacking. Years later, answering criticism that he had irresponsibly called for a separate monetary system for the Tennessee Valley, he declared that what he had in mind was simply a system he had instituted in Yellow Springs in the 1920s: "I suggested that individual small communities, or a few working together, set up a local credit exchange, with exchange credit coupons, to relieve this terrible economic paralysis" (Morgan 1974, 58). Barter systems were widely used during the Depression period, but it was odd to have a federal official publicly advocate barter in lieu of cash exchange.

At other times, he showed a stunning lack of political acumen. In a magazine article, he praised the people of the Tennessee Valley but wrote that the region was "a laboratory." He promised to offer state legislation to prevent the waste of good land. Under his proposed law, if land were misused, it could be taken by the state and "either sold to some one who will treat it properly or be planted as forest." He suggested further that Tennessee could reduce the number of its counties to one-fourth the existing number and "a large tax burden would be relieved" (quoted, McCraw 1970, 34–35). A reduction in business firms was also on his agenda. Speaking to an audience of Knoxville businessmen, he bluntly stated: "In most American cities there are at least four times as many merchants as are necessary" (quoted, McCraw 1970, 35).

New Towns for the TVA

A major triumph in Morgan's push for the new order, a jewel in the crown of TVA social engineering, was the creation of completely new towns. Housing large numbers of workers needed for the massive construction projects was an immediate problem. The directors, aware that temporary housing would be much cheaper than the model village proposed by Morgan, were hesitant to approve his plan. While the board considered it, the initial work force lived in barracks or commuted to their jobs over twisting mountain roads. Full approval was granted in July 1933, and Norris, Tennessee, so named by Morgan to honor the senator who had been instrumental in the fight for approval of the TVA, began to take shape. The town was to be the site for demonstrating many of Morgan's ideas, a frankly experimental effort to set an example for the nation of how life by proper ethical standards might proceed.

Norris incorporated many features of the greenbelt cities and its physical design alone merited much of the national attention it received. Surrounded by a 2,000-acre greenbelt, the town eventually contained over three hundred family houses, a dormitory for unmarried workers, and the business structures of an ordinary town of its size. Houses were completely electrified, and each had a four-acre plot available outside town for gardening. Compared to the ramshackle houses previously occupied by many of the new residents, the simple but comfortable houses, with indoor plumbing and electricity, were a considerable improvement. Rents were pegged at about 25 percent of a worker's income, and the town's businesses operated entirely on a nonprofit, cooperative plan.

It was the school in Norris, however, that caught the attention of the national press. "Of the numerous articles on the school, not one was in any way negative, and most reporters observed that the building served as a genuine community center, opening its doors in the evening for adult education and offering its 580-seat auditorium for community events, including church services and movies twice a week" (Talbert 1987, 118). Classes were arranged on the Progressive model, with an effort to incorporate real-life situations in the curriculum. The school's organization, from its curricular emphasis on melding the practical and the academic, including student development of businesses, to its stress on eliminating all forms of competition, bore the mark of Morgan's educational philosophy. Students operated a bank and made loans, ran the cafeteria and school store, and sold insurance—all as part of a cooperative. When school was not in session, the building was available for adult classes. With work organized into shifts of five and a half hours, a measure designed to increase the number of jobs available, there was time for adult classes in crafts, home economics, and, of course, ethical principles.[5]

Four years later, in 1937, the town had come upon troubled times. Morgan had planned for controlled industrial development to provide jobs, but the relatively high wages paid by the TVA offered little incentive for new industry in the area. Only the crowds of tourists who came to see the newly finished Norris Dam brought sufficient trade to the town's businesses. With the completion of the dam, the workers and their families moved on and the model village quietly turned into a bedroom community for commuters to Knoxville. After World War II, Norris, along with other TVA towns, was sold to private investors.

Moving On

Morgan attempted a number of innovations in the region, including the integration, with equal pay scales, of black and white workers. Aside from his ethical code and the experiment in community-building at Norris, he spread his vision of the new social and economic order in speeches and writings that gained national audiences.

But by 1937 he was reaching the point of forced resignation from the TVA. His interpretation of the TVA as the leading edge of a different social and economic order had time and again led him into sharp disagreement with his fellow directors, H. A. Morgan and Lilienthal. For his part, Arthur Morgan declared that he was following what he and Roosevelt had agreed was the spirit of the TVA. The heart of the conflict between himself and the other two directors, as he wrote years later, was that "the other members of the board held that no TVA development projects were legitimate unless they were individually and specifically described in the TVA Act. On the other hand, I was trying to implement the President's statement. Some of the most relentless opposition of the board majority was to actions directly in line with the President's specific illustrations to me of definite actions he had in mind" (Morgan 1974, 154–55).

Extensive differences existed among the directors on how to deal with the private utility companies in the region. Lilienthal, a veteran of the utility regulation battles in Wisconsin, held out for no compromise and no negotiation with private utility bosses. Arthur Morgan took the position that reasonable men should discuss the issue of furnishing electricity to the public and find a solution to the potential for destructive competition with private industry. He tried to establish discussion with Wendell Wilkie, whose company, Commonwealth and Southern, furnished electric power in much of the area.

Another issue had to do with a demand for damages by the owner of a marble quarry which would be flooded by a TVA dam. The quarry owner wanted a million dollars in compensation, although a survey by geologists and engineers concluded that the marble was worthless. Lilienthal was in favor of an out-of-court settlement, of probably less than a hundred thousand dollars, but Morgan was adamant "that not one cent would they give for something that is not worthwhile" (Creese 1990, 275). It was a difference in which compromise was unlikely. Morgan took an absolutist position against those who in his view were exploiters, a position that allied him with such other New Dealers as Rexford Tugwell.

Charges of dishonesty and irresponsibility went from side to side in the increasingly bitter dispute between Morgan and his fellow directors. Matters came to a head in 1938, as Roosevelt's Democratic Party prepared for a difficult election. Writing to the president in March 1937, Lilienthal and H. A. Morgan claimed that Arthur Morgan was "actively cooperating with Mr. Wendell Wilkie in such a manner as to prevent the Board from carrying out its obligations to the President and Congress" (quoted, Creese 1990, 275). They followed this in January 1938 with a nine-page list of charges. It "is not permissible," they wrote, for Morgan to make public attacks on their integrity in negotiating in the marble quarry case, or to fail to carry out decisions made by the board, or to "collaborate" with private utilities. As a majority of the board, "we believe," they concluded, "that Mr. Morgan's methods are wrong because the doctrine of 'rule or ruin' cannot exist alongside the doctrine of majority rule and minority responsibility" (quoted, McCraw 1970, 98).

Arthur Morgan gave his side of the story in a long letter to Representative Maury Maverick of Texas, a strong TVA supporter, in February 1938. The marble quarry affair, he wrote, was "an effort at a deliberate, bare-faced steal" and the entire board of directors knew it. Obviously referring to Lilienthal but without mentioning a name, Morgan wrote: "There is a practice of evasion, intrigue, and sharp strategy, with remarkable skill in alibi and the habit of avoiding direct responsibility, which makes Machiavelli seem open and candid. It took me a year or more of close association to be convinced that the attitude of boyish open candor and man-to-man directness was a mask for hard-boiled, selfish intrigue; so I am not surprised that Congressmen do not quickly see the situation from a distance" (quoted, McCraw 1970, 98). Morgan called for a congressional investigation to clear up the situation and sent copies of the letter to several other congressmen.

Morgan's accusations of misbehavior became bolder and each new development in the battle received front page coverage in all major newspapers. When a claims commission found that the marble quarry claim was worthless, Morgan told the press that the quarry case was "the kind of difficulty with which, as chairman of the TVA board, I have been faced in the effort to maintain good standards of public service." The "real difficulty," he said, was the impediments to his "effort to secure honesty, openness, decency, and fairness in government" (quoted, McCraw 1970, 99). In response Roosevelt released the nine-page complaint sent him by H. A. Morgan and Lilienthal; Morgan countered by publishing his letter to Maverick.

Now beset by growing congressional opposition to his New Deal programs and wanting no further bad publicity, Roosevelt decided to hold a meeting in his White House office on the various charges made by the directors. Morgan at first refused to attend, telling Roosevelt he thought nothing would be accomplished. (*New York Times* front page headline: "Morgan Defies Roosevelt!") Roosevelt responded with an angry telegram: "Meeting Friday is not called as you say to reconcile the differences between the board members but to enable me to get facts. You have made from time to time general charges against the majority members and they in turn have made counter charges against you. I want to get all of you together to substantiate these general charges factually. It is your duty as chairman and member of the authority to attend this meeting. Please advise" (quoted, Talbert 1987, 187). The message prompted Morgan's attendance, but he announced to the assembled news reporters just before the meeting began in the presidential office: "I am an observer and not a participant in this alleged process of fact finding" (quoted, Talbert 1987, 187).

The hearings took three days, spread over two weeks, and Morgan maintained an obstinate refusal to answer the president's demand for substantiation of charges made against Lilienthal and H. A. Morgan. On the third day, Morgan read from a prepared statement, concluding: "I cannot participate further in these proceedings" (Talbert 1987, 192). Roosevelt found Morgan guilty of failing to support serious and libelous charges against the other directors, and he declared that the chairman had obstructed the work of the

TVA and was "guilty of insubordination and contumacy" in refusing to answer questions from the president. Morgan had until the next day to either withdraw his charges or to resign.

Still holding that only a congressional hearing could provide a fair and proper forum for the investigation, Morgan ignored the president's ultimatum, declared that it was not in the public interest that he resign and that Roosevelt lacked constitutional authority to dismiss him, and boarded the train home to Yellow Springs. Two days later, on March 23, 1938, Roosevelt finally fired him.

Morgan's Tennessee Valley Authority "never really had a chance, not even in the strange days of the New Deal," says Talbert (1987, 193–94). As Morgan conceived it, Talbert's summation goes on, the TVA "was another benchmark on the road to Utopia. Nothing more. Not expecting success, he fought simply to continue the tradition of Utopian experimentation. That was the way he viewed his contribution. . . . It was part of the long-term effort to remake human society, another seed planted by a seedman in a long line of seedmen. His TVA was only a model, an example" (Talbert 1987, 194).

Engaged in his ferocious battle with the other TVA directors, Morgan still found time and energy to inaugurate the next in his series of experiments in utopia: the formation of Celo Community in the western mountains of North Carolina.

Notes

1. Lucy Morgan's tribute to her husband includes an "epilogue" by Arthur Morgan, pages 101–9. Morgan labeled his father "a poor provider for his family" (Morgan 1957b, 7). In the view of Morgan's wife, "the family life seems to have been rather a starving one in regard to the affections as well as to physical nourishment" (L. Morgan 1928, 17). Leuba's admiring biography of Morgan gives this portrait of the parents, no doubt provided by Morgan himself: Morgan's mother "was thrifty, kindly, neat, conscientious, and committed to her religious beliefs and to the right as she saw it. She attended church regularly. Smoking, drinking, and carousing were anathema to her. . . . His father, on the other hand, was easy going, dilatory, tolerant, and lazy; he was fond of his cronies, and of sitting, reflecting, chatting, and occasionally drinking, much to the embarrassment of his family. He was a religious agnostic—unreligious, but not anti-religious; he did not ordinarily attend church services. He was not neat or orderly. He made a precarious and only periodic living as a surveyor, sometimes filling in as a carpenter or as a laborer in the nearby railroad repair shop" (Leuba 1971, 22).

2. A further contribution to his rapid ascent to national recognition as educational reformer was Morgan's election in 1920 as the first president of the Progressive Education Association. The association's three vice-presidents were John Dewey, H. G. Wells, and Charles H. Henderson, the founder of an experimental school.

3. Note how similar are his ideas on democracy and community to those of John Dewey:

"American democratic polity was developed out of genuine community life, that is, association in the local and small centres where industry was mainly agricultural and where production was carried on mainly with hand tools." For Dewey, it was the "pioneer conditions" of early America that "put a high premium upon personal work, skills, ingenuity, initiative and adaptibility, and upon neighborly sociability." Even closer to Morgan's insistence on the fundamental nature of the small community, "It seemed almost self-evident to Plato—and to Rousseau later—that a genuine state could hardly be larger than the number of persons capable of personal acquaintance with one another" (quoted, Aronowitz 1993, 72–73).

4. Admitting that a comparison between More's Utopia and Inca society is "fascinating," one commentator slyly notes the "practical difficulties" of Morgan's idea: before 1515 explorers must have either "turned Cape Horn, or plowed 1,600 miles through the Brazilian jungles to Lake Titicaca, and then 1,600 miles back. After which they must have told the story to More in Antwerp, but to nobody else in Europe. This is odd behavior indeed." One might ask further "if the problem to be solved is worth the weight of the explanation involved" (Adams 1975, 230).

5. "Since we had reduced the working day to only five and one-half hours to spread the labor opportunities, there was much time for social and training activities. We built a combined store and post office and also a gas station. Since the members of the construction force for building a dam were of many different religious denominations, which might not be the same as those of the later, permanent residents, we built a single structure to serve as a nondenominational community church. We prevented saloons, gambling houses, and houses of prostitution from springing up, as they frequently did at other outdoor construction jobs. With these favorable living conditions, we were able to secure higher-caliber employees" (Morgan 1974, 89).

5. The Seedman's New Crop

As the nation remained in a deep economic depression, Arthur Morgan began to search for a suitable place for his new experiment in community. Some years earlier, while he was still at Antioch, he had been asked by one of his acquaintances, W. H. Regnery, a wealthy Chicago manufacturer, to suggest alternative uses for money Regnery had been contributing to the Chicago Boys Clubs. Already disillusioned with Antioch, Morgan "felt that it might be somewhat exploiting his confidence to direct his attention to Antioch, then my principal interest" (Morgan 1957a).[1] So he offered Regnery a chance to finance a new kind of community, to be populated by "young men wanting to get a foothold for themselves." Regnery, a firm believer in the conservative virtues of farming and traditional village life, offered to buy land for the project.

Before striking an agreement with Regnery, Morgan recalled later, he had "had a number of conversations" with Clarence Pickett of the American Friends Service Committee, in which they discussed their mutual concern with ethical matters. In the years prior to the Depression, both had been approached by young men and women who wanted "a considerable degree of freedom from the pressures and compulsions of the going economic regime, with the aim of using that freedom to try to orient themselves to the economic world in ways that would be in harmony with what they considered to be fundamental ethical considerations" (Morgan 1957a). Morgan's control of the TVA was under great strain, the Depression appeared far more serious than at first imagined, and Regnery eagerly offered financial backing. What better circumstances for starting an alternative community?

In his travels for the TVA, Morgan had learned of large tracts of land for sale in Southern Appalachia. Familiar with the mountain region and its people, he knew that the hardships of the Depression had led to very low prices for land. The climate of the region was moderate; the soil, generally poor, but it could be enriched.

More important still, the region was far from the centers of American economic ruin, the industrial cities. Isolation in this rural area could provide space for experimentation, for moving toward community self-sufficiency and autonomy. So Morgan limited his search to the mountain valleys of eastern Tennessee and adjacent North Carolina. After several months of investigation, his son found a 1,250-acre tract in the Toe River Valley, an isolated area of western North Carolina. Most of the land was forested and bounded on one side by a national forest. Regnery provided the purchase price of $27,375.

The project, now with tangible assets—land and three serviceable farmhouses—to match Morgan's vision and Regnery's promise of further financial support, was incorporated as a nonprofit educational enterprise, Celo Community, Incorporated. Morgan and Regnery appointed themselves and Clarence Pickett as the board of directors. In the articles of incorporation filed with the state government in 1938, provision was made for one of the three directors to be named by the American Friends Service Committee. As Morgan recalled twenty years later, this added "some insurance of stability of outlook and policy" to the project and served as protection should he and Regnery somehow lose control.

In the first years of Celo's existence, financial support was funneled through the Marquette Charitable Foundation, which had been established by Regnery; this insured that his contributions were tax-deductible. Control of affairs in Celo lay in Morgan's hands, with Regnery's advice and consent; the AFSC exercised no authority over the community.

Morgan's plans for his new community reflected both his idealistic vision and his often-stated impatience with incompetence and dogmatic attitudes. He held in highest esteem those he considered "practical idealists," a label he attached to himself above all. As he made decisions for the project, Morgan constructed tactful arguments to gain Regnery's assent. Below the genial surface of the letters and memoranda exchanged by the two men, however, there were sharp differences. Regnery was a conservative businessman, a staunch opponent of President Roosevelt and the New Deal policies. His support of the community venture rested firmly on his nostalgic belief that rural life and self-sufficient farming formed the bedrock of republican government. Morgan's view, expressed in publications over many years, that small communities, not cities, made decent civilized life possible, meshed with Regnery's willingness to support a revival of the pioneering spirit. Recalling their differences in 1957, Morgan wrote: "Regnery was inclined to see agriculture as the major occupation of the community. I thought of it as in the long run a minor interest, with specialized horticulture as having more possibilities than standard agriculture, and with other occupations as probably more important than either." With the decrease of Regnery's financial support over the next decade, even his peripheral involvement, together with his personal interest, in Celo rapidly diminished.

Since Morgan was *de facto* maker of community policy, his plans for Celo deserve careful scrutiny. A statement he made in 1936 justified the effort to build new communities:

> It is much easier for an individual or for a single family to maintain ethical and social standards if the community as a whole has the same standards, or at least understands and sympathizes with them. . . . In the unprecedented flux of American life there is a strong tendency for community influences to be dissolved, and for peoples' standards to become those of the great mass. . . . mass influences are tending more and more to displace community influences. It is doubtful whether increased fineness and distinctiveness of society will originate by mass movements. (Morgan 1936)

Certainly an experiment like Celo would at first be "very crude and require long periods of refinement," but the potential was high. Comparing his new project to the tiny Rochdale cooperative, he confidently predicted that a community of "normal, intelligent people" could work out "practical ways" of living together in a self-sustaining manner and thus show "what an all round community might be" (quoted, Mann 1957, 5, 6). One purpose "would be to train men and women to be leaders and builders of communities" (6).[2]

Celo might become a "master community" where "practical opportunities and locations and industrial possibilities" could be developed as a basis for founding other communities. Cooperation among a number of communities could then be carried on in recruiting members, economic exchange, and moral encouragement. Such linked communities could serve to revitalize American life on a grand scale.[3] Morgan, a serious student of experiments in community life, knew that "most communities which have survived and prospered have had a religious basis" (quoted, Mann 1957, 8). But a test of religious belief was not to be required for membership in Celo. Alongside the "craving for congenial society" and the necessity of making a living, "there needs to be a strong common purpose to try to get at the meaning of living, and willingness to undergo discipline and privation in order to serve one's highest purposes" (quoted, Mann 1957, 8). He might rule out religious uniformity as necessary, but his stern call for submission to discipline and willingness to endure privation could serve the same ends. Above all, Celo's members were to engage in a lifelong search for the "meaning of living."

Another of Morgan's topics was the quality of members. The young people who solicited his aid in the 1920s wanted alternatives to a life of moral and ethical compromise. They "felt like social outcasts" in the booming economic circumstances of the 1920s. To live where financial success was not the measure of men and women, where economic activity was congruent with high moral principles, was their primary goal. Morgan saw among such dissatisfied self-declared outcasts the promise of dedication and sacrifice required by the Celo project. We must have, he wrote, members "who have in common this quality of being willing to commit everything they have to the best purposes they know" (quoted, Mann 1957, 8). Success depended on the personal qualities of those who would come to Celo.

Morgan explicitly rejected *utopian* to describe Celo Community. The word meant to him, as he told me in 1965, "rigid, excessively visionary, and planned to the last detail. It ignores the necessity for change as the people involved grow in experience and wisdom." He carefully avoided prescribing detailed goals for Celo; he and the directors "had no formal ideology in mind" for the project. It was to be open-ended, experimental. Criteria for membership and descriptions of potential recruits also lacked specific detail. A broad range of interpretation of these general statements resulted.

Initial Settlement

Characteristically, Morgan looked to an acquaintance, the president of a small Seventh Day Adventist college in Tennessee, for promising settlers. Graduates from the school, in Morgan's view, had shown great success in creating small communities in their work as missionaries to economically depressed farming areas. Morgan admired the college for its "practical competence" (Morgan 1957a).

Three graduates were recommended by the college president as having the "pioneering spirit" needed in Celo. With their families, the three moved to Celo in early 1939. Morgan chose one man as salaried manager, another to set up horticultural experiments in exchange for free use of a house and a small stipend. The third family, their efforts to establish a "tourist camp" foiled by a local man's informal monopoly of that business, opened a rest home for the elderly.

Morgan's expectation that "while [the Adventists] might be embarrassingly orthodox, yet they would be paragons of harmony in their relations with each other" was not fulfilled. Within five months, the horticulturalist left in disappointment, his experiments with cultivation of various marketable vegetables inconclusive. The rest-home managers settled on a separate parcel of land owned by Morgan, under a private lease agreement. They soon withdrew from association with Celo and later purchased land nearby. (Years afterward, they insisted they had never belonged to the Community, although Celo's records list them as members.) By late 1940 only the manager and his family remained.

What was needed was a carefully chosen community manager to seek out new recruits for the project. Morgan assigned the existing manager, Bob Hoffmann, the job of "farm manager" and invited applicants for Celo's community manager from 4-H Club leaders in forty states. His letter explained, in the usual generalities, what he wanted: "The primary aim of this project is to make opportunity for a number of worth-while people to become self-supporting on land of their own, and to help develop a community whose members can fully respect each other and can cooperate with each other in developing the best possibilities of community life. Therefore the character and personality of the people who become part of the community are of great importance. They will need also to have practical common sense, and to work hard and exercise thrift."

In September 1940 Morgan found his man: Robert Lawson, who had extensive experience as handicrafts counselor for the Kentucky 4-H organization. Reared in the southern mountains, Lawson seemed an ideal candidate. As a "native of the region," Morgan recalled his assessment, Lawson "would talk the language of the [local] community" and thus improve relations between local people and Celo's residents. Just a few months before Lawson was hired, Regnery mentioned to Morgan his view of local people's misgivings: "There must be considerable doubt in the minds of some of the local people as to just what Celo Community, Inc. is trying to do; and, when their confidence in the project is once established it will be easier for all concerned" (WHR to AEM, 3/14/40).[4]

Lawson was instructed to select new members with great care, go slowly, take up to six or seven months to find a half-dozen suitable families. Morgan thought a few hard-working but impoverished Appalachian families, "who knew farming from the ground up," might provide good leaven for the college-educated idealists he foresaw as a future majority in Celo. Lawson brought in three families he considered "worth-while people" who wanted to be self-supporting. Not surprisingly, his new residents were all poor farmers from nearby mountain settlements. (One recruit was his wife's brother and family.) Lawson offered them economic security, with assurance that the Community corporation would furnish living expenses until they could support themselves. This was definitely not what Morgan had in mind. "Only one month on the job [he remembered later], and Lawson informed me that he had filled the quota of members I had set for him. When I went to see him a month or so later I found settled on the land a group of men, not one of whom could have the slightest understanding of the purpose of the undertaking, and not one of whom was a person of more than very mediocre personality. They did not last long" (Morgan 1957a). Nor did Lawson; he and his recruits left within the year.

The Adventist farm manager, who remained in Celo until after World War II, took a reading of community goals much like that of the dismissed tenants. When Morgan met a likely prospective member, usually through his contacts with Quaker and Humanist groups, he would suggest a trip to Celo for a first-hand look at the project. To these youthful prospects, Hoffmann, the farm manager, seemed to describe opportunities as limited to hired farm labor. Morgan complained: "I have the impression that when other people [besides myself] come to look into the situation, [Hoffmann] gives them no view of it except as a job of farm work, and fails to arouse their interest. I have got this directly from three or four people who have been there" (AEM to WHR, 8/27/41).

Morgan hesitated to spell out his ideas about what Celo should become. After an initial period of close supervision by the directors, primarily himself, he thought the Community should be organized as members chose, providing always for some form of democratic procedures. "Life is too complex and too large to fit into any formal ideology." On many occasions, he insisted that Celo was not open to members who advocate "any particular way of reforming society and who would plan to force their views on the Community" (Morgan 1957a). "It is not any particular dogma I fear in a community, but a dogmatic attitude" (quoted, Mann 1957, 58–59).

Any tendency toward unabashed commercialism, with residents considering themselves simply employees of the community corporation, brought forth Morgan's disapproval. He was determined that Celo not be a straggling copy of the parochial and morally crippled villages of the "prevailing society." For his third, and final, community manager, he turned to the Society of Friends to find someone closer to his own beliefs, one who might be trusted to interpret general statements as they were intended.

A Shift toward Utopia

Once more, Morgan called on an academic acquaintance for help. In early 1941 Celo's third manager, Peter Bullicott, was recommended by the president of a Quaker college. "It was perfectly easy to see the kind of person we needed as a leader," wrote Morgan in 1946, "and nearly impossible to find him" (AEM to CCI member, 4/16/46).[5] Bullicott seemed the answer; he eagerly agreed to come to Celo.

Bullicott and his wife lived in Maine where he led a Quaker meeting. Resolute pacifists, vegetarians, and dedicated promoters of consumer cooperatives, Bullicott and his wife toured Nova Scotia in the summer of 1941 (at Community expense) to investigate cooperative organizations. What they saw convinced him that Celo should become part of this larger movement.

The new manager and his wife, both reared in Quaker families in Philadelphia, were ill-prepared to face the harsh conditions of life in the Toe River Valley. In the midst of great natural beauty—forested mountains rising over six thousand feet to the west, and over three thousand on the east; clean mountain streams; a mild and healthful climate—poverty and privation were widespread among local people. There was no electricity in the valley, and the only telephone line ran to the national forest office several miles from the Community. Elementary education for local and Community children took place in a nearby one-room schoolhouse where a single teacher instructed about twenty children of all grade levels. High school, for the few valley children who attended, was twelve miles away. The nearest public transportation stopped over twenty miles from Celo.

In the short time it had existed, Celo Community had taken on an image among local people quite at odds with what Morgan had planned. From time to time, the farm manager hired local men to work in the Community's fields. Using new agricultural methods, and encouraging local farmers to adopt new techniques, the farm manager had turned Celo, from the perspective of those outside it, into a demonstration farm. Local men saw the project as a source of jobs; the Community was habitually referred to as "the company" among local families. As employer, Celo's farm manager expected minimal effort for higher wages than were customary or available elsewhere.

Dissatisfied with Hoffmann, Morgan brought in an assistant farm manager at the same time he engaged Bullicott. The new assistant, hired from a cooperative agricultural project in the Mississippi Delta, had spent fifteen years in India as a Presbyterian missionary. He and his wife were well educated (he at Cornell, she at Vassar) and dedicated to improving the spiritual and physical life of the poor. They immediately set about making the demonstration farm more efficient and tried to teach local people not only better farming but the virtues of punctuality and individual responsibility. Only a few months later they departed in frustration, their efforts at modernizing the valley defeated, as they saw it, by Hoffmann.

Hoffmann, it was reported to Morgan by the assistant, had not only failed to change local people but had taken on the attitude and habits of local men. The assistant wrote to Morgan that Hoffmann

> comes on and goes off the job at will. It is impossible to count at all on when he will work, when he will leave and what particular job he will do at any specified time.
>
> My concern is that when he is not regular and that when he stands and chats for an hour or two at a time either with the Community workers or with pass-ers-by who come along the road, the morale of the workers is bound to be affected adversely. They are all too inclined to stop their work frequently and visit. You can realize how awkward it is to try to correct the other workers when [Hoffmann] is the chief offender. (Asst. Farm Mgr. to AEM, 5/21/42)

Hoffmann and his short-lived assistant shared a conception of Celo that put emphasis on the Community's role as a catalyst for change among local people. Both as trained religious missionaries (one Adventist, the other Pres-byterian) and as social reformers, they sought to provide moral uplift to lo-cal people at the same time they showed how to improve the physical condi-tions of life. Hoffmann's way, to ingratiate himself with local people by imitating local modes of social interaction, was unacceptable to his assistant. Nevertheless, both men saw Celo as aiming at more than mere self-sufficiency and separation from local society.

Shortly after his arrival, the Quaker Bullicott set about changing this em-phasis, directly and indirectly. He had little interest in the farming activities of the Community. For him, Celo was an experiment in social life; econom-ic aspects faded beside this greater goal. Setting out a new Community pol-icy that jobs, when available, were to be given to Community members in preference to outsiders, he provoked another negative report from the farm assistant. It appeared to the assistant that, by preferring members over "good, faithful workers who tried to do their best," the new policy rewarded in-efficiency and waste by allowing Community residents to think of Celo as a private welfare agency, ready to make up personal deficits from apparently inexhaustible financial resources. But another result, he said, was that Bulli-cott's rule set up sharp distinctions between Celo and local people, thus in-creasing local resentment of the residents as "a clannish group" (Asst. Farm Mgr. to AEM, 6/11/42).

Intended or not, Bullicott's activities served to sharpen the boundaries separating Celo from local people. Only a few months went by before he had organized a "buying club" of residents, employees, and a handful of local neighbors. By 1943 the club expanded, with the purchase of a local storeowner's stock, into a cooperative store. Bullicott saw several advantages. It gave Community residents a way to obtain supplies, such as whole wheat flour and other health foods, which could not be had locally. It provided what Bullicott considered a vital first step in improving the diet of local people. He was horrified to learn that the daily breakfast for local people consisted of "sawmill gravy" (lard, water, flour), biscuits, molasses, and coffee. He recalled in 1966: "Why, those people had never even seen breakfast cereals. So we bought hundred-pound sacks of whole wheat cereals and stocked it in the co-op store. They would come in and ask what it was, and a few would buy it and, I assume, try it out. They seemed to have no conception of the relationship between diet and health, but we did have some success in teaching them."

Chiefly, however, the store expressed, for Bullicott and most Community members, a connection of the Celo project with what they considered the best alternative to an economic system based on exploitation. The very word itself—"cooperative"—was potent. One new member, writing excitedly of his plans for himself as a resident of Celo, told Bullicott of his hopes for installing a washing machine and thus "work out and equip a laundry on a cooperative basis" (Member to Bullicott, 5/12/43). If Bullicott was unclear about what was entailed, the member's next message set him straight: "What I had in mind was simply, to equip a laundry room which would be available for the use of our wives" (5/19/43), an idea to which "cooperative" added a measure of dignity and importance. The use of the term linked the simple idea of a common laundry room with a large movement with deep historical roots running back to the Rochdale battle of exploited workers against an unfair economic system.

Using the cooperative label for the community store also enhanced Celo's significance as social experiment. The instrumental feature of the project, jointly buying what could only with difficulty be purchased individually, was overshadowed by its expressive aspects. Bullicott recalled in 1966 that, in planning the co-op, he consulted with a farmers' cooperative in a nearby town: "Sure," he said, "they were affiliated with the national farmers' co-op. And they had a sign outside that said 'Co-op.' But they just didn't _talk_ like co-op people at all. Oh, they had rebates based on amount of purchases and so on, but they just didn't _act_ like co-op people."[6] The cooperative farmers did not see themselves tied to the same groups as Bullicott; they were not minions in the fight against the profit motive and economic exploitation.

Morgan visited Celo to find the buying club rapidly grown into a store with its own dilapidated building. It was promising evidence of a sounder footing for the Community, in his opinion, and he reported to Regnery that he had urged Bullicott to "work closely with Mr. Thompson [a local storeowner considered a Community friend] and try not to compete unnecessarily with him." The store's major value lay in the fact that it gave Community residents "something they can do in common" (AEM to WHR, 9/15/43).

As might be expected of a successful and conservative capitalist, however, Regnery took a less sanguine view. Piqued that Bullicott had not first obtained the consent of the board of directors for the cooperative, he predicted the store would "prove to be an expense and, even, a nuisance" (WHR to AEM, 9/10/43). The Community was too embryonic, as he saw it, to launch such nonessential projects. Elaborations of this kind should await a growth in population and the achievement of economic stability.

Regnery, still furnishing money for the project, fought for practicality. The Community, now playing host to small numbers of idealists, pacifists, and social activists of various ideologies, seemed to him to march in a direction far different from what had been planned. In spite of Morgan's assurances, his disillusionment grew. When news reached him of one new and completely inexperienced member's purchase of five hundred chicks in late summer 1943, he caustically remarked: "It would seem to me that a practical person would not buy livestock and poultry in the fall, unless he enjoys the pleasure of having them around him and the privilege of buying feed for them for six months or more" (WHR to AEM, 11/1/43).

Plans for small-scale industrial development in Celo added to Regnery's frustration. And gave Morgan optimistic hope. A "young manufacturing chemist in Chicago," involved in consumer cooperatives, visited Celo as a prospective member in 1943 and expressed interest in setting up a small chemical plant in the community. That the chemist was Jewish only strengthened Regnery's resistance. Morgan tried to mollify the Community's benefactor. "Since his name is Goldstein, I judge he is of Jewish descent, though I believe that his religious affiliation is Protestant" (AEM to WHR, 12/14/43). (Goldstein was a member of the Society of Friends.) Again, when Goldstein added two friends to his proposed chemical business in Celo, Morgan repeated his opinion: "Only the first [Goldstein] has any Jewish background, and he impressed me as not having Jewish characteristics" (AEM to WHR, 1/20/44).

Regnery sharply suggested that Morgan and the new residents in Celo might have gone too far: "I have only to suggest that at the time we planned Celo we had certain definite objectives in mind, in which we were all agreed; and I therefore feel that we should not at any time change these objectives unless by mutual consent and then only after giving a great deal of thought to the subject" (WHR to AEM, 12/17/43).

He was dismayed as well by Morgan's suggestion that membership be offered to a retired college teacher, a widow. Morgan's tendency to take in those who shared a belief in the need for cooperation in human affairs, regardless of age or ability, appeared to Regnery to scuttle the experimental purpose of Celo. For him the purpose was to determine whether selected young families could establish themselves in economic self-sufficiency on homesteads of ten or fifteen acres. Early in 1944 he made a final plea that they get on with the experiment:

> What do you think of the suggestion to make a definite trial this year as to what actually can be done with one or two tracts of land such as we have to offer at Celo? I have in mind planting those one or two tracts in accordance with the best experience now available. Of course, it would be necessary to hire labor for the purpose, but if a record were kept of the number of hours of labor required to make a crop, we then would have something definite to speak about whenever we attempt to interest settlers who come there. If on the other hand, it should turn out that our original ideas of about ten-acre tracts produce a living, plus [a surplus], are not possible, then it would seem in order to change our plans. (WHR to AEM, 1/5/44)

Such straightforward plans for careful testing would not prevail. Working to Morgan's great satisfaction, Community Manager Bullicott had little interest in tying Celo to trials of farm homestead efficiency. He wanted recruits reliably dedicated to cooperation and nonviolence.

A Wartime Pause

For the four-year span of World War II, Celo's membership increased little. Yet the Community's ties with large numbers of those interested in utopian and cooperative communities rapidly expanded, setting the stage for growth in the postwar period. Morgan was not dismayed at the slow pace in Celo; he found the same circumstances in his visits to similar communities elsewhere.

Traveling about the country, lecturing to groups of college students and pacifists, Morgan discovered the keenest interest in ventures like Celo among young men forced to spend the war years in Civilian Public Service (CPS) camps.[7] The inmates of these camps, having successfully persuaded the military draft authorities that they were bona fide conscientious objectors to the war, were assigned to public service jobs. Some worked in hospitals, some in federal educational facilities, and some in the national forests and parks. A

CPS camp occupied the buildings left by the Civilian Conservation Corps in the adjoining national forest, and several young men from the camp made regular weekend visits to Celo.

News of the Celo project spread in other ways than by Morgan's lecture circuit: when men were transferred from one CPS camp to another, through correspondence among those in different camps, and by notices in pacifist publications received in the camps. In federal prisons, where there were pacifists of a more absolutist belief who had refused to register for conscription, the communication network passed on information about Celo Community.

Morgan was encouraged, but he restrained his enthusiasm in his messages to Regnery. Stressing the agricultural expertise of some in his audiences, he wrote: "There is a very great variety in the personality and character of the men in these camps. Some of them are theorists or dreamers or unstable persons or extreme individuals, but among them I also find some very stable, well-balanced and intelligent persons. Some men of this latter class have grown up on farms, and some of them are persons of very substantial personal quality whose fathers are successful farm operators, and who themselves could run farms efficiently" (AEM to WHR, 8/25/42).[8]

Although pacifist groups occupied the hub of this communication network, Celo's members and supporters had links to people of other interests. Two reform issues stand out: the effort to eliminate discrimination against minority groups, particularly African Americans, and the quest for health improvement by the use of vegetarian diets, avoidance of tobacco and alcoholic beverages, and so on. Groups committed to creating utopian and cooperative communities—their numbers and vitality somewhat diminished with the post-Depression economic prosperity and the onset of war—were also involved. War, for most of these groups, resulted from the national concentration of power. Their alternative was the construction of autonomous communities or, for some, world federalization as an institutional basis for world brotherhood. A peaceful world would be only the first and obvious result of the existence of numerous new communities, utopian or cooperative; a completely new social order would, in time, follow. Whether a particular group formed to further the ideal of pacifism or to publish more general critiques of existing society and plans for its improvement, an antiwar attitude was part of the ideology of all.

When the nation shifted to defense and wartime production, putting an end to the Great Depression, Celo's attraction as employer for local men diminished. Many people left the Toe Valley, drafted into the military or finding work in defense industries. Fervent patriotism took hold in the valley and underlay a growing suspicion about the intentions, morality, and national allegiance of the "quare" folk who came to Celo Community. The boundary between local people and Community grew more solid and impermeable.

Pacifism, particularly an open opposition to United States involvement in World War II, was the essential issue in the withdrawal of local support of Celo and the arousal of hostility toward the Community. In large part Bullicott's public expressions of an antiwar attitude drove the wedge between local people and Celo.

Reports of Bullicott's relations with local folk reached Morgan through Lawson, the former Community manager, who spent his summer vacations in a cabin in the valley. Confining his association to local people, he found them incensed about Bullicott. According to Lawson, Bullicott chose any occasion to exhort local people not to contribute to the war effort. To buy war bonds, Bullicott declared to a local gathering, "is a waste of your money" (Lawson to AEM, undated). Another time, the local 4-H Club decided to collect scrap rubber as a group project, and the county farm agent asked Bullicott to lead the collection drive. Bullicott had been the club's adult sponsor for several months, but the scrap rubber drive led him to refuse any further association. He did not leave quietly but delivered an impassioned antiwar lecture to the children.

Given Bullicott's penchant for presenting his opinions as the only morally acceptable position, damning others as ignorant and immoral, Lawson feared that "some hot-headed mountain man" might lead a mob of vigilantes into the Community to wreck equipment, burn buildings, and injure the residents (Lawson to AEM, 9/6/42).

The rising dislike for the Community turned on other matters as well. Bullicott commonly wore short trousers, which to local people seemed appropriate only for small boys. His habit of working without a shirt, and of walking the public highways attired only in shorts, proved even more startling. Public exposure of the body was sinful, by local mores. Such a view was not confined to religious extremists and was not easily ignored. Even in the mid-1960s, complaints of indecency were lodged against a summertime labor crew of adolescent boys who removed their shirts as they cleaned highway ditches in the valley.

Other members of Celo were also partial to scanty clothing, vegetarian diets, and beards. Lawson summed up the reaction of local people: "The stocking up of the Community with folk who are 'queer' in eating habits, religious worship, and business dealing, to say nothing of unusual beards, and etc., is not conducive to good fellowship with native folk. The native folk are wondering if Celo Community is trying to be a colony of 'freaks' or 'misfits.' Something will have to be done to again get the confidence and respect of the folks around here" (Lawson to AEM, 9/6/42).

Morgan lost no time in reprimanding Bullicott. Only four days after Lawson's ominous warning, Morgan analyzed his Community manager's attitude: "I have observed a somewhat dogmatic attitude on your part toward pacifism and toward some other issues. You think there is no doubt about your being right. That is almost evidence of a weak belief that does not dare to face the question objectively. Also it tends to lead to actions which are unnecessarily offensive to people of different views" (AEM to Bullicott, 9/10/42). Bullicott agreed that he was dogmatic, but from the perspective of either "reason" or Christianity, he replied, pacifism was the only tenable position. And it was his duty, furthermore, to explain his beliefs. He responded to Morgan's admonishment: "I do not ask people to believe as I do but if they bring up the matter of war, I do believe that I should try to help them understand what I believe. They may not accept my view, they may not wish to be reasonable about the matter, but I think they may have a better understanding of it if I speak than if I keep quiet about it, especially when it is known that I do not agree with them" (Bullicott to AEM, 9/24/42). If only the local people, he went on, "would be willing to express their ideas to me so that I could quietly explain some things," friendship between them and Community residents might blossom.

Noting that there had been, in the early prewar years, some friendly acceptance of Celo Community by local people, one local man recalled (in 1966) the sudden eruption of hostility: "When the war come along, people just turned against the Community. Bullicott and some others started talking about being conscientious objectors and not wanting to help the war effort, and people just decided they didn't like Celo Community any more."

How pacifist ideas were presented to local people was only part of the problem. Not only did they find pacifism strange, they were puzzled by the Community members' blatant refusal to obey government dictates. They shared a view that control over state and federal government, especially the latter, was out of their hands. It was a feeling that persisted forty years after the war. "You can't do nothing about it nohow" was an often-repeated commentary about government action. To cope with the restrictive applications of federal law in the course of daily life, local people simply tried to avoid being caught for illegal behavior. Hunting in the national forest took place under cover of darkness; cutting marketable timber on government land was carried out with elaborate measures of secrecy. Military deserters hid in the coves and hollows of the Toe Valley, protected by geographical isolation and the acquiescent silence of kinsmen and neighbors. From time to time, federal investigators tried to discover the culprits responsible for setting fire to the national forest, only to meet a wall of blank stares and professed ignorance. Hence, while the power of distant government agencies was unquestioned, and their authority frequently admitted, legal restrictions impinging directly on local activity were evaded as occasion demanded.

A local man, justice of the peace for the valley in 1942, remembered how astounded he had been at one incident of Celo Community's open defiance: "Bullicott was a conscientious objector when the war come along. I took a paper down there to him to get Celo Community to sign up their farm for the war effort, and he wouldn't sign it unless I took out the part that said it was for the benefit of the war effort. Why, I couldn't do that! It was a *government* document!"

When Community pacifists directly confronted government authority by refusing to be drafted, locals found no way to fit this behavior into accustomed categories. Watching the CPS camp move into the national forest, seeing Community residents leave for internment in similar camps, they concluded that pacifists had federal government protection. Action against the Community might be punished by arrest and imprisonment. This knowledge, according to local informants, deterred those in the valley who spoke of burning Community buildings and driving out the pacifists.

Objection to war and steadfast refusal to join in projects for the war effort stamped the Community residents, in the eyes of most local folk, as cowards. "There don't nobody *want* to fight in a war," said one local man in 1966, "but sometimes you just *have* to go and do your duty as a man." Another told me: "If a man don't want to fight for his country, then he ought to get out of the country and go somers else. He can't sit around here and have the benefits if he don't want to pay for it." On rare occasions when members of Celo chanced to hear locals' opinion of them as cowards, they sought to discuss the matter and pointed to the sacrifices required of conscientious objectors in forfeiting the financial benefits of military service. They stressed the obligation of pacifists to react passively to insult and contempt. In at least one case, the argument was rebutted by violence: a member's sincere protestations met a local man's fist. But hostility generally took the route of avoidance of contact by local people.

The very purpose of Celo Community's existence confounded local folk. Their confusion grew as they watched the Community change in membership and goals. Reflecting on his years in the valley, Bullicott told me in 1966 that the most frequent question he encountered from local people was "Why are you here?" "I would patiently explain to them, but they never seemed to understand what I was talking about. There wasn't a week that went by in the first year I was there that somebody didn't ask me why we had come into the valley." It did not clarify matters when Bullicott, in superheated optimism or exasperated disgust, told some locals that Celo's members were "building heaven on earth." Blasphemy of this sort served as another mark of the unsavory nature of the project.

Failing to receive satisfactory answers to their queries about Celo's purposes, local people arranged the scraps of information they had into a coherent pattern. They began to classify Community members as German spies and saboteurs. Rumors circulated, in this time of intense patriotism and swelling hostility, about buried "spy equipment," code books, shortwave radio sets, and caches of explosives in the Community. Bullicott's installation of a gasoline generator and a shortwave radio receiver provided the germ for fantastic tales. To help put in the equipment, the manager hired several local men, and they spread word of the new radio. It was unique in the valley; even simple battery-powered radios were rare, and few people had ever heard of gasoline-powered electric generators. Twenty-five years later, stories of Celo's wartime assistance to Germany still passed from one aged local to another.

Dissension in the Community

Disharmony within Celo added to the discrediting of Bullicott and the pacifists. Hoffmann, the farm manager, exploited his friendship with local men to cast suspicion on Bullicott and changes in the Community that he disliked. Following Morgan's earlier order, Hoffmann geared his work in the valley toward closer association and cooperation with locals. He was quite well liked by them. In recalling the wartime years, local folk carefully distinguished Hoffmann from other members. One recollected in 1966: "Bob Hoffmann was a full-blooded German, but he was born in this country, I think. Anyway, he was a patriotic man, and he didn't go along with Bullicott and the other people down in there that wanted us to lose the war."

Perhaps the clearest indication of the change in local attitude, however, was the planning of a consolidated school for the Toe Valley. A telegram from Community Manager Lawson to Morgan in early 1941 was the first mention of the proposed school: "County board of education plan to build a ten-room elementary school. They have selected site on Community land. . . . Need 3 to 5 acres, will exchange present school building and ground [one acre abutting Community property] for new site. Work to start immediately. . . . I approve plan. If satisfactory wire at once authority to negotiate with board of education." With Regnery's agreement, Morgan approved the exchange. It appeared to be an excellent opportunity for teamwork between locals and Community members. Not only could reform in local education practices be brought about, but a modern school, in Morgan's view, would aid in attracting well-educated families to Celo. Morgan arrived in the valley and extracted an agreement from local officials for Celo's board of directors to name two or three of the new school's teachers. Before construction could begin, however, war broke out and plans were shelved.

Not until 1951 did the consolidated school open; the five one-room schoolhouses in the valley closed. Just after the war, Celo offered a five-acre site for the school, but by then alienation between the Community and locals had gone too far. Already in 1942, Lawson saw the situation clearly: "The consolidated school was lost to Celo Community because of such [Bullicott's antiwar] talk and actions." A local politician, when asked (in 1966) about the school and why a far more expensive site was chosen instead of accepting the land offered free by Celo, recalled Celo Community's position as not only inexplicable but probably dangerous: "That Community just didn't seem the right place to put our school. Them people was just strange, and there didn't nobody want to build a school right in there next to them, with the children going to it ever day and all."

Toward Democratic Decision-Making

At the close of the war in 1945, the Community's population rapidly increased with the arrival of men released from the CPS camps. To make room for them, the Community membership, more and more in control of day-to-day activities with the departure of Bullicott in 1945, instructed the few remaining tenants to vacate Community houses by the beginning of 1947 (CCI, 7/1/46). Even earlier, members decreed an end to the cutting and selling of timber on Celo's land. Henceforth, "timber and other Community resources should be reserved for members, and as far as possible be fabricated in the Community, instead of being sold as raw materials" (CCI, 11/14/45). Logging operations, under the inefficient and possibly dishonest direction of Hoffmann, had been the last source of jobs in the Community for local men. With these and similar decisions, Celo's new members marked the formal conclusion of the Community's era as "the company."

In the new political structure, the position of farm manager was eliminated. Hoffmann was elected the first Community chairman because of his experience, and he tried to continue to set Community policy single-handedly. Distressed at his authoritarian demeanor, Celo's membership simply ignored his orders. Morgan wrote Regnery: "Bob Hoffmann continues to be a source of division. He has a few personal followers, but there is a feeling among most of the members that he is dictatorial and frequently makes disparaging remarks about other people. In my opinion Bob is sincere, but has a habit of talking too much, and has a habit of making decisions affecting other people without keeping them informed. I believe he has improved decidedly in attitude, and is genuinely interested in the Community, but is not tactful" (AEM to WHR, 1/21/46). By the time Morgan wrote his letter, Hoffmann had resigned as chairman. Within a month, he and his local allies staged an "invasion" of Celo.

Sixteen local men marched into the Community's meeting on January 28, 1946, to demand that "Celo Community accept no more conscientious objectors as members, and that C.O.'s now in the Community leave within fifteen days." None of the several local war veterans in the group spoke, although the ultimatum was presented on their behalf. After delivering their demands, the men left abruptly. No "conclusive explanation for the visit was arrived at in the . . . discussion" that ensued. Bewildered, the members considered the possibility that the locals were drunk, but they agreed only that "the threats were not likely to be carried out except by men under the influence of alcohol" (CCI, 1/28/46). An appeal to the Community's lawyer in the county seat resulted in a strongly worded letter to the leader of the intruders. This called their bluff, and no further threats were made.

The invaders resorted to such desperate measures when they found Community employment closed to them. But Hoffmann bore special animosity toward some of the members who had questioned his honesty in the management of logging on Celo property. In any case, for several years, Hoffmann's increasing estrangement from Bullicott and his resentment of the "new look" in Celo had led him to cast about for ways to drive out the members and, along with other disgruntled employees, take over Community land. Hoffmann found it an easy chore to collect the small force when he draped his plan in the noble cloak of patriotism. Except for the veterans, most of whom apparently went along for a lark, those concerned were on the economic fringes of local society and badly needed jobs. Hoffmann's complicity in the hostile action was shortly uncovered and he left Celo in August 1946.

The last Community tenant, a local man found to have been allied with Hoffmann, was persuaded by Morgan to leave before year's end. According to Celo's member-historian, "With Bob had departed the last of the entrenched adherents of a managed agricultural development; Nate Oliver [the last tenant] did not possess the intelligent pertinacity which might have rendered his parasitical tenure secure and was already alienated from the Community even though he hung on until 1947" (Mann 1957, 87).

Added to their store of common experience as a self-conscious minority, the Community members, only one of whom had come to Celo before 1943, now had plain evidence of hostility among their nearest neighbors. The invasion incident was taken as typical of local sentiment. All that was required for a violent attack, they thought, was the appearance of another cunning leader. But a recurrence of open conflict was actually unlikely. Several men who had been asked to join Hoffmann's gang and "get shed of them Germans once and for all" declined because, as they recounted the event in 1965, they thought the Community was under government protection. After all, the links between the Community and the men at the nearby CPS camp had been obvious and, even if the pacifists left, others would no doubt replace them. "And I just never did like to start something I knowed I couldn't finish," concluded one local informant. The low esteem in which most of the invaders were held by local people, too, evoked more censure than approval. Certainly it was wrong for Celo's residents to "go around here talking down the war when our boys was over there fighting it," but it was just as wrong to attack them. To most locals, the wiser course was to avoid contact with the Community and its members.

The removal of Oliver and Hoffmann erased, at least temporarily, the lines of conflict and factionalism within Celo. Only one local family remained in the Community, and it was well known that they had brought upon themselves the pointed disapproval of kinsmen by joining. As far as others could tell, the family accepted the general beliefs of the membership and, most important, the family head spoke of himself as a convert to pacifism. The threads of friendship and kinship previously strung between the Community and local people were reduced to the strained ties of this one family with their relatives.

Community boundaries, clarified by Bullicott's wartime dissent and the policy decisions made by the members, grew even stronger after the invasion. Organized opposition by representatives of local society, as they were seen by the Community members, affirmed Celo as a distinctive social entity. They shared a victory in this brief skirmish; what they were doing entailed possible danger and would not be an easy task. Defeating the enemy had been simple and quick; pacifist methods of dealing with conflict proved to be not only moral but efficient.

Together with the end of the salaried management system, the rapid growth in membership after the war, and the waning of Regnery's influence, the "invasion" ushered in a period of vitality and eager dedication not seen before in Celo. The way was cleared for truly utopian adventure.

Notes

1. Unless indicated otherwise, quotations from Morgan in this chapter are from a typewritten manuscript, "Celo Community: Notes from Memory," which Morgan composed in 1957 (cited as Morgan 1957a). The manuscript is part of Celo Community's documents file.

2. On the occasion of Celo's twentieth anniversary, Leonard Mann, the physician-member of the Community, compiled a history of Celo. Much of the information contained in Mann's manuscript was based on the writings and oral recollections of Morgan. The manuscript is part of Celo's file of documents.

3. Comparable visions of linked communities can be found in a number of utopian writings, including Skinner 1948. Some modern communities have successfully established close ties, notably the Walden Two groups: Twin Oaks, East Wind, and Acorn.

4. References to letters between Regnery and Morgan are abbreviated as: WHR = William Henry Regnery; AEM = Arthur E. Morgan, with dates as month/day/year. The letters are in Celo's file of documents.

5. As stated in the "Note on Sources and Style" in the frontmatter of this book, CCI is the abbreviation for Celo Community, Incorporated, the Community's legal foundation. It was the preferred term of members when they referred to the legal status of the Community, to the authority of joint decisions, and to the Community itself as a corporate continuing entity. Hereafter, I cite the minutes of Community meetings as "CCI" with date of meeting, mirroring Community usage.

6. The cooperative store to which he referred had been formed with Arthur Morgan's encouragement as director of the TVA, although Bullicott was unaware of this.

7. Civilian Public Service camps were sponsored by the three historic peace churches—Quakers, Mennonites, and Church of the Brethren—who directed them under the surveillance of the federal government.

8. At one point, Morgan suggested that Celo might usefully maintain its cropland, attract the interest of potential members, and provide worthwhile public service by becoming a CPS camp. Sensing that the notion might easily raise the hackles of local people, who were already suspicious, he let the proposal die.

6. Bloom and Harvest

Now in control of the Community's daily affairs, members began to establish patterns of meeting and decision-making that would remain for decades. These early steps toward self-government, rules of land tenure, and methods of taxation were often tentative and frankly experimental. Members held regular sessions each week. This was later varied, as business warranted, from one period to another, but scheduled meetings were never fewer than one per month. Rules of parliamentary procedure were not followed, and differences of opinion were settled by long periods of discussion, by postponing issues when agreement could not be reached, and by invoking periods of silence when argument became heated. Postponed matters were discussed in casual conversation between meetings.

Land Tenure and Taxes

The Celo Community Holding Agreement, accepted by the members in 1950 (with revisions in 1965), and henceforth the instrument of land tenure, was a contract between member and Community granting the holder-member "possession, occupancy, and use" of a plot of land in Celo, "subject to such zoning, standards, regulations and restrictions as may be adopted and prescribed by the resident members of the Community." It was specifically "not a deed" but a "cooperative agreement between parties which have a mutual interest in the development and welfare" of Celo Community (see Appendix). Signing the agreement, a holder indicated a willingness to "forgo some elements of private control in order to promote [all members'] welfare."

Upon leaving Celo, a holder would be reimbursed by the Community for improvements on the holding at half their appraised value, to a limit of $4,500. That is, improvements (buildings, drainage, fences, etc.) with a value of $9,000 would bring the same compensation as those totaling, say, $20,000; neither could demand more than $4,500. These limitations were increased upward in the 1965 revision of the Holding Agreement, and again in 1974. By that year the Community had become financially secure enough to increase the repayable percentage from 50 percent to 60 percent of appraised value, to a maximum of $15,000. The amount of immediate payment to departing members went from the 1965 limit of $1,000 to $1,500 and the time limit within which the remainder would be paid was reduced from ten to six years. Landholders paid the Community for their plots, signed the Holding Agreement, and accepted the stipulated restrictions on use of the property. They also agreed to pay annual assessments for taxes and other Community services. Most new members were granted a loan from a Community fund to pay for their holdings.

The Community's tax system, designed to promote equality, consisted of a "unit" (household) tax and an income tax. Fifty percent of the annual budget came from equal assessments on each household; the remainder was raised by taking an "equal number of days' wages from each [member] sufficient to make up the required sum" (CCI, 2/11/49). County real estate taxes, assessed on the Community as a single unit, were divided among the households. The income tax could be satisfied by cash or by labor on Community projects. With population rapidly growing, there was much demand for work on repair of roads, clearing of brush, and so on. Cash income was low in most households, and this lightened the financial burden. At the same time, it fostered cooperation, since labor contributions were made in organized groups on special "work days." When employment outside Celo increased in the early 1950s, members' time for participation in work parties was limited, and they abandoned this provision. Like almost every instance of making general regulations, the members reserved the right to make case-by-case exceptions, in this respect, to "adjust" the amount of tax required of particular households. (An example: one household's tax was waived in 1952 when the husband became seriously ill and the family income greatly reduced.)

The tax system underwent modification in 1975. A substantial increase had occurred in the number of single-adult households and the membership agreed that each nondependent adult "shall be assessed equally" and that rather than "meeting the assessment one half by head [formerly 'unit'] tax and one half by ability to pay, all adults will be taxed equally" (CCI, 2/5/75).

In the same year, they changed the policy for paying taxes on Community property not allocated to individual holdings. This portion of the annual county tax bill had previously been met with income from sales of Community hay and timber and from interest on Community funds. After 1975 it would be shared among individual holders. Further, as national inflation rates began to rise in the late 1970s, they set a new policy for the increase of the cost of landholdings which bound increases to inflationary increases by 10 percent increments (CCI, 5/3/78).

Being a member came to be synonymous with holding land. The usual course was to live in the Community for six months, sometimes more, as a trial member. At the end of this probationary period, full members decided whether to accept a trial member, to ask that the trial term be extended, or to refuse membership. It was unstated but assumed that households would consist of nuclear families. Further, it was generally expected that single adults would eventually marry and establish a family "unit." Although there were infrequent cases of cohabitation by unmarried adults, it was not considered a normal or long-term arrangement. Absentee membership, quite common in the beginning when the project welcomed support of any kind, was abolished in 1952. Ending one's membership in Celo meant that the Holding Agreement was "automatically terminated."

Several features of the Holding Agreement deserve comment. The members accepted Morgan's view that "the relations [between Community and individual member] we had in mind were of a new sort." The members held up their Holding Agreement as a unique document, the very cornerstone of the Community. In its balance of individual and group interests, the contract confirmed the intention to create experimental alternatives to existing social relations. As a moral agreement, it demonstrated their conviction that the correct basis of human association was mutual trust, a moral basis. The kind of voluntary cooperation they wanted could not be induced by the threat of coercion they saw lurking behind all legal contracts. Singling it out as unique, a distinctive feature of their venture, they applauded themselves as experimentalists in social order.

Economic Plans and Projects

The economic ideal of the members was to set up in Celo, either alone or, better, in partnership with other members, a novel enterprise which could provide a modest living and an opportunity for doing nonexploitative work. Sometimes necessity led members to work for a few weeks at manual labor.

One man cut and hauled firewood for a local mining operation. Another, when he first came to Celo in the early 1950s, worked with construction crews on local highways.

Farming, of course, was an attractive way to make a living, and was preferred by most Community residents. Yet their inexperience as farmers, in most cases, and the poor roads in the mountain region made this unprofitable. From time to time, some of them tried growing vegetables for market, but none succeeded for more than one season. An elderly local man remembered (1966) the sight of two Community men returning from a failed marketing trip. Their truck was almost as full of yellow squash as when they set out, and they paused on the river bridge and dumped the vegetables in the swift water below. "Hit looked like that whole river was full of little goslings!" chuckled the old man. Planting and tending gardens remained important for all.

Several projects provided an adequate but not luxurious income. Celo Mountain Products, a woodworking and carpentry business, involved four members as partners. During its existence from 1947 to 1954, the group at one time or another employed most of the Community's adult males. Growth in Community population kept them busy constructing houses within Celo. The five houses built by these men were paid for with funds brought into the Community by new members. That is, the Mountain Products partnership was indirectly dependent upon outside sources of money. When the early spurt of new recruits subsided and finally halted about 1952, the woodworkers had to find jobs outside.

A smaller number of members worked part-time with Celo Knitters, a hand-knitting business. Its originator had obtained from a fellow CPS inmate (later a member of Celo) an antique loom, and the two men formed a partnership in 1947. Hand-knitted hosiery was produced under the direction of one partner, while the other secured orders in New York. The first and largest sale was to supply argyle hose for the cast of a Broadway musical, *Brigadoon*. Smaller orders came from Manhattan haberdasheries. There were perhaps greater long-term possibilities here than with building houses for new members, but the knitting supervisor made less than $1,000 annually. His part-time workers earned far less.

The symbolic significance of Celo Knitters is reflected in its description as a "cottage industry." Its owners depended on several other ventures of an economically marginal but ideological vital nature. Banking all of his income save about $600 per year, the supervisor kept a small herd of milk goats, canned food for winter use from his own extensive garden, and occasionally worked as a casual laborer. He reflected in 1966 that he longed to feel himself close to nature, and he looked for work involving physical labor. Agriculture appealed to him, as it did to most members, as a way to bring holism to his life. The ideal was to make work and leisure inseparable; to make work a pleasure by doing a variety of satisfying tasks.

Of a different sort entirely was Laurel Cove, a religious retreat. Located on one member's landholding, the retreat, according to a promotional brochure of 1948, "is a place where people may give time for prayer, study, and work that may assist them to find greater meaning in life, and a deeper spiritual awareness." Three one-hour periods of daily prayer were interspersed with three-hour work periods. "Work at Laurel Cove is for spiritual exercise, a relaxation for the body and mind from hours of work and study, . . . for gardening and for improving the physical facilities of the place." Although the retreat attracted a number of young people from outside Celo, together with some new members, it was cut short after only two summers by the untimely death of its leader (see Brooks 1994, 27–55, for details of Laurel Cove's operation).

The lack of money in Celo gave rise to another scheme. A "labor pool" was formed and notes printed from linoleum blocks in denominations of one and four "hours." Crude imitations of ordinary currency, the notes read "Celo Community, Inc. / Good for One Hour's Labor by the Undersigned," with space for date and signature. The labor exchange was another attempt to extend equality beyond abstract belief; it presumed that members were equal in their productive capacity as well. The exchange displayed, too, an uneasiness about using money. It could so easily be turned to usurious—that is, immoral—purposes. Still, members very soon acknowledged that people do not work with the same speed, reliability, or skill, and the labor pool was given up after several instances when labor notes were not satisfactorily honored. Equality, it seemed, could not be pushed to every corner of Community life; it worked best when members concentrated on the equality of the "inner person."[1]

Like utopian communities before them—Oneida, Shakers, Modern Times, and others—Celo witnessed a steady effort to find alternative means for building and mechanical devices. In the late 1940s, one member requested Morgan's aid in patenting his invention, a "rotatable fire engine ladder." No further mention of the patent or ladder exists among Community documents. Another devised a passive way to fill and vacuum his small, hand-dug, concrete swimming pool. It was gravity-fed (at 50–55 degrees F.) from a spring two hundred yards above the house and cleaned and drained by manually starting siphon action through a tube dropped down an incline near the pool. The director of Laurel Cove developed, with other members, a lightweight building block by combining cement and sawdust. At least one house was constructed with the blocks in 1949; thirty years later it was still secure and watertight. The same members made a recipe for permanent floor covering of "newspapers run through a hammer mill and mixed with melted asphalt, which could then be troweled onto wood or concrete floors. The finished surface was linoleum-like." The material was used in several Community houses (Brooks 1994, 30).

Watching events in Celo from afar, Morgan thought his project an excellent alternative to such tightly communal groups as the kibbutzim and the Hutterites. In those groups, he wrote in a 1955 essay, "when the initial zeal of the organizers wanes, their growth stops, except perhaps by births within the community." But Celo had set out on a path of continuous growth. Morgan continued,

> Security, and freedom of self-determination, both are values. A good way of life will try to recognize them both in right relation. It does not lie in giving a monopoly of loyalty to one of these and suppressing the other.
>
> Recognition of both these elements was the course taken at Celo Community. . . . there was no prescription as to the degree or intensity of communalism, but it was left for the community to find its way by experience. At one time the community owned a herd of cattle. It was decided that this activity had better be left to individual initiative. The community owned its own agricultural machinery, but came to the conclusion that this would be used more effectively and more economically if owned by one or more individuals. On the other hand, the community has a cooperative store. It has locally organized group medical service. The land is owned by the community, but lifetime leases are given to members. Any matter affecting the common interest, such as timber cutting and mineral extraction, either on unoccupied community land or on the individual holdings, is controlled by the community as a whole, even though carried out by individual initiative and responsibility. The community has "work days" when the members as a whole work for their common interests. It maintains a "capital fund" from which loans are made to meet the needs of members. . . . Thus a pattern is taking shape which seems to fit the desires and needs of the community members. It combines much community of effort with much freedom. (Morgan 1955, 30)

By the time Morgan composed this laudatory description, dissension and conflict had already prompted five families to leave. Disillusionment spread among those who remained. Striking a satisfactory balance of individualism and communalism had proved very difficult. To arrive at consensus on the desirability of, say, cooperation and simplicity as characteristics of personal and community life posed few problems. When members applied belief to specific circumstances, however, strong disagreement arose. Conflict over the control of a health center built in the late 1940s and, more generally, over the extent of communalism in the Community, provided the background against which members considered leaving Celo.

Health Center and Defection

Celo Health Center, built to enhance the Community's attractiveness for recruits, was established in 1948 under a corporate charter separate from that of Celo Community itself. Initially the same board of directors served both corporations, but the day-to-day management of the health center soon came under the control of a physician, hired by Morgan, who became a Community member. Within a few years, the directors of the Community corporation changed to include member-residents, but the health center remained distinct, with directors usually named at the physician's recommendation.

Putting the health center, the grandest of all Community projects, under the charge of one member, the physician, appeared to many of Celo's residents to run counter to their expectation of joint authority in common undertakings. In addition, some began to think of the physician as Morgan's personal agent, sent down to keep the Community on the path of practicality. They had not been consulted when he was hired, and they had no voice in the center's affairs.

What intensified this resentment was the requirement, informal but effective, that each member find his or her own way to make a living. This meant that many of them had to work outside Celo, at jobs that were often personally unsatisfying. The physician, presented with ready-made economic means, contradicted this rule.

There was also the physician's strong and consistent support for financial conservatism that distressed other members. He considered it financially irresponsible for the Community to invest in jointly owned buildings except when a departing member's house was purchased under the Holding Agreement. Several efforts to reach consensus on the construction of communal buildings—for example, to house a cooperative chemical business—were blocked by the physician and his supporters.

Growing dissension in the early 1950s, primarily turning on the arrangements the Community made with disappointed defectors, clarified the different conceptions of Celo. Two unstable factions emerged. One, with the physician as spokesman, comprised those who wanted to strengthen the Holding Agreement by abiding strictly by its terms in negotiating settlements.

From their perspective, this would further a definition of the Community as a group of people voluntarily bound by a moral contract. In opposition stood those who sought ways to increase the number of cooperative projects in Celo. They frequently spoke of the need for dealing with defectors with "love" and "generosity," rather than by the arid and materialistic terms of a written document. For them, the Holding Agreement's significance paled when compared with the much weightier bonds of love and friendship among the membership. In the extreme view of a few, the Agreement even impeded closer bonds. For this faction, the Holding Agreement, as a moral obligation, was but a small, tangible indication of their commitment to working cooperatively toward common goals. They could not accept the opposition's idea that the Agreement was "one of the main foundations of the Community."

Opposition to the "businesslike" faction led by the physician was centered in Celo's Friends Meeting, where a majority of the Community membership gathered on Sunday and during the week for discussion of social issues. But there were, as well, moderates in the Quaker group, whose regular support could be counted upon by neither faction. When the number of moderates decreased, leaving to pursue careers or to join other experimental communities, the gulf between the factions widened.

Committed as the members were to the expression of individual differences, their dislike of confrontation led them to allow conflict to remain unspoken and to undertake communal projects only as smaller groups. This meant that one faction could insist on individual and family autonomy, and the other could experiment with various forms of communalism. Here, in this tacit agreement and the projects facilitated by it, the expression "a community within the Community," a phrase in common usage during the period of my fieldwork, 1965–67, appears to have originated as a way to distinguish the two factions.

If one selects a particular series of events which precipitated general disenchantment and brought on a gradual redefinition of the Community, an unavoidable choice is the defection of four families to the Society of Brothers (Bruderhof) in 1954. Those who left Celo for the Society of Brothers were all part of a group, "a community within the Community," formed to found a boarding school. Preliminary to building their school, they were experimenting with a "common purse" scheme to share their income. Until the four families departed, there still seemed to be hope for achieving the kind of intense cooperative living they had expected in Celo. Eight adults (in five households) decided to quit Celo and join the Brothers. Four of the five families in the common-purse group left. Having once tried to solve their dissatisfaction with urban life by withdrawal into Celo Community, so they sought in the Society of Brothers relief from the dissension and difficulties of life in Celo.

A loss of this proportion capped an increasing frustration among the members as they discovered that control of the health center would probably remain in the physician's hands. Several families left before 1954 after repeated and heated arguments on this issue. With the defections to the Bruderhof, and others immediately following, Celo in 1958 was left with only twenty-one adults. The project stood on the brink of extinction. The Community chairman, in his annual report for 1958, admitted that the general feeling was "one of depression if not discouragement." Taken together, the defections of the early 1950s "just demoralized the Community, I think," a remaining member sadly told me in 1966. "We lost some of the best members and it threw a lot of doubt on what we were doing here." Not least in the sense of defeat was the fact that among the departing families were ten young children.

One measure of their doubt was a provision written into the Community's bylaws (adopted in 1956) that foresaw the possibility of collapse. If the membership dropped below twenty, a "time of emergency" would be declared and the directors would assume full control of Celo's affairs. With a unanimous vote of the board, the Community could be dissolved. Corporate assets would then go to one of three specified nonprofit organizations (including the American Friends Service Committee) and landholders would receive deeds.

Building a Boarding School

Despite their reduced numbers and their doubts about the Community's viability, the members did not abandon the plan for a boarding school. Together with the single family left from the common-purse group, Morgan's son and daughter-in-law came to Celo and provided the necessary leadership. For the six years from 1958 to 1963 they organized and directed summer work camps for Quaker college and high school groups. Land was cleared and school buildings erected. The Arthur Morgan School opened in 1962 with sixteen students. Organized as a separate unit under the same corporate charter as the health center, it felt little influence from the physician.

The Morgans' plan to locate an experimental school in Celo was immediately welcomed. Community members offered a large tract of Community land for the school's use. The school presented a chance to revitalize a battered Community spirit: the school's brochure later boasted, "the school is needed here. Celo Community needs it, to achieve meaning and cohesion, perhaps even survival." The school became more and more a part of Celo Community. Every member became involved in one way or another, some as teachers; others managed the school's business enterprises, supervised camping and hiking trips, or, in the physician's case, monitored the health of the students. From the outset, the school's round of activities—movies, folk dances, occasional communal meals, work parties, and so on—were well attended by almost all Community members.[2] A close relationship existed between the Friends meeting and the school: most students attended services on Sunday, school teachers belonged to the Friends, and visitors to the school frequently attended Sunday Friends service.

After the low point in the late 1950s, with extinction a clear possibility, the opening of the Morgan School stimulated new activity in Celo. The summer farm-home camps operated by one family and involving several others grew in size; family camps sponsored by the school added to the roster of regular visitors to the Community. Summer camp experience frequently led to later enrollment in the Morgan School. With the school came a printing press, which, for the first few years, turned out and sold "nature-inspired" writing paper and notepads. The first book published at Celo (in 1962) was *A Manual of Simple Burial,* by Ernest Morgan (Arthur's eldest son), and by the 1970s Celo Press was issuing several volumes a year with the aid of donated money, time, and labor.

By the middle of the 1960s, when a renewed interest in communes struck the country, a new kind of visitor stopped off in Celo. College students, searching for alternative lifestyles, could find Celo listed in a number of directories of intentional communities (for example, *The Modern Utopian* [1967]) and they began to add the Community to their summer tours. The federal government's programs to eliminate poverty—the War on Poverty— led to lengthier sojourns in the mountain villages for college-age VISTA (Volunteers in Service to America, a domestic Peace Corps) workers. Similar efforts were mounted by church-affiliated groups. Many of these young people discovered in the Community a welcome respite from their labors, a place for discussion with people much like themselves, where they were welcomed to the Quaker meeting and invited to share meals in members' homes.

Caught up in the nationwide protest against the Vietnam War, most of Celo's membership took active roles. A few lived in "voluntary poverty," keeping their income below the level at which they would be liable for federal income tax and thus avoiding involvement in financing the "war machine." A number of them participated in the large protest rallies staged in Washington in 1965 and subsequent years. One family decided to withhold their payment of the 10 percent telephone tax that had been added as a means of financing the war. All fed their knowledge of the war and protest movement by reading pacifist journals and passing them on to other members, by gathering to hear reports from visiting activists, or by private correspondence with protestors over the entire country.

During the two years of my fieldwork, Celo was a bustling place, in spite of the low membership, empty dwellings, and sense of uncertainty. Official monthly meetings, attended by the greatly reduced membership, required little time, but informal occasions for association were frequent. One could expect invitations to a member's home to hear a report from visiting members of a community in British Columbia, or to another's home to see slides of a member's visit to an experimental community in India. Some residents shared transportation to nearby states to pick peaches or to distant farms to purchase organically grown produce. Films and lectures by visiting pacifist leaders alternated with folk dances at the Morgan School, monthly potluck dinners followed Quaker meetings every first Sunday, and Community workdays periodically brought together most members to clear paths and repair vacant buildings.

Daily life in Celo was steeped in egalitarianism and informality. All residents used first names to refer to and to address each other. Children used adults' first names casually and unselfconsciously; students in the Morgan School called teachers and staff members by first name. The clothing worn by all residents was informal; men, women, and children wore cotton slacks or short pants and T-shirts.[3] Only on rare occasions did one find women in dresses and men with neckties—usually when attending formal events in the county seat such as high school parent association meetings or county political conventions. Both men and women repaired roofs, cut brush, painted houses, cooked, and hauled firewood. It was not a calculated attempt to ensure gender equality, however, since most activities were carried out with the conventional division of labor: women did most housework and cared for small children, men cut and split firewood, and so on.[4]

Seating arrangements reflected a similar concern for equality. Members arranged themselves in Community meetings in a circle; gatherings in their homes assumed the same pattern. The final selection at the periodic folk dances at the Morgan School was the hora, in which participants are linked into a circle and dance with increasing speed.[5] This pattern was not accidental. As demonstrated on many occasions, the desire for circular seating arrangements was quite urgent and deliberate. For example, a casual gathering in a member's yard to share homemade ice cream was anxiously halted by the host until the chairs and benches were drawn into the customary circle.

Revitalized Utopians

A recently formed commune settled in the valley in 1969 and established friendly relationships with Celo's residents. Within a year or so, the commune requested to be taken in as members of the Community. Their offer of merger was refused, on grounds that Celo's policy was to accept (or reject) new members on an individual basis. When the commune disintegrated soon afterward, several members stayed in the valley and were accepted as trial members of Celo.

The growth in communes throughout the nation continued into the 1970s, gaining momentum, and the number of visitors to Celo grew. At the same time, the population of the Toe River Valley increased, reversing a twenty-year decline. A sizable part of the population growth came from back-to-the-landers. Some who had lived in the valley as VISTA volunteers returned to buy land and build houses. Others were searching for a site for homesteading. Some had learned of Celo from publications of pacifist organizations or various magazines addressed to an interest in experimental communities. In some cases, those who wanted to homestead in the valley lacked sufficient money for land and applied for membership in the Community, combining an economic and ideological purpose.

The result for Celo Community was what seemed a flood of applicants. Discussions about membership, particularly the acceptance or rejection of applicants, covered different aspects of the issue, but centered on the problems of housing and the criteria for acceptance. By 1973 all houses were occupied, and the question of whether trial members should be allowed to live outside Celo for their probationary period was addressed. Although a few exceptions were made to the general rule that trial members should live within the boundaries of the Community, there were other issues at hand. For instance, if trial members lived nearby, should their contribution to the maintenance of Community property and the payment of taxes be the same as those who resided on Community land? If current members had accepted more trial members than they felt capable of absorbing into full membership, then what criteria should they use for choosing some, rejecting others? This was already the situation for 1973: four new members accepted, ten trial members awaiting a decision. Struggling with the problems of sudden popularity, Community members tried to find "some way to take the hurt and the feeling of rejection out of being turned down for membership, seemingly inevitable in a group with selective membership" (CCI, 4/2/75). Beginning in January 1974, the Community declared a moratorium on new trial memberships. Over the following years, the list of trial members declined as career plans changed and jobs elsewhere became available to several, and the appeal of permanent membership faded for others.

Gradually, as the decade wore on, the membership's emphasis on its purpose as "a vigorous physical experiment in land management and usage" took precedence over other goals, including that of creating an alternative community which would be widely emulated. Celo began to advertise itself as a "community land trust" and thus asserted its position in a category of increasing relevance in a period of environmental protection, ecological movements, and efforts to preserve resources which were generally acknowledged to be nonrenewable.

Notes

1. Labor notes, of course, were not unique to Celo. Apparently the first use was at Owen's New Harmony in 1826, followed by the several experiments led by Josiah Warren, including Equity (Ohio, 1833–35) and Utopia (Ohio, 1847–51). What may have been the florescence of utopian labor exchange, however, occurred in Warren's final effort, Modern Times (Long Island, 1851–63) (see Wunderlich 1992, passim). Later, labor notes turned up at Ruskin (Tennessee, 1894–99) (Egerton 1977, 64–86).

2. For an idealistic and romanticized picture of the Arthur Morgan School, drawn from brief visits, interviews with teachers and students, and the school's promotional literature, see Gorman (1969).

3. Style of clothing and hair often carry heavy significance as symbolic indicators of character. Visitors to Oneida in the mid-nineteenth century were frequently shocked to find community women outfitted in an early version of bloomers (ankle-length pants) and wearing their hair bobbed (Klaw 1993, 38). The local furor raised by the Celo manager's bared torso and shorts was paralleled at Black Mountain College, where, at about the same time, the college community was charged with nudism, godlessness, and free love, based on local people's observations of students decked out in shorts and "wearing sandals that revealed *bare feet*" (Duberman 1972, 38). An engaging argument for the meanings of different hair styles is made by Leach (1958).

4. This seems to have remained the pattern for most modern utopian communities. See Wagner (1982); and Chmielewski, Kern, and Klee-Hartzell (1993).

5. The hora was the favorite dance in the kibbutz studied by Spiro. He describes the dance and analyzes its significance as follows: The hora "is a group dance in which the participants, who are linked to one another arm-on-shoulder, are united in a large circle. The group thus becomes a unity, in which each individual faces the center and can see every other individual. The unity of the group is expressed spatially and physically, but kinesthetically, as well, for the momentum of the dance creates a centrifugal force which

threatens to thrust the individual from the circle; but his centrifugality is counterbalanced by the centripetal force emanating from the entire group, and he is drawn again toward the center by the entwined arms of his fellows on either side. Thus the dancer experiences a sense of freedom and abandon, but it is a freedom checked at every step by the pressure of the group, whose sense of unity is enhanced all the more by the rhythmic beat of the feet and by the monotony of the never-ceasing repetition of the song. Thus can the group both create and express the hysteria of its individuals" (1970, 58).

PART 3

Worlds Apart:
Inside and Outside

7. Constructing Agreement

CELO COMMUNITY was one of a number of utopian settlements either founded or renewed by pacifists released from prison and CPS camps after World War II. Macedonia in Georgia, Bryn Gweled outside Philadelphia, Tanguy in rural Pennsylvania, Glen Gardner and Kingwood in New Jersey were some noteworthy examples (see Miller 1990 for an extensive list). Although their social arrangements differed—for instance, in the extent of communal activity and joint ownership of houses and other property—all these groups sought to construct new social and cultural frameworks and to serve the world as models of a better life.[1]

Celo's new members, like those of other communities, classified themselves as outcasts from American society. Not only had their wartime experiences given them solid assurance of their status as a minority, but their rejection of conventional social life had been strengthened by prolonged association with others of similar belief. Pacifism was central in their ideas about how human life should be carried on, but their sense of injustice was not confined to an abhorrence of war or the resort to violence. They sought new ways of living on a broad front.

Locked away in camps and prisons because of their pacifist beliefs, themselves and their families often ridiculed for their pacifist creed, it is not surprising that the new members, their wives, and children found Celo compelling as a place to share social life with others of presumably similar views. More than any specific blueprint of the society they envisioned, however, the members stressed the repugnant aspects of American life they meant to escape. Celo was no exception to the tendency of utopian community-builders to confine their visions to very general and undetailed prescriptions.

To serve a term in a CPS camp—and even more in a federal prison—required considerable financial sacrifice. No wages were paid in most cases, no allotments granted for dependents, no special privileges awaited at war's end (Pickett 1953, provides an overview of the management of the CPS camps). For the most part, those who joined Celo were between twenty and thirty years old; war had prevented them from putting firm roots in occupation or career. Although some had attended college, they had little money to continue formal education, and no hope of postwar training benefits. If conscientious objectors had held good jobs before the war, there was no guarantee that they be reserved for them afterward. Even had they wanted a good position in the national economy, public prejudice against them would have left slim opportunity. Or so was their perception.

Why Come to Celo?

With any deliberate attempt to establish a new community, or to form a new group of any kind, the question of motivation arises at once. Why did these people come to Celo? What possibilities did they expect to find or create there? One can approach answers to these questions through the recollections of those who threw in with Celo in the years 1945–50, and by examination of statements made when they applied for membership. What this reveals is both similarity, a sense of shared belief, and diversity in how practice might reflect those beliefs.

"There was a lot of interest and talk in the CPS camps about community," recalled one member (in 1965). "We felt a kind of brotherhood, a spirit of community, in the camps that I didn't want to lose." According to the former CPS and prison inmates who arrived in Celo during 1945–50, a desire for preservation of close fellowship was joined with an impatience to get on with something significant and worthwhile. Tasks assigned them in the camps had "often appeared futile and lacking in any immediate importance" (American Friends Service Committee 1945, 10). Their requests for transfer to various private social work had been summarily rejected; their skills and idealism deemed useless.

Celo Community's lack of rigid ideological tests was appealing as a call for diversity and experimentation; Morgan had said as much in his lectures. On many occasions, he continued to insist that Celo was not open to those who advocated "any particular way of reforming society and who would plan to force their views on the Community" (Morgan 1957a). But membership, as a publicity flyer (written by Morgan) noted in 1942, "requires something more than a desire to improve one's economic status. An interest in community building is essential." Besides the "craving for congenial society" and the necessity of making a living, "there needs to be a strong common purpose to try to get at the meaning of living, and willingness to undergo discipline and privation in order to serve one's highest purposes." Clearly, it was an offer to trade physical comfort (perhaps only temporarily) for the pursuit of higher moral and ethical goals.

One member explained his early days in the Community. He and his family came, he told me in 1965, "because there were some people here who were thinking about important things, it seemed to us. There were different kinds of people here, and it was exciting to help build a community. It was unfinished, with people having a hard time getting along, economically. There was a lot of fellowship, though, in that poverty. We could all laugh about it together."

Another CPS graduate, who left Celo after more than ten years, also saw it as "a place where I could go on living in closeness and harmony with people who shared some of my ideas." All sought a niche where behavior need not compromise beliefs and where they could commit themselves to a project of great moral usefulness. Merely to retire from a world that had shunned and punished them would have been a selfish act, one forbidden by their self-conception. Personal advantage must be sacrificed, whenever necessary, to the higher purpose of serving others.

A somewhat less positive reason for joining was suggested by an ex-member. Some years after leaving in disillusionment and frustration, she published a brief memoir of her time in "Winterstar," as she called Celo. As to motives for joining, she declared: "I think that nearly everyone came to Winterstar against the fist of some fear or anxiety. For most, it was the fear of 'normal' life after the rigors of prison or war. Winterstar was a refuge and their stay there a time of healing" (Greenbough 1959, 14). Fear and anxiety? Perhaps it was more distaste than fear of what they might expect in conventional, "normal" American life. Regardless, the postwar members' view of themselves certainly seemed to fit Morgan's expectations, spelled out in a Community information pamphlet in 1945. He believed, he wrote, "that the chance to participate in working out a program and polity will attract intelligent people of pioneering spirit and discourage those who want to settle into a ready-made pattern."

When they assumed control over Community affairs in the final years of World War II, Celo's members began to define themselves and their community-building project. They set down two aims which voiced their desire to combine mutual aid and individual autonomy. They wanted to create a "community of independent neighbors" and to "develop a Community where every person can have a sense of belonging" (CCI, 6/7/44).

With a view of the Community as a place to express personal beliefs, and an awareness of differences among themselves despite an assumed agreement on primary goals, they were inclined to consider Celo a protective shell within which a number of economic and social approaches could be worked out. They came to Celo to avoid excessive conformity and preferred to keep separate households. If a communal arrangement were decreed for the entire Community, they feared, some might use Celo's joint resources parasitically, leading to dependence upon the Community for survival. Whether from personal disappointment, such as one member's expressed dislike for the "close living" he had experienced in the CPS camps, or from a more abstract notion of preserving individual freedom of action, there was general agreement that the Community should not be entirely communal. The decision pleased Morgan, who had gloomily portrayed for the members the Community's past failures in various communal schemes.

The deep antipathy to conformity, a symbol of much that they hated in American society, was a major consideration in limiting common ownership and activity. An example of what Community members saw as a necessary balance of individualism and cooperation was provided by Arle Brooks's comment, written the year before he joined Celo: "We must deliberately create an environment in which individuals are not forced to conform, but may have the freedom of creative choice; yet where there is a stable influence which would aid one in making choices" (Brooks 1946, 7).[2]

Yet to make Celo into an ordinary community, where each household might remain unrelated to its neighbors, would extend autonomy and individualism too far. Dislike the demands of conformity they did, but the members still held as a major goal the achievement of harmony: among themselves in Celo, between themselves and the local mountain folk, in the worldwide "brotherhood of man," and between themselves and their nonhuman environment. They were reticent about declaring their commitment in the Community's official documents, but members referred to this ideal, in interviews and written notes, time and again. Statements published by other communities, from whom Celo sought assistance in writing the Community's bylaws, were explicit about the same sentiments held by Celo's members.

The 1948 annual report of Macedonia Community, founded in 1937 and, like Celo, undergoing a replacement of its population by former CPS internees, put the notion of harmony this way: "The most important thing to us here is not the business activity of the place but the special quality of relationship among living things. The larger entity which is Macedonia Cooperative Community is composed of smaller entities: the micro-organisms that are enriching our soil; the grass, trees, and plants growing in that soil; and the animals and people who feed on the products of the soil" (Macedonia Cooperative Community 1948, 3).

Bryn Gweled (Welsh for "hill of vision"), a cooperative enterprise begun in Pennsylvania in 1940, also felt rapid growth with a postwar influx of pacifists. As for tolerance of diversity, indeed the encouragement and cultivation of it, the retrospective declaration published in 1956 expressed the aims of Celo as well. Men and women in Bryn Gweled, its members wrote, "wanted to live harmoniously among friendly people, where the beauty found in nature was as little spoiled as possible. They wanted to see their children grow up accustomed to playing freely with other children of any race or creed. They wanted to know that their neighbors, by whose children their own would inevitably be influenced, felt similarly on questions of human evaluation, and tolerance of the opinions of others" (Bryn Gweled Homesteads 1956).

Celo and similar settlements of the period were peopled largely with pacifists released from prison and CPS camps, and their efforts were based on a firm rejection of conventional America. From their perspective, they had been thrown into jail or held in CPS camps because they refused to compromise individual belief. A political minority, they had personally known persecution. Intolerance for diversity of belief and behavior, coded as an overwhelming demand for conformity, was coupled with economic exploitation as two detested features of life outside the communities. Celo, according to a pamphlet written by members in 1950, "is not an attempt to escape the problems of the world. Some necessary escape it does offer, members believe, from commercialized distractions that hinder cultivation of lives capable of creating peace. Such cultivation is the central problem which like-minded persons are invited to share. . . . As to the future, the pattern [of community life] remains flexible, leaving individuals and small groups within the Community free to experiment with more specialized patterns."

Taking advantage of their respite from conventional social and cultural modes, the members set about experimentation. The ideal was to construct, for oneself and one's family, an existence of rounded participation in all facets of life. By fashioning a balanced and complete life, one might come nearer the goal Arthur Morgan had set, to discover the meaning of life. Preston Morrow, a member of the Community from 1950 to 1954 and quite representative in his ideals, told me in 1966 that he came to Celo,

> as we all did, in my opinion, to get close to life, real life. Working up there in a Philadelphia office as I was, there was never any chance to have anything but secondary experiences. Life seemed too remote, too many things got between

me [and life] and I thought I had no connection, no roots in, the kind of life that was genuine. I wanted some primary experiences.

When you get down in your garden and work with your hands—that's a primary experience. When you build your own house, or when you make the kids' toys out of whatever's available, that's a primary experience. We even had one baby at home, for the experience. Then, when Arle Brooks died, the men in the Community all got together and made a plain coffin; we managed the whole thing ourselves. I think it's important, for kids especially, but for adults too, to have those primary experiences: to find out for yourself how things are born—people and plants and animals—and grow and die. That's the only way you can get right down to the core of real life.

Novel approaches in agriculture, in the construction of members' houses, in the formation of committees and the composition of Community documents, in working out ways to eliminate social conflict, in setting up schemes for sharing labor and doing away with monetary exchange, in devising different kinds of mutual aid: almost every part of Community life in these postwar years was suffused by a self-conscious search for new techniques, for "a better way."

It was an exhilarating time, full of promise and hope for achievement. The tone of bold exploration emerged quite clearly in a report by a religious social worker who surveyed Celo in 1947 at Morgan's request. She explained:

> It is a group of folk who, for the most part, have wanted to escape from the mass discipline of mass industry but I had the feeling they had not yet learned the more difficult discipline of disciplining themselves. Again, some of them are so anxious to discover all of life for themselves that they are not even willing to accept the best scientific principles as these are discovered to date by persons much wiser than they. This revealed itself through the failure of many of them in producing good garden crops. On two occasions when I asked if the persons in question had used certain well known planting and cultivating practices, I was told that there was a search for a better way.

Their drive to discover life all anew for themselves should not surprise. Their youthfulness, prolonged by the interruptions and occupational aimlessness of wartime internment, might account for some of the firmness of their commitment and their vigor in trying to build a new world. Their links to occupation or career were weak or nonexistent. Ties with their childhood homes and families of orientation had been severed and those to families of procreation, with the multiple responsibilities thus entailed, just beginning. Most of them were at a personal stage of in-betweenness. They stood, as Erik Erikson observed for youth in general, "between the past and the future," both in individual life and in society, where ideologies "offer . . . overly simplified and yet determined answers to exactly those vague inner states and those urgent questions which arise in consequence of identity conflict" (Erikson 1960, 39).

For a few of Celo's new members, the road to a liberal, reformist outlook had opened only during their time in CPS camp. Howard Goggin, to mention one case, seems to have been transformed. Recommending Goggin for membership, his CPS supervisor remarked, "Howard was a conservative chap with very little social vision. During the time he was in camp he made exceptional strides in developing a liberal attitude on social and economic problems. He became tolerant of many things which he did not countenance when he first arrived in camp. In fact, it is my impression that Howard has become so ultra-liberal that he would be intolerant of people who hold the same prejudice he formerly held."

But more was at stake here than just personal yearning for a better life. The postwar world appeared to hang between past and future, old and new, finished war and incomplete peace. Erich Kahler, writing in the *American Scholar* in 1946, expressed the sense of many Americans that a new age had dawned:

> The appearance of the atomic bomb has not created a substantially new situation, but it has nevertheless completely changed the world. The state in which mankind finds itself now is no different from what it was before Hiroshima; it is one that long ago crept up on us unobserved. . . . Entangled in . . . gigantic mass relationships, the individual sinks to hopeless insignificance, impotence, and ignorance. In the tumult of our daily life and business in a metropolis, where press and radio, with their ceaseless waves of urgent news, sweep away even the experiences of yesterday—in this overwhelming turmoil, no sort of connected memories, and hence no coherent knowledge, can be built up. (1946, 167, 170–71)

It is clear that, in Celo no less than in similar settlements of the period from the mid-1930s through the 1950s, the intention was to create new social and cultural forms as examples for the world. Morgan hoped for Celo to become a "master community"; members of other communities saw their work as experimental beacons to better worlds. For example, Tanguy Homesteads, a Pennsylvania group begun in 1945, hoped that "a community such as ours may serve as a humble example, pointing the way to a better civilization" (Tanguy Homesteads publicity 1950). And the less radical settlers at Melbourne Village in Florida, to whom "Dr. Arthur Morgan, formerly of Antioch College and T.V.A. acted as consultant," intended "to demonstrate the

American way of life *at its best* so convincingly that groups in other parts of the country will be inspired to increasingly fruitful experimentation along similar lines" (Melbourne Village 1950, 1; emphasis added).

Consensus Decision-Making

As they set off in their search for the new, the experimental, the unique in housebuilding, diet, and sharing of resources, the Community's members worked within the shelter of Celo. If individuals or family groups preferred to adhere to, say, vegetarian diets, they had wide latitude to write their own rules. One could limit oneself to eating only fruits, nuts, and vegetables or one might go further and avoid the use of animal products entirely. One vegetarian family in Celo (in the early 1950s) wore only canvas shoes and belts, kept no pets, and did not eat eggs, since sustained egg production requires killing male chickens. It was when decisions were made, courses of action set, for the entire Community that members' freedom was limited.

Consensus, sometimes translated in Celo with a Quaker phrase, "sense of the meeting," was the means chosen for decision-making in Community meetings. The desire for a harmonious and unified membership was politically embodied in the rule of consensus. Through consensus, all were equal, all involved in each decision; once a decision was taken, no sour minority would survive to weaken Community solidarity.

The failures of the United States, in the Community members' view, formed an integrated pattern. Their way of looking upon all life as a whole, with the ideal as "balanced and rounded," focused on competitiveness as a basic evil in existing social arrangements. From competition arose exploitation, conflict, violence, and, of course, inequality. On the political plane, competitiveness was rule by majority, a technique based on (and generating) a kind of social atomism. When decisions were made by simple numerical majorities, the individual voter was an isolated, powerless digit. Their experiences in political minorities reinforced their ideological position that democratic methods invariably produced a tyrannical majority and a disgruntled, ineffectual minority.

In politics as in all else, they held out for harmonious unity: they aimed for an organic combination of human beings, between them and nature, and among all facets of individual existence. Each person was part of a larger whole; in political matters, each member should be firmly attached to the Community.[3]

Consensus as the means of making decisions for the Community as a whole was the most enduring effort in Celo at achieving harmony among the members. It was the centerpiece of their efforts to come to agreement on basic principles. Agreement not just upon how to make a new society, but also on the meaning of what they were creating.

In selecting consensus as a key feature of their enterprise, they were very much like other American utopian groups regardless of historical era. In recent years, for instance, Alpha Farm (established in Oregon in 1972) displayed its members' awareness that consensus has far wider implications than the making of joint decisions. They described themselves in 1991: "Consensus, our decision-making process, is also a metaphor for the ideal world we seek to create here—and so help create in the larger world. We seek to honor and respect the spirit in all people and in nature; to nurture harmony within ourselves, among people, and with the earth; and to integrate all of life into a balanced whole" (Fellowship for Intentional Community 1990, 169). From his analysis of 120 contemporary communities, Zablocki concluded, "Legislative assemblies have always been rare among communes. Voting has never been a popular way of deciding the outcome of divisive issues. Consenual [*sic*] meetings of the whole, seeking to come to a common mind, have been the norm. . . . Consensus itself is the most prominent goal among communitarians. . . . to find a group of people with whom one can agree about fundamental values and goals can . . . become an end in itself" (1980, 47, 200).

Very soon after installing consensus as a method for reaching decisions, Celo's members found themselves with a problem that proved the most persistent and difficult in the Community's existence. A number of issues arose from their use of consensus to make decisions.

The definition of consensus itself posed a difficulty. If it is defined, on the one hand, in the Quaker usage as the "sense of the meeting," then unanimity would not appear to be required. Yet if, after long discussion and, presumably, the adjustment of views by compromise, a clear sense of the meeting is not apparent, what action can be taken? Does the group then resort to an implicit form of decision by majority/minority procedures? If so, then how large a minority can be tolerated without rending the assumed fabric of harmony and unity?

On the other hand, making consensus synonymous with unanimity brings on the possibility of halting decision-making altogether. If consensus prescribes unanimity, a single person can block decisions. Not only does the group face inaction, but such a definition easily threatens another kind of tyranny: the tyranny of a minority. To avoid such a situation, how can a disagreeing minority be persuaded of the wisdom of the majority's view? What happens, finally, if all attempts to persuade fail; what if there remain hold-outs?

Making decisions by consensus is inherently problematic for any group as devoted to harmonious relationships as were Celo's members. Taken as a matter of moral and ethical principle, consensus requires agreement on fundamental values. Logically, it demands unanimity. Keith Graham, a British philosopher, apparently taking "utopian" to be hopelessly idealistic, argues for the inevitable failure of consensus. He writes:

> Consider the following Utopian suggestion. In any form of collective decision-making, decisions which issue from the will of a minority or a majority are a moral affront. The individual has a moral duty to follow the dictates of his or her own conscience. If we assume, therefore, that any member of a collective actually has a preference that some particular state of affairs should exist and (what is no doubt a larger assumption) that he holds this preference as a matter of bona fide moral conviction, then the institution of some contrary state of affairs will thwart his will: it actually prevents him from conforming to the requirements of morality. True, if it is the majority's will which prevails then fewer unfortunates will end up in this position than otherwise, but some will nevertheless. Accordingly, collective decisions ought to be based upon unanimity. The right to impose ought not to be the prerogative of any social group, whatever its numerical relation to the remainder. The only way for the autonomy of the moral subject to be preserved is for the whole community to act in concert. And since such acts are to be the expression in the outside world of moral conviction arrived at in the inner sanctum of conscience, it must also be a requirement that the whole community think in concert. (Graham 1984, 49)

Of course, not all matters that require decision spring from "bona fide moral conviction," and thus the potential for compromise is greater in some circumstances than in others. Acknowledging a wide range in utopian communities' efforts at the "subordination of individuality to the communal will," Zablocki found that issues of low ideological significance might be decided by vote. He posed eleven hypothetical situations to members of his large sample and found that "it is the least ideological of the situations (deciding what color to paint the walls of a common room) that evoked the most claims that members would decide the issue by voting" (1980, 250).

Confronted with the necessity of making decisions, Celo's members used several techniques to overcome or ignore differences among themselves. Standing committees were formed to craft proposed courses of action—a particularly useful way of dealing with practical (and time-consuming) matters like renting unused portions of Community cropland, repairing empty houses, and keeping track of finances. Some questions failed to gain consensual agreement and were turned over to special committees, where discussion of significant but troublesome matters continued. In addition, Celo's members made many decisions that were contrary to the general rules and principles they had fashioned. Marked as exceptions in the Community's records, such choices were accompanied by a reaffirmation of the rules. The Community's historical documents provide a rich source of specific examples of these practices. An examination of each technique should clarify the challenges the members faced with their insistence on adhering to the consensus procedure.

Standing Committees

Committees proliferated in Celo, with purposes ranging from maintenance of the Community library, to planning for a child-care center, to keeping financial records, to providing hospitality for visitors. Meetings of all committees were open to the entire membership, and each brought regular reports and proposals to Community meeting. Although the proposals were usually accepted, they were thoroughly discussed and sometimes returned to a committee for further study. Two committees, property and finance, were most significant: they endured longer and were consistently busier than others. Hardly a single Community meeting passed without a report from each of the two.

The Finance Committee maintained financial records for the Community, issued regular reports, granted or recommended loans to members, and proposed changes in Community investments and interest rates for loans. An example of easy agreement occurred when the co-op building, by then organized separately from the Community, was severely damaged by a flood in 1977. The Finance Committee recommended a year-long moratorium on rent payments and a ten-year loan from the Community. The proposal was quickly and unanimously approved (CCI, 12/7/77). In ordinary times, however, the members insisted on reaffirming their rules even as they approved exceptions. In a committee report of 1973, for example, the chairman "brought up Bill's request for a business loan. He wanted to borrow $450.00 for a truck and pay it back over the next six months. After a discussion it was approved, although it isn't the usual procedure" (CCI, 5/2/73).

Devising proposals for long-term financial management, however, was the special task of the committee, as the following plan illustrates. They suggested that Celo "set aside money from the sale of forest products to help pay taxes on unallocated land. We need a regular income from our land, at least

$1,000/yr. and we will be eligible for a tax reduction if the income is from farming and timbering" (CCI, 2/1/78).

Even more active than the financial group was the Property Committee. Charged with the maintenance of Celo's jointly owned real estate, mainly unoccupied buildings and unused cropland and forests, the Property Committee met at least once, often several times, a month. They decided rental rates, established property values for purposes of settlement with those who had left Celo, scheduled Community workdays for the repair of roads and buildings, and came up with ways to protect and improve Celo's land. Serving as the Community's property guardians, the committee zealously took on matters large and small. For example, they attempted strict enforcement of the rule requiring the Community's prior approval for rental of members' houses to nonmembers, as the following reports reveal. To a Property Committee meeting in 1971, Barbara Miller introduced the "possibility of renting her pottery building to Tom Bleck, of Detroit, to use as a pottery. The matter will be considered if and when Barbara or Tom make official inquiry. This does raise the problem, in principle, of community members renting property on a long-time basis to non-members" (CCI, 8/18/71). Later, Barbara formally requested approval to rent the building and the Community agreed, but only after considerable discussion and only on a month-to-month basis (CCI, 9/1/71).

Action without proper authorization was dealt with summarily. Advised that a nonmember had rented and already moved into an absent member's house, the members decreed that the nonmember "is asked to come to the next property committee meeting to put in a proper request and discuss it with us" (CCI, 5/1/74).

By far the knottiest problems for the property committee had to do with the use of fertilizers and chemical herbicides. These issues struck the moral chord of a large proportion of Celo's membership; they could not be dispensed with as mere practical matters. One can sense the feeling of relief when events postponed decisions on these divisive topics, as shown in these excerpts from minutes of meetings in the mid-1970s. "Objections to the use of chemical fertilizers [on Community hayfields] were again voiced and the issue was sent back to Property committee, giving authority for it to make final decision at its next meeting" (CCI, 4/2/75). But by the next meeting, the fertilizer question was temporarily laid to rest, leaving the weed poison dilemma unchanged. A local farmer

> will cut the hay lands twice, apply no fertilizer, and pay 30c/bale. The money realized can be used for lime or whatever later soil tests indicate is needed. This avoids a decision on the use of non-organic fertilizers at this time. There was

further discussion continued from Property Committee [meeting] on the use of 2,4,5,T, the pressing need to control poison ivy and multiflora rose versus very intense feelings by some that the chemical is too dangerous to use at all. Present policy is to allow individuals the use of 2,4,5,T with great caution and requiring the posting of sprayed areas. There will be a moratorium on this policy until the next Property meeting, to allow time for gathering any new facts that should be considered. (CCI, 5/7/75)

Eventually, they decided against the use of 2,4,5,T, but only after protracted argument and investigation.

Recording Dissent

From time to time the sole obstacle to consensual action was the dissenting view of a single member. These situations could be avoided, and frequently were, by casual discussion outside official meetings. It then became clear that a dissenter stood alone, and he or she might remain silent in meetings. If the potential dissenter felt strongly enough, however, he or she could voice disagreement but, in a magnanimous gesture, request that objection be entered in the Community record without holding up the group's decision. One such event came early in the years of self-government. The members found themselves with surplus funds and discussed how to use the money for loans to individual members. The proposal that gained favor immediately was to set interest rates on loans at the same percentage as the Community received from its savings account in a local bank, at that time 3 percent. Arle Brooks, a man of deep religious conviction, declared that to charge any interest whatever would be usury. After long discussion, he remained a minority of one. Not wanting to frustrate a decision supported by all but himself, Brooks abstained, requesting that his view be recorded (CCI, 4/5/49).

There were repetitions of this procedure, with variations, through the Community's history. When members considered naming a new director to the Community's corporate board in 1973, for instance, one objected to the man proposed because he was divorced. Sensing himself in the awkward position of single dissenter, he announced that "if he is the only one that feels this [way] he won't stand in the way of his [the prospective director] being elected" (CCI, 4/4/73).

Six years later, the same member objected to accepting a trial member because she lived with a man to whom she was not married. Again a lone dissenter, he asked "us to think about it for a month and come back for a discussion of the issue. If after that discussion other members still feel she should be granted trial member status, Dan said he would not block consensus" (CCI, 2/7/79). A month later, opinions were mixed. One person, a liberal-minded Methodist social worker, thought "Joyce's trial membership was not the appropriate occasion for the Community to become judgmental." Dan's solitary objection, however, was joined by other members who shared his conventional view of marriage. Several declared that "although they had nothing personal against Joyce they were against unmarried couples living together. Other people felt that we should look at a person as an individual, not at their status. . . . Consensus was reached to accept Joyce as a trial member and that people who still had questions would get further clarification during her trial membership period" (CCI, 3/7/79).

Affirmation by Exception

By far the most effective technique for evading the restrictions of consensus was to grant exceptions to established policy and, at the same time, note explicitly that the policy remained in force. Numerous uses of this technique are found in the Community's records. The likelihood of drawn-out argument on issues of membership and leaves of absence were frequently forestalled by making exceptions. Such crucial matters lay at the very foundation of the Community's existence. In circumstances which demanded that each family provide for its own subsistence in a region of low economic opportunity, Celo tried to balance its rule that members should be Community residents with the grim prospects faced by all.

Henry Nilsson, for example, found that he could no longer provide for his family by building houses and rustic furniture. In resuming his previous career as a Protestant minister, he was unable to reside in Celo. Since he planned to return to the Community upon retirement, he asked for a leave of absence. Given the special circumstances, his request was granted in 1961. Leaves of absence, according to Community policy, could be granted and renewed for only one year at a time, so Henry's leave came up for routine renewal every year for the next two decades.

Facing similar problems, some members resigned their membership and left to pursue new careers. But a committed few, forced to make a living at some distance from Celo, wanted to maintain their holdings in hopes of returning in the future. By 1972 a variety of special arrangements had been made with absentees; the situation approached chaos. Because of this complexity, those at the meeting "reiterated their intention to abide by Community policy with regard to absenteeism rather strictly in the future—that is[,] to grant leave of absence on a yearly basis only" (CCI, 10/4/72). Having thus provided for stability and continuity, they immediately moved on to make "adjustments for individual cases," including four special exemptions for lengthy absences.

Rapid growth in membership in the 1970s put added pressure on the policy that trial members should live within Community boundaries. Two kinds of solution were found for the problem of housing shortage: allowing potential members to live outside Celo and granting permission to build within the Community before full membership was achieved.

One case of this kind came before them in 1977. Two families who wanted to join as trial members could find no housing available within the Community. The members considered the problem and "agreed that the principle be retained that applicants be considered for membership only if they live in the Community, but that exceptions will be made if there is a definite schedule for building or renting on [in] the Community" (CCI, 10/19/77). Similar decisions were taken several times during that decade, each time with a reminder that the "principle" remained unchanged.

Another solution—building a house in Celo before permanent member status had been bestowed—entailed some risk. Nevertheless, some applicants were either confident of acceptance or willing to take the plunge. A trial member asked in 1970 for permission "to start clearing land for a house, get electricity, etc. before the end of his trial membership" and "was cautioned that he might lose all improvements if he had to move away 'unexpectedly.'" His petition was granted, although as usual this was noted as an instance of "flexibility . . . without setting a precedent" (CCI, 10/7/70).

Making an investment without assurance of permanence was less hazardous for other applicants. A double exception was made for Carl Halsbeck, who had held member status during the early 1950s. He left to attend graduate school, then to teach for some years, but he kept his ties with Community members, always intending to retire in Celo. By the late 1970s, he was ready, and he applied for trial membership for himself and his wife. "They were received with enthusiasm, particularly by those who know the Halsbecks well. Questions centered around the CCI policy of not accepting or encouraging applicants past 60. Everyone seemed to feel that this rule need not apply to the Halsbecks in view of their unusual vitality, zest and appetite for constructive new projects and particularly in view of Carl's having been a highly valued member of long standing who has maintained an unflagging interest in CCI" (CCI, 9/7/77).

After some delays due to illness, the Halsbecks arrived and asked if they could build a shed to live in while they were trial members. They agreed to "leave this structure with no payment" if they were rejected as full members. "This is an exception made in the knowledge that Carl Halsbeck was a former member." Still, the decision upset some members who voiced their "reluctance" at the making of yet another exception to established rules (CCI, 4/5/78).

Despite the careful affirmation of principle that accompanied each special arrangement, adjustment, or exception, the obvious failure to toe a consistent line irritated them. And they firmly expressed a determination to adhere to established plans even in relatively small things. When the finance committee, for example, reported at one point that it had increased the interest rate on loans "to keep up with inflation," the members approved the single loan made under the new rate, but they "emphasized the need to follow the established procedures for loaning and borrowing or else to change the procedure" (CCI, 4/1/70). At the next regular meeting, they officially changed the interest rate for all loans (CCI, 5/6/70).

Diversity and Consensus

The very diversity among the members, of which they were so proud, set snares on their way to consensual decisions. Over and over, they preened themselves on their individuality and difference. Conversations with sympathetic visitors (including ethnographers) often centered on contrasts they saw between their experiment and an undifferentiated mass society beyond the local region. Periodically, discussion at Community meetings turned from routines of land rental and making loans to a stocktaking of their past and a restatement of aspirations for the future.

One of these occasions arose at a particularly low point—1967—in Celo's history. With the Community's membership reduced to twenty-nine adults, its demise already anticipated, and contingency plans for disposal of Community property securely in place, the remaining members bravely assessed their situation: "Although there are probably as many shadings of opinion as there are members, all have high sights and high ideals that have not visibly lowered in the 15 or 20 years that some people have been striving toward them." Looking back over the history of the project, they calculated it a "major strength" of the Community "that there has been no incorporated religious or philosophical dogma." The Community, beyond its basis as a landowning cooperative, "has been a vital mixture of ideas and people." Whatever its future course, Celo's "body of membership should be as lithe and free of encumbrance as possible" and "continue to encompass and profit from the varieties of age, experience, outlook and physical vigor available to it" (CCI, 3/1/67).

Underneath their treasured diversity, perhaps making it possible in the first place, in their estimation, lay common goals. The members concluded this celebration of variety with a reaffirmation of shared goals: "The common bond among members is a desire and willingness to keep on creating a human community that is better than any randomly chosen suburban one—in its physical setting, social conscience, and potential influence on its neighbors" (CCI, 3/1/67).

The reference to alternatives as "randomly chosen suburban" communities underscored their vision of conventional America as a mass society where ethical compromise and domination by urban centralization was unavoidable. Nonetheless, a commitment to perseverance in constructing an example for the world, however firmly held, does not guarantee agreement on concrete matters. Practical problems might be left to committees, radical notions might be registered as individual dissent as the group proceeds to decision, but there were some problems more difficult of solution. Chief among these were decisions about membership: acceptance of new permanent members (as opposed to those on trial) and settling accounts with members who left, especially those who departed in anger or disgust.

Notes

1. Bassett credits the Quakers with substantial influence on communities existing in the 1950s. His compass, however, is too wide, including Quaker-inspired communities together with those which simply included some Quakers among the membership: "If one visits the comprehensive or partial co-operatives now functioning in America, he will find Friends or Friends' ways in several of them: Macedonia and the Society of Brothers in the first category, and among those attempting more limited co-operation, Bryn Gweled, Celo, Canterbury, Hidden Springs, Kingwood, and Tanguy Homesteads. The communitarian spirit lives on among Friends, not only because of the pertinence of latter-day monasticism in the atomic age, but also because there is a reservoir of communitarianism in their religious beliefs. The Friends are a Society, out of which will intermittently come those hardy members who are called to try the way of mutual education, mutual criticism, open worship, and mutual aid" (Bassett 1954, 99).

2. Unlike most names of Celo's members used here, Arle Brooks is not a pseudonym. In an autobiography published in 1994 by Celo's press, his widow, Arthelia, devotes a lengthy chapter to Arle's life. Her detailed and fond record would make mockery of any shield of anonymity; it would be a disservice here *not* to use his real name. See Brooks (1994).

3. The idea has been clearly stated by the Gandhian social philosopher Narayan: "Modern western democracy is based on a negation of the social nature of man and the true

nature of human society. This democracy conceives of a society as an inorganic mass of separate grains of individuals: the conception is that of an atomized society. The brick with which the present edifice of democratic polity is constructed is the individual voter and the whole process of democracy rests on the arithmetic of votes. The individual casts his vote as an atom of society, not as a living cell in organic relationship with other living cells. It is not living together that is expressed and represented in the institutions and processes of democracy, but an abstracted individual" (quoted, Bailey 1965, 3). The entire argument was expressed—piecemeal, far less succinctly, but just as impassioned— by Celo's members. Ultimately the argument rests, as Bailey observes, on the proposition that "Conflict is not inevitable and a part of human nature: it is the product of wrong institutions" (1965, 4). That is, it is part of a belief in social perfectionism.

8. Consensus: Recruits and Defectors

ONCE THE MEMBERS controlled Community policy (in the late 1940s) they decreed that members who had served a trial period of six months could be taken into full membership by consensus.[1] This was interpreted as consent by unanimity. For those entering Celo from CPS camps and prison (in one case as a military veteran who had converted to pacifism while serving in the navy) consensus was easily secured. In addition to the conscientious objectors and their families, two single members arrived in 1948 from Black Mountain College, an experimental educational community located fifty miles away (see Duberman 1972 for a historical analysis of the experiment).

But the consideration of membership for one family involved the Community in bitter dispute for over two years, culminating finally in acceptance by majority vote. In the process, Celo was almost destroyed, the necessity for unanimous agreement on new members was discarded, and the stage was set for the departure of half the membership. It was a pivotal moment in the Community's history. To understand the consequences of this event and why it bore so heavily on the Community's future, we must examine the specific issues. Much of the historical detail revolves around the health center built in Celo in 1948, its management, and the development of factions in the Community.

To make the Community more attractive, Regnery agreed to pay for the construction and equipment of a small health center. Federal regulations made it easier to obtain war surplus construction materials and medical supplies if a separate corporation was formed. Although the directors for the new organization, Celo Health and Education Corporation, were initially the same as those for the Community's parent corporation, the health center was a separate entity. Once a physician was found, the directors turned over to him the day-to-day operation of the center.

The new physician, Leonard Mann, had fled Nazi Germany in the 1930s, graduated from Harvard Medical School, and spent the war years in a North Carolina hospital as a Public Health Service officer. Morgan learned of him through distant relatives who had assisted Mann in emigrating to the United States. As Mann's wife recalled in 1966, her husband was so distressed at what he considered the rampant commercialism of medicine that he was "already toying with the idea" of giving up medical practice to go into business growing trees and shrubs in some isolated rural setting. Then he met Morgan, who offered him the position in Celo's new health center.

Space in the health center's two-story brick building was assured for the Community library, office, and meeting rooms. Part of the center might be used for Community purposes, but its management was clearly separate and firmly guided by Mann. Putting control of this grandest of all Community ventures outside the hands of members struck some as a violation of the steady progress they had made toward autonomy and self-rule.

An immediate success, the health center rapidly drew more patients from the mountain region than Mann could handle. With the directors' approval he hired another physician, Nathan Gordon. Gordon and his wife joined the Community, took a holding, and built a house. Great plans for extending services in preventive medicine and low-cost hospitalization were made. The large number of patients cut down on the time the doctors could devote to Community workdays, and a shortage of cash made it difficult for Community members to meet the schedule of the "pre-payment health plan" they had devised. A plan was worked out in which the two physicians would provide free medical services in lieu of their share of the cash and labor assessments levied on all members. Cooperation among center, Community, and local people outside Celo seemed promising.

The hopeful scene was soon spoiled. Friction between the two medical men emerged almost from the day Nathan Gordon joined the staff. Gordon's specialty was plastic surgery, and his emphasis was on treatment more than prevention. Mann grasped Gordon's philosophy of medicine—"always eager to perform surgery for the slightest reason," Mann recounted in 1966—as representative of American medicine and thus defective. While Gordon tried to reassure his patients with thorough (but often expensive) testing and a variety of medicines, Mann stressed better diet, simple diagnosis, and minimal use of drugs. Gordon's departure was a foregone conclusion; the directors accepted Mann's call for his dismissal.

Even without Mann's shove, it is doubtful that Gordon would have long remained in Celo. He and his wife had no experience of, nor apparent yearning for, life outside cities, and his desire to add medical specialists to the center's staff indicated that he was not likely to be satisfied as a generalist, the only medical role practicable in the region. His career plans became clear in one of his letters to Morgan: "I am seeking a university appointment. . . . I like to teach and to do research and wish to devote a major part of my time to one or both, with the remainder spent in the practice of plastic surgery" (4/3/51). Upon leaving Celo, Gordon became a consultant to a drug firm in New York.[2]

The sentiment against Mann and his control of the health center swelled with Gordon's removal. Part of the membership, led by Eric Evanson, one of three chemists operating a mail-order drug business in Celo, saw Mann as arrogant and high-handed. Evanson held intense feelings about prejudice against minority ethnic groups. When he learned that Gordon was leaving the Community, he immediately proclaimed that Gordon, a Jew, had been the victim of the anti-Semitism that lay at the very root of Celo Community. It was clear to everyone that Regnery, the financial angel of the Community, harbored a conventional bias against Jews. By accepting Regnery's support and yielding to his authority, according to Evanson, the Community implicated itself in anti-Semitism. To these charges, Mann retorted that Regnery's beliefs were personal and had not damaged Celo. Such defense could, in Evanson's view, only come from a fellow anti-Semite. If other members agreed with Evanson, they did not make their opinions public.

Stepping into his usual role as mediator, Morgan arrived in Celo and held long discussions with Evanson. Although he was quite familiar with Regnery's anti-Semitic views, what seemed to offend Morgan most was the virulence and dogmatism of Evanson's attacks on Regnery. Morgan left, and Evanson stormed into the next Community meeting to resign his membership. It was refused, and the members jointly composed a conciliatory letter to Morgan, arguing that Evanson "meant only that Mr. Regnery's generous contribution and participation and the Community members' daily work and struggle were complementary to each other, and he [Evanson] did not mean to put one in opposition to the other" (Members to AEM, 6/6/50).

For the next several years, the contest over control of the health center continued. Only in 1952 was a Community member named to the center's board of directors. The gulf between Mann's and Evanson's groups widened; peace was restored in one dispute after another only by those whose consistent support could be counted on by neither extreme.

While members sought more authority over management of the health center, amid charges of "fanatic dogmatism" (Mann against Evanson) and "cold materialism" (Evanson against Mann), another battle took shape and threatened to tear apart the entire project. It was a contest over the status of Mann's sister and her husband, both postwar refugees from Germany and residents in Celo since 1948.

Paul Wetzel, Mann's brother-in-law, had served as a captain in the German army during World War II. He was not a member of the Nazi party, but his association with militarism, and the taint of Hitler's racial imperialism, branded him—in the eyes of Evanson and a few others—as undesirable. Mann told me in 1965 that he wanted merely to give the Wetzels a temporary home; he did not intend to propose them as Community members. For his part, Paul Wetzel planned to stay in Celo only long enough to find permanent employment elsewhere. To him and his family, the Community was just a stopover on the road to a new life in America.

Living in Celo, however, meant being a member and taking a holding. The few exceptions to status as member-holder were the rentals of Community housing by parents of several members and the two instances, regarded as historical accidents, of members who owned their plots outright. Not Mann, but another member suggested that the Wetzels be accepted as members. The family's time in Celo had shown most members that, contrary to Evanson's assumption, the Wetzel family was not Mann's tool. They were friendly and outgoing in their relationships with others in Celo. They willingly took on their share of Community work, and they seemed to be well suited for life in this remote valley. Paul ran the Community's cooperative store for a small salary, his children went to school with other Community children, and both adults participated in workdays and Community meetings. In short, their presence as nonmembers was anomalous.

Membership for the Wetzels struck Evanson as the final confirmation that Celo had lost its bearings. From his perspective, a sharper contradiction could hardly be imagined: a former German military officer embraced by a group dedicated to nonviolence and tolerance. Add to this insult the danger of greater power for Mann in Community decisions, with a sister and her husband ready to do his bidding. Finally, Mann's stint in wartime government service (in the Public Health Service) certainly paralleled Wetzel's job in Nazi Germany. No, it would not do.

Membership for the Wetzels soon merged with a broad range of dissatisfactions and frustrations; it assumed the trappings of a showdown. The denial of membership to Mann's sister and her husband became a crusade, a way to demonstrate to Mann the power of other Community members.

The Wetzel question was discussed for almost two years, allowed to lie quietly for a time under a general ban on membership decisions, then taken up anew. Arguments raged over the goals of the Community in general, the criteria for membership, and, at last, over the consensus techniques for reaching decisions. In a situation of deadlock, to which the Wetzel membership rapidly brought them, the members postponed a decision and carried on lengthy discussion. Then they broke into smaller groups of four or five people, to give greater opportunity to air individual opinions. The religiously devout members held prayer meetings to seek divine guidance, and one remembered (in 1966) that "even Leonard [Mann] was in there confessing his sins. It looked like we might be able to cooperate with each other after all." An atheist, Mann was not likely to confess sin, but he did show contriteness. In a letter to Regnery he wrote: "As you know I tend to a certain violence of expression which had frequently been harmful to the cause of Community harmony. I am trying hard to improve on this and hope on their side the other members of the Community will show tolerance for occasional lapses" (Mann to WHR, 12/11/51).

These heroic and persistent efforts failed to yield consensus. Months of exhausting discussion had reduced the members to a state of suspicion, bitterness, accusation, and counteraccusation; to clear the air of hostility assumed highest priority. Frustration even led Evanson's wife to suggest that Celo be split into two separate communities. A decision by vote seemed unavoidable.

Evanson was confident that the Wetzels would be rejected and Mann's sway thereby diminished. "Everyone I talked to," he told me in 1965, "was against the way Mann was trying to run the Community as a personal empire, and they all thought this would just give him more power." But he overestimated the strength of the sentiment against the Wetzels; they were taken into membership by an 85 percent majority vote. Reporting to Morgan, the Community secretary noted that it had "been one of the big questions whether or not to continue the practice of seeking decisions by unanimous consent, or whether to provide for a percentage vote if consensus fails" (Secretary to AEM, 4/29/52).

Accepting the Wetzels was, for some of them, an act of charity: "they had no place to go, and we simply acted on a human basis—most of us, that is— and refused to toss them out," recollected one of the prayerful members (1966). Surely, if this attitude were widely held, the decision-by-vote could have been marked as an exception, as one of those case-by-case special adjustments. But there is no indication, either in Community records or members' reminiscences, that it was ever thought to be less than an announcement of principle. Henceforth, admission and expulsion of members would be put to a vote, and would carry by the same 85 percentage.

Dealing with Defectors

Evanson, already disillusioned with the Community, considered the inclusion of the Wetzels the final step toward betrayal of Celo's purposes. He withdrew from all participation in Community affairs and asked for a two-year leave of absence. The members granted his leave, and Evanson left his house in Celo in the care of his parents. At the end of two years, he wanted a renewal of leave and the members politely demanded an explanation for such a "special arrangement" (Members to Evanson, 12/8/54). Evanson responded by declaring that he had "no intention of returning to the Community to live in the near future" but would come for short visits with his parents. He expected them to live in his house as long as they needed it (Evanson to Members, 12/8/54). He now sought a "special holding agreement," to retain his holding but as an ex-member. This was seen as an effort to separate membership from residence, which the Community refused to consider. Community members invoked the procedures of their Holding Agreement and invited Evanson to join with them in the initial move toward a financial settlement: naming a committee to appraise his holding. As of the end of 1954, with the expiration of his leave, Evanson was declared to be no longer a Community member (CCI, 1/17/55).

By the terms of the Holding Agreement (the version of it in effect at the time he joined), Evanson was entitled to immediate payment for the value of the holding and improvements up to $900. In addition, if his holding was not taken by another member within a year (at his price), the Community was obligated to pay him 50 percent of the value above $900. The stumbling block was the appraisal of his holding. Centering on a different conception of "equity" arising from a change in the Community's appraisal of members' holdings, the argument involved a difference of about $1,700. But far more was in contention: the Community's insistence that profit through speculation was immoral.

An appraisal of Community houses, including Evanson's, in 1947 was based on construction costs without regard to appreciation or market value. This method followed Celo's policy that neither holder nor Community should reap financial profit from exchange of holdings, and reflected the conception of the Community as independent of the conventional economic system. The prevailing assumption was that the Community and its members were immune from fluctuations in market value of real estate and thus could ignore the immoral principle of the national economic system that allowed speculative profit.

Later, in the early 1950s, appraisals were radically increased to bring them into line with the county tax assessor's estimates of value. This was done to allow equitable sharing of real estate taxes among the Community members. In changing the appraisal method, there was general agreement that the price of holdings would not increase for those who had begun with the older system. (That is, the loan they were repaying to the Community for their holdings would remain the same.) Evanson had one of these holdings. The apparent growth in value of his holding, resulting from the large difference in the earlier and later appraisal, was the foundation of Evanson's dispute with the Community.

Evanson's insistence that the lion's share of the increased value of his holding rightfully belonged to him struck the members as a demand for speculative profit, and they resisted. It had never been the intention of the Community to use market value as the basis for appraising holdings, they agreed, and any use of market value in the past had been only for purposes of apportioning shares of county real estate taxes among individual households.

The attempt to settle with Evanson dragged on for years and reached a conclusion only at the end of 1957. The intervening years found the members spending almost all their spare time in meetings, discussion groups, mediation encounters with Evanson, or in doing research on their documents. It was an issue that consumed enormous energy and time. Charges of bad faith and greed flew between Evanson and Community members; accusations of "materialist" and "fanatic" reappeared among the members; prayer groups again looked for divine inspiration; ominous threats of further defection surfaced. Evanson's resort to communication through his attorney alerted them to the possibility of a court battle. This move fed apprehension in the Community that the Holding Agreement's unconventional features—"neither a deed nor a lease"[3]—might be found legally invalid. To many of them, litigation was another form of violence, and they opposed any use of legal action, defensive or offensive. One of these families announced a willingness to resign from Celo: "On the matter of litigation, we believe that, like war, it closes the door to friendship and love, and creates further hatred. . . . if the community feels that we hamper it too much in this matter, we are willing to resign" (undated memo). To the contrary, proclaimed a small but vocal minority, we should abide strictly by the terms of the Holding Agreement, to the point of a court test if necessary. Indeed, a legal decision did not disturb them, "because it might be good to know exactly where our holding agreement stands." Only the time was not ripe; the "strained situation" and the principled objection of some members made litigation inadvisable at the moment.

When they found it impossible to come to a unified position in open meetings, either of the full membership or in smaller groups, they tried other tactics. At one point, each member submitted a written proposal for dealing with Evanson, and the proposals were discussed at great length. The only apparent agreement among them was that the Community had made several fair offers and Evanson was greedily trying to come out with an unjust "profit." One member's proposal pungently captured the general hardening of views. Evanson, he wrote, should approach the Community directly and participate in setting up a board of arbitration: "I am against what seems to me trying to offer my lord some more roast squab and having him turn it down because the arrangement of the parsley displeases him. From now on, he helps cook it or he eats it raw."

After several years of enervating dispute, most members considered it imperative that the matter be laid to rest, almost without regard to cost. They appointed one person to conduct a poll, in which each resident member was separately interviewed. As expected, a large majority of members came out for compromise, although the proposed terms differed widely. It was the comments appended to the poll's tabulated results, however, that revealed what the controversy had done to Community harmony. It became clear that the amount of money was not a main concern. Even put into simple cost-benefit terms, as one of them analyzed the matter, protracted argument was not worth it: "If you count all the hours that go into all the meetings, it seems that a little extra money isn't worth the time and energy . . . I can't get awfully excited about the amount of money. The human relations are more important. . . . To spend endless time to save a small amount of money doesn't seem worth while. In your own business you frequently pay more money to get things done" (CCI poll, 12/56). Most thought it best ended quickly because "it causes so much disruption and taking sides and accusations within the community." Another said: "We should close it because it is a source of accusation, spoken and unspoken, poisons relationships, is bad for us and we ought to get rid of it. If we have done things that are foolish in our stewardship, let's pay for it, learn from our experience, and put things on a sounder basis" (ibid.). For several of them, financially the sky was the limit, the highest goal to restore peace and harmony. "I would be willing," said one member, "to go as high as [Evanson] wanted—whatever it is—because I would rather give people what they want than to have hard feelings. I would rather be the one to suffer than have the other fellow do it. It is possible to do this without thinking the other person is right" (ibid.).

In the end, the Evanson matter was turned over to a special committee "given full authority to negotiate a settlement . . . limited only by their conscientious concern to consider the opinion of each Community member" (CCI, 12/3/56). Evanson got part of what he demanded as a share of the increase in value, and more than the Community thought fair. At least the matter was laid to rest.

Judged solely by the surviving documentary record, the negotiations assumed impressive proportions. Added to the records of poll interviews and individual statements of opinion, there are numerous letters to and from Evanson, and several closely argued papers justifying the Community's position. After a diligent search through Community records for evidence, one member circulated a treatise of seven single-spaced, typed pages, in which she presented a series of complicated arguments on everything from the predictable attitudes of defectors to the concept of "equity" and the distinction between holder, renter, and owner.

Leaving for Careers and Other Communities

The years of wrangling over the Wetzels' membership and Evanson's departure put Celo in crisis. Several members had decided to forge new careers and left with financial settlements arrived at, for the most part, in an atmosphere of mutual respect. More significant, however, was the exit of eight members (in five households) who experienced a religious conversion and joined the Society of Brothers. As members of three of these converted families told me in 1966, they foresaw only continued strife and dissension in Celo. The prospects of finding in the Community that sense of closeness and cooperativeness for which they had struggled appeared very dim. The Society of Brothers offered a new world of security and peace for those like themselves who were willing "to turn away from all loveless self-interest and all that excludes the life of one's fellows" (Society of Brothers 1952, 41). At last a thoroughly communal life, a goal to which these members had already dedicated themselves and tried to achieve within the bounds of Celo, came to them as a definite possibility. In Mann's report of their withdrawal, the emphasis on religious motivation was combined with an accurate assessment of their economic hardship. He wrote Morgan and Regnery that the major

> motivating forces behind the decision to join the Bruderhof [Society of Brothers] appear to be religious, the forces which generally lead people to embrace a monastic way of living. Celo Community has of course never been primarily a religious community and that appears to be Celo's greatest shortcoming in the eyes of the converts. . . . Under the circumstances it is not at all surprising that the Bruderhof would have a strong appeal to this group, all the more so because

of the material difficulties which they have encountered here in Celo. Geograph-
ically they have been somewhat separated from the remainder of the Community and had formed something of a smaller community within the larger.
(Mann to AEM and WHR, 5/29/54)

Further details about the relationship of Celo and the Bruderhof are offered
in chapter 9.

More important for the present discussion is to attempt an understanding of the anguish voiced by those who remained. The outlook for Celo in
1958 was bleak indeed. Only twenty-one adults remained. A ghost-town air
hung over the Community. Eight houses stood empty, silent memorials to
rejection of the Community and loss of hope in its future.

Joined to the physical evidence of uncertainty, the remaining members
held a solid inventory of recriminations and denunciations from their former
comrades. Even before departure, those who left revised their perception of
the Community and their relationship to it. They became convinced that
their expectations of what could be accomplished, by themselves in Celo and
by the Community as an organization, were doomed to only partial and
unsatisfactory fulfillment or outright failure. Economically most of them
were doing poorly. Those who sought refuge in the Society of Brothers looked
on Celo as a pale imitation of what could be done. If sacrifice were necessary, why not make it in a fully developed communal group with firm assurance of common beliefs?

Settlement of accounts with ex-members fed the conflict. Actually, little
difficulty appeared in paying off those who went to the Brothers: enjoined
by their new creed to act in a loving manner, they were encouraged by the
society to make rapid settlement. All proceeds went to the Brothers' common treasury and the former Community members took whatever was offered so long as it was immediately paid. Other cases, however, were not so
easily dismissed.

Defectors usually looked upon their work in Celo as largely unrewarded.
They had undergone sacrifice, had labored long and hard, and the result fell
short of their expectations, both moral and material. Appraisals of their
holdings, and the subsequent offer of compensation by the Community, in
almost every case, were less than what they anticipated. From their perspective, the Community was unfair and was trying, intentionally or not, to cheat
them. Without any independent evaluation of their holdings—a committee
inspected the property and arrived at the evaluation figure used in the settlement process—the entire process of settlement appeared to be abandoned
to the vagaries of individual opinion. The compensation offered was too low.

For their part, the remaining members took the ex-member's objection as an attempt to milk the Community for more money. Evanson, for example, was said to have aimed at "getting all he can, rather than recognizing Community interests and practices" (undated memo).

Argument between Community and ex-members about the amount of compensation arose even in cases that were otherwise free of acrimony. Leaving for a new career in teaching, one family responded to the Community's settlement offer by accusing the membership of collective irresponsibility and immaturity. (At issue were the different bases for appraisals of holdings that plagued them in the cases of several departees, including Evanson.) The newly minted teacher lectured the membership:

> It is clear to me that legally the full amount [of appraised value] is due us. It is cloudy whether it is morally ours. It is clear to me that it is legally and morally not the Community's. Let me explain this last. I feel it is weak for Celo to try to avoid paying for a past mistake. The Community should have the responsibility to make decisions, which may mean mistakes will be made. Responsibility assumes willingness to accept consequences of decisions.
>
> Now the Community is being immature. It is using its impersonal corporate status to grab a thousand or two bucks which seem to be slipping through its fingers. And this is being done by social coercion. As individuals, no one of the members would think of doing such a thing. (Ex-member to CCI members, 7/27/53)

The Community secretary offered his own moral lesson: "As I see it . . . you have a moral right to your profit according to the prevailing U.S. code of business ethics. My own code is different from the prevailing one in many things, including this one" (CCI Secty. to ex-member, 7/31/53). Distance between members and ex-members grew with each step in such negotiations. The terms of their Holding Agreement put them in the position of picking at an open wound, exacerbating it with the salt of added abuse.

Beyond these often petty, sometimes bitter, debates stood opposed conceptions of Celo itself. Disillusioned defectors, by far the more characteristic, saw the Community as identical with its remaining members. In this view, Celo was a group of individuals with whom he or she had clashed and had rejected. Negotiating a financial settlement simply continued the conflict that had precipitated the departure. For those who remained, on the contrary, the Community was a corporate group. More than an assortment of individuals, it was an enduring entity in which membership fluctuated but the essential purposes remained. During the Evanson controversy, one member spoke to this point: "I do not think that finding a solution that will be conciliation to [Evanson] is of paramount importance, and that it is more important to establish the fact that it is the Community, not ourselves, that we are trying to protect, that the Community has an integrity and a continuation of purpose that is worthy of being protected" (undated memo).

This imputation to the Community of a stability and endurance lacking in its impermanent membership explains in part the members' customary hesitancy in making or changing policy that was presumed to be permanent. Carefully specifying that particular decisions were exceptions to general rules, they underlined this conception of Celo Community as distinct from its membership. Toward recalcitrant ex-members, this allowed them to take an unimpeachably moral and altruistic stand. It was as if they proclaimed to those who refused to accept their offer: We act not as individuals, but as stewards of property that is not ours to give away. If you did not hold such animosity toward us, as separate persons, you could easily see the justice of our position.

Most defectors, however, saw the Community, defined as its existing members, making less than fair offers and thereby deprecating the effort put into improvement of a holding. Difficult cases were sometimes settled by the Community's provision of additional payment as a gift. In a typical outcome of this sort, members declared themselves willing to go a step further because "of hardship in this case" (CCI, 4/27/53).[4]

Perhaps the best illustration of the assumption that Community and membership were not the same was the arrangement made for settlement with one of Evanson's allies. Dissatisfied with the Community's offer, he applied for "non-resident membership permitting the retention" of his holding. This was of course rejected. The eventual solution adroitly evaded the alternatives of strict obedience to the Holding Agreement, with its potential for long-term discord, or of allowing a special exception, with the insinuation that principle had been abandoned in exchange for tranquility. A buyers' club was formed of those members willing to use their own money to make up the difference between what the Community had offered and what the ex-member demanded. Repayment depended upon the eventual sale of improvements on the holding to a new recruit. Contributions to the buyers' club were made in secret "to avoid any possibility of causing division in the Community" between "those who contributed and those who did not, either because they could not or did not wish to" (undated notes). Hence, a satisfactory conclusion was reached without "making [an] exception to the terms of the Holding Agreement, since [the Community's] financial involvement in the settlement would be limited to that provided in the Holding Agreement" (CCI, 5/6/57).

The loss of trust in the Community that was typical of defectors is well illustrated in a statement made by one of Evanson's friends at the beginning of settlement negotiations with him. In his opinion,

> the Community had drifted toward "statism," increasing the emphasis on the Community, at the expense of the individual, and . . . this drift threatened the security of all members. . . . He did not believe that the provision in the Holding Agreement, which allows a former holder one year to sell his holding at his own price, was adequate protection, since he thought it likely that Celo Community would encourage a prospective holder to delay purchase until this year had passed [and the holding could be bought from the Community at a lower price]. (CCI, 4/1/57)

Casting their arguments in a moral idiom, each side could deny any involvement of self-interest and thus continue to regard themselves as upholders of abstract justice. For the sake of living in Celo, the members had made sacrifices, economic and social (e.g., the poorer educational opportunities for their children, the lack of urban intellectual stimulation), and consequently felt a strong sense of personal investment in the Community. What Lewis Coser has noted for radical groups in general might usefully be applied here: "Through introjection of the group's purpose and power and through projection of his own self into the group," the Community became for each member "an extension of his own personality" (Coser 1956, 114). To break the tie with Celo Community was emotionally painful for disillusioned defectors, and they soothed the pain by blaming separation on faults in the remaining members, rather than on changed views of themselves or on a desire for advantages lacking in Celo.

Those who stayed took a defector's attacks on the honesty and fairness of the group as personal assaults, reacting more fiercely than if the attacks had been aimed at an organization demanding less personal involvement. The attacks they received from their former partners in community-building were taken very seriously. Indeed, such reproach, cast as it was in the idiom of morality, struck at their conception of themselves as principled men and women.

The Challenge of Consensus

Reaching decisions by consensus, as we have seen, posed great challenges for Celo's members. When problems were not cast as matters of moral principle, agreement was ordinarily arrived at after brief discussion. Practical issues—arranging for mowing of Community fields by local farmers, for ex-

ample—could be dealt with by broad grants of authority to standing committees. Or the members might declare an exception to the rule, thus concluding a particular issue while explicitly preserving an established policy.

Problems put into moral and ethical terms, however, offered little hope of
easy and harmonious solution. Foremost among these was membership:
whether to admit someone as a permanent member, how to dissolve ties with
those who chose to leave. Every situation of this kind that began with disagreement soon escalated to discord and rancorous dispute. These recurring
battles demonstrated how far the members were from harmony and consensual belief, and each time revealed their deep aversion to confrontation.

They were well aware of their strong dislike of argument, and comments
on this collective and individual attribute were abundant. An extensive analysis of their approach to decision making appeared in 1978, in the aftermath
of a membership fight. After rejecting an applicant by a negative vote of over
30 percent, the members spent much time and energy debating the rejected
person's request to remain in the Community as a long-term tenant.

A statement written by one member and circulated through the Community during this period provides a description of how one woman perceived
the struggle for consensus. All the available evidence supports her opinion
that her experience was far from unique. She wrote:

> We disagree deeply and fervently, with stomachs churning and tears flowing and
> pulses racing (though hopefully others' responses aren't as intense as mine).
> Supposedly we have a process to temper such disagreement, a process called
> "consensus." Using this method, we talk and listen to one another and conflict
> melts away leaving us with a collective synthesis more profound than any in-
> dividual voice. But we all know it's not that easy. I don't think my experience
> is too atypical. I speak up in a meeting and someone challenges me and I stop
> listening and start defending myself (either inwardly to myself or outwardly to
> others) . . . or I withdraw to avoid conflict and walk away feeling frustrated and
> thwarted.
>
> Note another familiar pattern. An individual comes to a meeting with a pro-
> posal. A few challenge that proposal (sometimes in an intimidating manner).
> Many sit squirming uncomfortably. The less aggressive individual backs down
> or time runs out and perhaps the proposal disappears into oblivion somehow
> not seeming worth the fight. Energy dissipates.

Why did they find it so difficult to reach agreement? Why did they become
so agitated and disturbed about openly debating their differences? Part of the
answer to these questions lies in their assumption that despite their cherished
diversity, they shared basic beliefs. When disputes manifested a rift, they were
baffled and felt threatened. If the argument was with an ex-member, no long-

er one of the group putatively sharing common beliefs, they tended to impute selfish motives to their opponent. Open debate was also difficult because most of them were pacifists and interpreted argumentation and confrontation of any sort as violent behavior. It was, like court action, a kind of "psychological violence."

Even more important to them, however, was their conception of their behavior as derived from firmly held moral codes. They saw their actions as principled actions. After all, each of them had joined the Community because of strong moral conviction. The members had worked to maintain the project as a setting where moral action was expected and ethical compromise was unnecessary. Not only did they consider their behavior motivated primarily by moral concerns, their personal identity rested on their beliefs. They sought to occupy only one "master role—that of a man [or woman] of convictions" (Nahirny 1962, 401n). Further, they tended to regard other people in much the same manner, as first of all vessels of belief. Most of them were strongly inclined to "respond to ideas and beliefs as if these were qualities of persons" and to "relate to one another in the light of ideas and beliefs rather than in the light of personal qualities or specific functions which they perform" (Nahirny 1962, 401n, 398).

This attitude, an "ideological orientation" to use Nahirny's label, has been observed among numerous radical groups (Nahirny 1962; see also Shils 1958; Bittner 1963; Kornhauser 1962). To be sure, considerable variation existed among Celo's membership in the extent to which they displayed this outlook. Nevertheless, the evidence derived from Community documents and fieldwork clearly demonstrates a strong inclination in this direction.[5]

Ideally, Celo's members pledged total commitment to the Community and each other. The contrast of Community life with an outside "world of conflicting interests, half-measures, and self-seeking" (Shils 1958, 464) was keenly felt. One insightful member described for me in 1967 her distress at partial commitment, segmental participation:

> It simply makes it harder for you to have a sense of identity, because all relationships are mutual, and what you are is what you are in relation to somebody else, the people you're working with. But you're with different people, between home and church and business, especially if you work in a hard-driving, competitive business with very competitive people. The values of the different groups are different and you're required to put on a different face for each one. The next thing you know, you don't know who you are. I don't think that's an extreme picture—it's the way a lot of people live.

She found it exceedingly stressful to shift from one social role to another. Far more satisfactory for her was to assume the single, unambiguous part of woman of high moral conviction and to base her behavior on principle.

In circumstances like those obtaining in Celo, where individuals were so closely identified with their moral convictions, compromise did not come easily. Dispassionate examination of proposals which spring from principle requires a separation of proposal from the proposer, a willingness to pretend that the ideas in debate are, only temporarily perhaps, disembodied. When the discussants are identified primarily by their moral principles, disagreement assumes the shape of assault. Those who are defined and define themselves by what they believe, as Celo's members tended to do, experience disagreement as a doubt cast on their validity as moral beings. If one accedes to compromise, it is as if one has abandoned part of one's personal identity. To compromise in making collective decisions is, then, to give up part of one's identity, one's very self. Given these conditions, even in the modified and varied way they applied in Celo, maybe we should not dwell on their failure to reach consensus in a timely fashion. It is a wonder significant decisions were possible at all.

The Quest for Harmony

Assessing the goals of communities like Celo, Zablocki is emphatic in concluding that the "state of consensus (a situation in which all are content with and actively supportive of the agreed upon decision)" is "the primary aim of all but the least ideological of communes. It is the sorely felt need of the befuddled as well as of the convinced. It is expressed in the unwillingness of some communes to make decisions in the face of even token minority opposition. It is expressed in that the lion's share of time that commune members spend together is always given to the decision-making process" (1980, 249n; 250–51). Celo's membership displayed a strong tendency in this direction, particularly in the period just before the serious loss of members in the early 1950s.

The main reason for joining Celo was to associate with like-minded people, to gather with those of common purpose. Members sought, as they plainly said in the early years, a sense of belonging. For most of them, this meant the achievement of harmonious relationships among themselves as a group of dedicated reformers and congruence in their individual lives between act and moral principle. If one's behavior is based on principle, then belief and behavior become one. The ideal should become real. Further, group activity should reflect shared belief.

Quite willing to admit that perfection, either in a personal existence of unblemished principled behavior or a social and cultural order without shortcomings, was beyond their grasp, Celo's members still considered working toward the goal not only worthwhile but obligatory. If their action as Community members must entail the ethical compromise and moral equivocation they perceived in conventional social life, why bother with the inconvenience and economic discomfort of living in Celo or any community like it? It was the greater possibility of basing action on belief, with the emphasis on shared belief, promised by the Society of Brothers that impelled some families to switch their allegiance from Celo to Bruderhof. Firmly anchored in Christian communalism, the Society of Brothers offered a divinely ordered situation in which the close bonding of practice and preachment appeared to suffuse daily life. By comparison, at least from the perspective of those searching for a thoroughly principled life, Celo ran a distant second.

Other defectors saw Celo more and more headed toward conventionality, destined to differ from suburban America only in minor details. A career in teaching or chemical research appeared to offer opportunities to serve mankind with fewer difficulties than they experienced in Celo.

The very emphasis on individuality and diversity among the Community's members set limits to whatever unity they might expect. Whenever they tried to set down their shared purposes, the result was some form of the conclusion reached in 1967: "a desire . . . to keep on creating" a better community (CCI, 3/1/67). A clear and detailed statement of common goals eluded them, yet the absence of specifics could not be ignored.

From the earliest flush of utopian enthusiasm in the 1940s, they returned again and again to the quest for common purpose. The effort took several forms. On a number of occasions they divided into small discussion groups and brought suggestions to the entire membership for further discussion. Individual statements were circulated among the membership, then discussed in Community meetings. From time to time, they polled themselves to find how thoroughly they agreed with lists of descriptive statements.

A survey of this kind was conducted in 1950, to "describe what Celo Community is at the present time," to "make clear to prospective members" what sort of community it was. It was not expected that unanimity would be found for any of the survey's fourteen statements, but they "hoped to get a majority opinion." Responses came very near to unanimous approval of such statements as "we stress cooperation rather than competition" and "we value willingness to work with a group at some personal sacrifice." But diversity reigned when they considered "we discourage the use of intoxicating beverages." Greater solidarity was found for "we place no premium on sophistication or formal education" than for statements that called for approval of a "simple standard of living" and then went on to peg simplicity at specific income levels.

In short, Celo's members could wholeheartedly commit themselves to common beliefs that were couched in general terms. When it came to specifying how a particular generality might be put into practice, they faltered. The 1950 survey unanimously endorsed the statement of principle: "we want the community to be inter-racial." Marching toward this lofty goal, however, led them through the thickets of trying to adapt peacefully to the conventional prejudices of their local neighbors without compromising their moral principles.

A racially integrated work camp was planned in Celo in the summer of 1946, under the auspices of the Fellowship of Reconciliation (FOR), a pacifist organization. Members were apprehensive about the reaction of local people to the project. The work camp director assured them that "care would be taken not to make an issue of race; that probably few if any Negro campers would be taking part," and preparations proceeded (CCI, 2/25/46; see also minutes for 10/13/45 and 1/21/46). In the end, the prospect of compromising their principles by staging a camp that officially welcomed African Americans while privately hoping none would come proved too much. The venture, they decided, "might better be postponed until an inter-racial camp consistent with FOR principles could be planned with confidence" (CCI, 3/11/46). Three years later one member asked in Community meeting if the others "felt it wise to have Negro guests." The consensus was that guests would be acceptable, but "the Community is probably not as yet in a position to offer strong enough protection to a possible Negro family" as members (CCI, 8/5/49). Racial integration did come to Celo in 1962, with work camps to build the boarding school. African-American students attended the school beginning in the early 1960s, and the Community welcomed an African-American man as trial member in 1977.

By this time, however, they had become resigned to their dissimilarity of purpose. "Perhaps that very diversity we promote makes it more difficult to understand and trust one another," suggested one member in 1978 (the same woman who analyzed the wrenching effects of disagreement). She went on, "Some of us are committed to Celo as stewards of the land, others are here to pursue human relationships within the community with many gradations along the spectrum. There are few activities that [we] do with one another as an entire community, perhaps also because of this diversity. It would seem much easier to work for unity if we all felt committed to some common purpose larger than ourselves." Surely they invited recurrent flare-ups of disagreement by extolling the virtue of diversity among themselves. With that emphasis, the search for commonality often became secondary.

Notes

1. Trial membership was not a troublesome issue. It was open to almost anyone willing to spend a half-year on probation while members decided if they found the person compatible.

2. Gordon stayed on for two years after losing his job in the health center, commuting to a veterans' hospital fifty miles away.

3. This phrase appears in "Brief Explanation of CCI's Holding Agreement," an undated document included in *About Celo Community* [1988], a compilation of official community documents and miscellaneous material relating to Celo: "The Holding Agreement is neither a deed nor a lease but a legal *contract* defining the legal relationship between Celo Community, Inc. and the Holder in regard to the use of real property within the Community when taken as a Holding." In the official "Summary of Celo Community Procedures and Rules" (see Appendix), the legal distinction is reluctantly made: "A Holding Agreement is not only a legal agreement but a personal moral obligation. It is a special type of agreement, different from the usual type of lease as well as from a deed; however, if it must be defined as either lease or deed, it is considered a lease."

4. For those who took on new careers, the Community gradually became less important and their commitment to its purposes declined along with their investment of time and energy. One of these had worked for two years in a chemical factory, commuting long distances to his job, before leaving Celo. He recollected (in 1967) that "somehow, without even realizing it, I had begun to think of my job in that factory as a career. I was more of a chemist than a Community person." This was one case in which settlement was immediate and mutually agreeable.

5. As an ideal type, the notion of "ideological orientation" provides a useful approach for understanding the perspective of Celo's members. The key features of this orientation, according to Nahirny, are: (1) totality—a view of group members as solely holders of belief; (2) dualism—an intolerance for ambiguity and a conception of the social world as divided into two parts, good and bad, damned and blessed; (3) impersonality—an inability to see others as combining "personal ascribed qualities and performances"; and (4) lack of affectivity—an absence of "direct affective disposition toward human beings" (Nahirny 1962, 401–2).

9.   Defining Utopia: Celo and Its Neighbors

Celo's problem of self-definition, in deciding what common purpose if any bound the members together, came closest to solution when they considered themselves in contrast to their perception of the "outside world." For them, the "outside" had several components: America as a mass, centralized, competitive society; local mountain people as a rapidly disappearing group of sturdy but often misguided pioneers; and other utopian groups and experiments as sources of new members and moral support. Each provided useful contrasts with themselves.

Just as significant as Celo members' contrast of themselves with local mountain folk was the local view of the Community and its residents. Both served to reaffirm the boundary of Celo Community and maintain it as a locally isolated and distinctive group. Following a brief account of the Community's outlook on the national society and a longer description of its relations with outside allies, most of the discussion in this chapter is devoted to the reciprocal images of each other held by locals and utopians. The chapter closes with a consideration of Celo's redefinition of itself in the late 1970s.

American Mass Society

Sometime in the mid-1960s, one of Celo's older residents drew up a list of contrastive features of "community," including but not limited to Celo, and American society. Not every member would have agreed with all his terms, but the list serves very well as an outline of the ways Celo's members saw themselves as unlike the mass society they had forsaken.

Non-Community	Community
Competitive	Cooperative
Punitive	Rehabilitating
Emotional	Rational
Consuming—receiving	Producing—giving
Responsible only to those present in space and time	Responsible to past and future generations
Childlike	Parentlike
Dependent	Independent
Warlike	Peaceful
Nondiscriminating between fact and fancy	Discriminating

The traits of non-community had produced and reinforced a mass society that was seen as a vast landscape of rotting urban centers linked by expanses of suburbs as alike as peas in a pod.

Since isolation and withdrawal from this mass society could never be complete, the issues that motivated public policy and dominated public discourse had direct influence on Celo. The strident pacifism of the 1940s and the search for peace in the atomic world of the 1950s shifted to involvement in the civil rights efforts and nuclear disarmament movement of the 1960s. What most agitated Celo's residents in the 1960s, however, was the Vietnam War. They traveled to Washington to participate in peace marches, held prayer vigils, withheld part of their federal taxes, and engaged in a variety of attempts to protest the war and bring it to an end. At war's end the national issues of preservation of the environment, the elimination of nuclear power plants, the search for renewable sources of energy, and the battle against pollution also excited Celo. They began to experiment with alternative sources of power, to install solar heating devices in their homes, and to search for ways to eliminate pesticides and other dangerous pollutants.

Even as the Celo members opposed national policies, however, they found ways to benefit from them. The health center had been built by obtaining government priority for materials in the post–World War II years of scarcity, and fifteen years later the restricted sale of military surplus goods was turned to the uses of their Arthur Morgan School. The school's administrators managed to have it listed as an acceptable purchaser of surplus jeeps, compasses, massive stewpots, and other equipment at very low prices.

Perhaps the largest boon to the Community, stemming from the military conscription laws of the Vietnam era, was the availability of a new generation of conscientious objectors. Young men who had been classified as conscientious objectors to the military draft became available for alternative service. The Morgan School quickly took advantage of this opportunity by applying for the service of some COs to teach in the school. It was a bargain well struck; the school obtained the services of appropriately trained young teachers and counselors at very low salaries and the conscientious objectors were afforded a chance at employment in a worthwhile cause. All the while, Celo and its school could maintain the contrastive conception of themselves as engaged in morally useful tasks, even as they used the tools and talent that only national war policies made possible.[1]

Outside Allies

From the beginning, Morgan had promoted the linkage of Celo with other communal and utopian ventures. His lectures in the wartime Civilian Public Service camps and on college campuses bore fruit, not only by drawing new members to Celo but also by stimulating recruits to found and join similar communities at war's end. Relationships of Celo with these communities provided new recruits and support of other kinds. Community residents had a large number of outside acquaintances or friends. Some belonged to other utopian groups, but there were many who carried on radical political activities in other ways. Celo's members regarded as ideological confederates those who desired to bring about nonviolent social revolution and who tended to dramatize the opposition to their efforts on the part of conventional Americans.

The ties of Community residents and their outside acquaintances were sustained by personal visits and correspondence, circulation of specialized newsletters and magazines, and joint participation in conferences, peace marches, and public demonstrations. Residents contributed money to pacifist organizations like the Fellowship of Reconciliation, Peacemakers, War Resisters' League, and the Committee for Non-Violent Action. A few served on editorial boards of the publications of these groups, and many of them attended conferences sponsored by pacifists. Articles describing Celo appeared in pacifist journals, and in such utopian magazines as *A Way Out* and *The Modern Utopian*.

Over the years of its existence, Celo was described in numerous lists of communities and radical organizations, including most recently the *Communities Directory* (Fellowship for Intentional Community 1995). Each summer, a number of the Community's many visitors came after learning of its existence from these publications. Some visitors strengthened ties created with individual Community residents on an initial trip by returning to participate in the summer camps or to enroll their children in the Morgan School.

The Community's involvement with other utopian settlements can be illustrated by the activities of Celo and its residents in aiding a besieged group in the 1950s. Koinonia, a religious community in rural Georgia, was under assault from its local neighbors, both by economic reprisal and armed attack. The interracial nature of Koinonia, and especially its function as a headquarters for civil rights organizers in the area, was the focus of local displeasure. In this crisis, Celo Community sent a small cash loan. Further, as a personal gesture of support, one woman from Celo went to Koinonia to assist in its mail-order pecan business. While she was there, she insisted upon taking a turn as night watchman and was fired upon by a carload of local assailants. As she disarmingly related her experience to me in 1965: "There was actually little chance of being hit by a bullet and even if you are, you're not likely to be killed. Nevertheless, I decided not to alarm my family by telling them about the incident and didn't realize that Dorothy Day, who was with me, would write it up for the *Catholic Worker*. When my daughter found out by reading the *Worker*, she joked about it and said to me, "'You forgot that it's a small world, Mother!'"[2]

Both the Community and its school attracted some visitors who can conveniently be called "transient utopians." To cite one example, two visits were made to Celo in the period 1965–67 by a man who, on each visit, led discussions in the Quaker meeting, gave short talks on nonviolence and race relations at the school, and stayed for a few weeks in a resident's household. He had lived in several utopian settlements—Tuolumne Farms in California, Koinonia and Macedonia in Georgia, the Society of Brothers in New York— but refused to join any of them. Like Celo's members and residents, he was well acquainted with many people in the civil rights and peace movements all over the nation and joined with them at times on picket lines and demonstrations. On his travels, this itinerant herald wore a sandwich board inscribed with slogans similar to the one he arrived with in Celo in 1967: "Jesus Taught Us to Love One Another / Try It." Another visitor, also a veteran of life in several utopian projects, repaid the Community's hospitality by teaching a short course in Esperanto at the Morgan School. In earlier years, the Community was host for the Peace Pilgrim, who stopped off for a few days as she walked across the nation to promote nonviolence.

Participation in radical reformist activity outside the confines of the Community took on greater significance when its population dwindled in the late 1950s. Links to these outside groups furnished a means for members to express their dissatisfaction with existing social institutions and to work for change. With the uneasy peace that prevailed between them and their mountain neighbors, they estimated that staging demonstrations in the local area might bring about open hostility and violence. Better to celebrate Hiroshima Day, for instance, by sending a delegation from Celo to ceremonies in urban centers. Little would have been gained by a display of opinion on the local scene; as they saw it, no one would notice anyhow.

Maintenance of personal relationships with individuals outside the Community allowed members to dramatize their efforts and transform them from the ineffectual acts of a small band of dissidents into potentially momentous innovations. Much of the communication between residents and their allies took the form of reaffirmation of verbal symbols: "nonviolence," "community," "personal responsibility," "world brotherhood," "cooperation," and so on. Whenever they tried to explore the meaning of these symbols, it often became evident that the presumed agreement did not exist. A liberal Catholic priest, visiting the Quaker meeting in 1966, for example, was thought to share the Quaker residents' belief in pacifism. In discussing with him the Vietnam War, however, it soon developed that he fully concurred with his church's concept of "just war." It was only this particular war, an unjust one in his opinion, that he opposed. As one of the Quakers said to me, "He just holds material values above human values, that's all—he's for war to defend property rights."

There was another, crucial aspect to these relationships with ideological confederates, a facet related to the very purpose for which Celo was created: that of making an alternative social order as an example to a diseased world. Residents were aware that, outside a narrow spectrum, their experiment in community was not widely known and thus might readily be labeled isolated. They tended to equate isolation with selfishness and escapism, and they regarded both attributes as immoral. Involvement in the great issues of our age, they said, was the moral duty of every human being. Even recognizing that residence in Celo provided a respite, perhaps only temporary, from the immense pressures for conformity and compromise in American life, they could not close themselves off from the problems of the world outside.[3] To do so would have been tantamount to admitting that their motives were only self-indulgent hopes of personal improvement. As Celo's "hope for success in history"—to borrow a phrase from Bassett (1952)—dimmed in the decade of the 1950s, doubt grew about their reasons for remaining. The members seemed to ask, If we are not here to light a beacon for mankind, then why continue? Their guilt was not sufficiently assuaged by opinions even as adulatory as that from a Quaker visitor's letter in 1959: "I think that the Celo community is world-shaking. In [George] Fox's day, one dedicated Friend could shake the land for 20 miles around. But in this day of rapid communication, a community like that at Celo can shake the whole world . . . at least give it a tremor. Louise and I had a renewing experience at Celo."

By committing their reform efforts to purposes beyond those possible in a small community, Celo's members were not despairing when they contemplated the lack of imitation of their community-building endeavor on a larger scale. Hedging their reformist bets, so to speak, and spreading their labor in several directions, they could count on some success, however small, while they prepared themselves for a measure of failure. Having admitted to themselves that Celo Community wielded slight influence, they still were not forced to see their continued residence in an isolated locale as selfish and escapist. In this way, their outside involvements provided one means of easing the burden of escapism (Hicks 1971).

The Coming of the Brothers

Multiple benefits accrued from the Community's ties to the far-flung groups of the like-minded, but there were hazards as well. The devastating loss of members to the Society of Brothers (Bruderhof) in the early 1950s gave evidence of how perilous the ties could be. Celo Community, along with other struggling utopian communities, lay in the direct line of fire as the Society of Brothers took careful aim at establishing colonies in the United States.

Founded in Germany in 1928, the Society of Brothers is a communal group of religious pacifists, a modern incarnation of Anabaptists whose beliefs are very like those of the Hutterites. The Brothers escaped Nazi militarism by moving to England in 1937 (Arnold 1964; Durnbaugh 1991). On a farm in the English countryside, they added local converts to their membership. Facing the wartime internment of their German members, they accepted the help of American Mennonites in trying to move to the United States. In spite of the intervention of Mennonite and Hutterite leaders and the AFSC's Clarence Pickett, who arranged a breakfast meeting with Eleanor Roosevelt, concern with the coming election of 1940 prevented President Roosevelt from openly assisting in the immigration of avowed pacifists. Finally, with the aid of the American Mennonite officials, they gained refuge in Paraguay and arrived in South America in 1941 (Durnbaugh 1991, 71–74). By 1942 they had over 350 people, including children, in their Paraguayan community (Society of Brothers 1952, 10-11).[4]

Wartime prejudices receded by 1951, when the Brothers, restive in their South American isolation, embarked on missionary work in the United States (Peters 1965, 176). Agents visited many of the utopian communities in North

America, presenting their case and gaining converts. Although they shared many beliefs with the Hutterites, the Brothers' tolerance of movies, folk dancing, and amateur theater productions violated Hutterian rules of austerity. A connection with the Hutterites, dating from 1930, was dissolved in 1952 (ibid.).[5] It was these very signs of intellectual liveliness and sophistication, however, that appealed to people in Celo and similar communities.

Three colonies of the Society of Brothers were formed in the United States, combining people from the Paraguayan settlements with new American converts, many from existing utopian communities.[6] Celo lost five families to them. Kingwood, a small communal settlement in New Jersey, disbanded in 1953 when five of its six families joined the Brothers. Macedonia Community was engulfed in 1957; its toy industry became the economic mainstay of the Brothers' new colonies (Zablocki 1971, 94, 98). Other communities, including affluent Bryn Gweled (near Philadelphia) and embattled Koinonia Farm, felt the wave of conversion and loss, but less disastrously. By 1956 fully one-third of the adult Brothers had been gathered from other communities (Tillson 1958, 47–52).[7]

For the Society of Brothers, living in a utopian community was no experimental affair. "We dare not experiment with community life," reads one of its statements of belief. Communal life for the Brothers was "the one and only way of unconditional love towards, and fellowship with, our fellow beings of God's mankind. . . . [It is] God's perfect way of love for all men." Their "call to that true repentance which must turn from the old life of personal endeavor and isolation to the true life of community one with another in the love that is of God" (Society of Brothers 1952, 40) could hardly have fallen on more receptive ears than those who heard the call in Celo Community.

The fallout for Celo was not entirely negative. A few years after losing members to the Society of Brothers, Celo gained from the same source. An elderly widow and a family with three children came to the Community from the Brothers. And, at the same time, the single surviving family from the takeover of Kingwood, a couple with two children, joined Celo. All these new residents had known each other in two or more previous utopian adventures. As the wife in one family declared in 1966: "Why, Fred and I haven't lived in a normal, ordinary community in sixteen years of marriage." They had threaded their lives through a series of communal groups, shifting from one to another as disillusionment deepened, or as groups dissolved or were swallowed into one another. Of Celo's twenty-nine adults in 1966, six were utopian "repeaters" (the term is from Bassett's discussion of nineteenth-century utopians; Bassett 1952, 203). Association and links extended beyond the United States, to Costa Rica, where one member went from Celo to join a

Quaker community, and to England, where developments in community-building were carefully monitored by people in Celo.

From their links with allies, Celo's members drew moral support, recruits, and a strengthened sense that their efforts were significant and not mere escapism. "America" was the background against which they defined themselves. But the closest and most conspicuous contrast available to them lay in their day-to-day interaction with their local neighbors, the mountain people whose families had lived in the Toe River Valley long before Morgan discovered it as a setting for utopia.

Locals and Utopians

Almost from its inception, Celo Community had found ways to separate itself from the local folk. Morgan's vision included Celo as a center for raising the standard of life in the valley, both in economic terms and in stretching the social and intellectual horizons of the mountain people. Put off by the direct method of change—that is, of inviting locals to membership—Morgan quickly turned to idealist sources, hoping at the same time to find his prized "practical idealists" in sufficient numbers.

The 4-H Club executive chosen to manage and find settlers for Celo in the initial period, John Lawson, recalled for me in 1965 his experience with Morgan. He irritably described Morgan as "a dreamer, an idealist," who wanted to "set up a little community that was entirely self-supporting." Morgan told him at the outset, he remembered, that Celo "was not to be like the local community. We want the butcher, the baker and the candlestick maker in this new community." Yet, for anyone "making a good living somewhere, there's no reason he would be here in the Community with this bad soil and bad economic prospects." Those who came were "mostly misfits who couldn't make it elsewhere." Lawson still did not seem to understand, twenty-five years later, that the building of a self-sufficient, self-sustaining community of misfits and outcasts was precisely what Morgan had intended.

Morgan's tendency to romanticize the mountain folk as strong, independent pioneers who possessed practical skills worked out over long periods of adaptation to their environment led him to look forward to good relations between his new community and the local people. That mountain people were not yet enmeshed in the demoralizing economic system of a homogeneous mass society, together with the physical isolation of the valley, made the locale attractive for Morgan's purpose.

The difficulty for local people was in defining Celo Community, in absorbing it into some appropriate category. At first the Community offered jobs and, as described earlier, became known as "the company," a category that placed Celo alongside coal mine and sawmill operations, somewhat like a private form of New Deal government employment. As war approached and defense jobs became widely available, the Community's position as employer rapidly diminished, to the relief of the founders. Regnery abhorred this view of Celo, "as though some private company had come into the area and could supply employment" (WHR to AEM, 4/11/40). Neither he nor Morgan intended for the Community to be put in this position, which seemed too close to the government work programs they both disparaged.[8]

If not a company, a source of jobs, then how was the Community to be understood? It was not a church, another institution with which local people were intimately familiar. It was not a family; its recruits came from all over the nation, many unknown to each other before their arrival in the valley. It was, and remained, an enigma.

Kinship was the paramount factor in social relations in the valley, as it was throughout southern Appalachia (Batteau 1990; Foster 1988; Hicks 1992; Pearsall 1959). As Beaver suggests, "Kin ties connect community residents into a system that gives personal identity through the expression of common roots, common ancestry, shared experience, and shared values; kinship also provides an idiom for people's behavior toward one another and is one of several bases for the actual formation of groups" (Beaver 1992, 57). With some exceptions, neighborhoods consisted of households linked by kin ties. As many local people contended (1965), "Everybody in this whole country [the valley and adjacent areas] is kin to everybody else." Households from which no kinship tie extended to others in the valley were rare and required explanation: "Old Zeke Wilson come in here with the road-building gang thirty-five year ago. He just liked it and stayed, I reckon." Kinship, a knowledge of who is related to whom (and how), along with an awareness of current rifts and alliances among them, formed the backdrop for all social relationships.

In occupations that were important at various periods until the 1970s—logging, gathering evergreen branches for sale to florists, small-scale mining of mica and feldspar, subsistence gardening—work crews were ordinarily composed of kinsmen. Certain careers, especially teaching in public schools, were expected to be pursued by members of particular families.

Kinsmen had diffuse rights and obligations to each other which extended far beyond the nuclear family of parents and children. Refusal to honor these obligations often led to correspondingly general breaches. Once in the open, conflict was difficult to confine to specific issues or situations. The fear of beginning new disputes, and of renewing or encouraging the persistence of old ones, underlay the local custom of trying to avoid controversy or overt disagreement in social interaction.

Not only among kinfolk did techniques develop for preventing conflict. Relationships outside the network of relatives tended to be viewed through the lens of kinship; the model for social relations was a kinship model. Social relationships among local people were not predicated on segmental, partial interaction. To every encounter, locals brought an established set of relations extending throughout local society; each person's private history, known to all those with whom he or she was in frequent interaction, figured in each encounter.

Over the decades of Celo's existence, changes in local social life occurred, but the importance of kinship and its ramifications persisted. Celo Community remained outside local society. Strangers when they came, strangers they remained.

Open hostility to the Community was rare; the abortive attempt to oust its pacifists in 1946 was a singular event. But suspicion—of members' goals, their intentions, and their activities—remained among local people.

A number of events and issues served to define the Community and its members, from the point of view of local folk, as intruders. Lacking a satisfactory answer to the question, Why are they here?, local people seized on bits of information to construct a coherent picture of the utopians. They set about solving the puzzle of this odd group among them. Several issues afforded room for interpretation of motives and identity, including the Community's joint ownership of a relatively large tract of land and how the members acquired it, the role of pacifism, the Community's involvement in local schools, and the Community's position on racial integration.

Land Ownership

That Celo Community's right to land in the valley was contested became evident in a variety of statements made to me during fieldwork (1965–67). Many people outspokenly charged Morgan with unfairly buying a large tract of land, sometimes described as "the best land in this whole valley," at bargain basement prices. The clear insinuation was that the Community, from its beginning, had somehow taken wrongful advantage of local people's ignorance and poverty. Yet the same men who offered this view of the Community's sharp trading bemoaned their own lack of foresight: "Why, I could've bought that whole boundary [tract] for the taxes just a year or two before Old Man Morgan come in here and snatched it up."

The notion was expressed to me many times that Celo Community intended to hold the land in order to sell it for a huge eventual profit. Meanwhile, "they don't pay taxes" on their real estate, said one local farmer, "because it's set down as a church. But there's no church on the property and the church don't own it any more."[9]

The Community's use of the land, as observed by locals, provoked the sharpest commentary. Local politicians in 1966 made great efforts to lure a small industrial plant to the valley, and Celo's land was suggested as a possible site. But, as one man said, shaking his head, "You know them people ain't gonna sell none of that land and there ain't no industry gonna build on leased land." Others remarked: they "just sit on their land"; they "won't allow anybody to cross it" for hunting; they refuse "to do anything with it—won't sell it, won't build tourist cabins on it, nothing but just sit on it!" Although of a milder sort, similar commentary was evident in 1979.

It was not the Community's legal right to its 1,250 acres that was at issue in these (and many similar) observations. What was denied was a *moral* claim to the land. People outside the Community talked derisively of Celo's property as lying fallow, unavailable for any use beneficial to local folk, yet the existence of a 400-acre tract, owned by a local family and put to even less cultivation than that of Celo, evoked no antagonistic comment. The 400 acres belonged to local people who had a clear right, legally and morally, to use, disuse, or misuse it as they pleased.

Pacifism and Conspiracy

The most important events in formulating a definition of the utopians as alien, not just to the valley but to the entire nation, surrounded the announcement of the Community's opposition to World War II. The Community manager's ardent profession of his pacifist beliefs, and the association of the Community, as members and visitors, with conscientious objectors, promoted local people's classification of the entire enterprise as "German." For many, Celo was a den of German spies: the residents' use of a shortwave radio and electric generator provided sufficient evidence that they were in league with the nation's enemies. This label stuck to the Community until the national enemy was redefined as "Communists," in the postwar era. Again, there were bits of evidence to make the Communist tag plausible.

A Community member, for example, taught in an extension program of the state university, set up in the county seat to accommodate military veterans in 1948. He was asked his opinion of the wisdom of a "preventive strike" against the Soviet Union as a quick and clear-cut solution to the Cold War. The utopian answered to the county school superintendent (who controlled the college extension) that the idea was foolish. He went on to assert that the Cold War was the result of nationalistic greed, and thus was as much the fault of the United States as any nation. The only solution, he maintained, was a nonviolent attitude. The conversation, embellished as it was recounted in offices and stores, reached the furthest rural fringes of the county and gave definite proof of treasonous sympathies. A representative of Celo, he had confirmed the unpatriotic beliefs widely imputed to Community members. Soon thereafter he lost his job.

A decade later, in 1960, another Community member was dismissed from a position as elementary school teacher in the Toe Valley. He was told he was terminated by the rule of "last hired, first fired," since a decrease in the local population had mandated a reduction in the faculty. His credentials, however, were superior to those of several other faculty and, by state law, he should have been given precedence. According to my informants among local people in 1966, the reason for his discharge was actually the confirmation of his Communist affiliation. Damaging evidence came from his unorthodox manner in the children's daily devotional period. Rather than stick to the customary daily Bible reading, he occasionally read inspirational poems and taught religious folk songs. Hence, he was branded atheist. Even worse was his encouragement that the children write letters to men on foreign ships, as part of a program to promote better international understanding. Distorted by the reports of children to their parents, and by the transit of the story through school employees, this became proof that the teacher maintained radio contact with Communist ships at sea.

In the county seat, a town of fifteen hundred or so, an outspoken group of political and business leaders displayed (in the mid-1960s) even greater dislike of the Community. Here, where the regional daily newspaper was widely read, letters to the editor from Community members served as a recurrent source of commentary. "I just feel ashamed for our county whenever I pick up the paper and read what one of those people has written against this country. There's just no way out of it: they *must* be Communists!" a hardware dealer told me. His sentiments echoed through similar statements from businessmen and government officials.

The conspiratorial view of Celo was stronger among the better educated and more prosperous locals. A young storekeeper in the valley explained why Community members so often applied for teaching jobs in local schools. Referring to a period in the early 1950s when four Community members simultaneously held teaching jobs in an adjacent county, he declared: "We could all see that what they wanted was to get in our schools here in *this* county and teach their [subversive] beliefs to our children." Certainly, he agreed, they would rather have had positions in the valley's school, with the chance to work nearer home. But, he insisted, there was a sinister aspect to their motivation. "People in this county were just determined not to let them into our schools and teach Communism," he concluded. This man was neither stupid nor ill-educated. A graduate of the state college, he represented modernity and progress among local people. But his conception of Celo was framed in the same terms one heard from barely literate local farmers. The image of Celo as strange, alien, and very probably treasonous grew sharper as one incident after another passed through the gossip network, gathering layers of ominous conjecture as they traveled.[10]

Seldom did the boundary separating locals and utopians allow the locals' view to penetrate to Celo's membership. Keeping them largely unaware of the intensity of local suspicion of their political ideas, the insulation of the Community combined with the local custom of making derogatory remarks only out of the hearing of the subject, his or her friends and kin. The Community members could therefore continue to regard themselves as leaders in local society, while local people cheerfully accepted their aid if it appeared innocuous and silently moved to block assistance they deemed dangerous.

Leadership, Religion, and Schools

Local people at times received Community members' offers of assistance in public projects—for example, volunteer labor and cash contributions for improving school facilities—with gratitude. It was, from the locals' standpoint, neighborly aid, an idea especially prevalent in Celo's earliest years. Celo's members, however, insisted on offering "leadership" to local folk. Where existing leaders were so ill-educated and self-seeking, in Community members' evaluation, they felt summoned to guide their neighbors to the amelioration of social ills. With a transparent but doubtless unintended condescension, the Community secretary gave Morgan this report in 1952:

> Several members of the Community are having an opportunity to give leadership in the larger community. Dave Hutchins is teaching public school music three days a week at Bear Creek, where Everett Galt teaches. Jean Nilsson is giving private lessons in piano three full days a week at the local school, and Pat Hutchins is teaching group singing there once a week. With the encouragement of some parents of Boy Scouts, the troop recently received permission to meet in the new school building; meetings have been resumed under the leadership of Carl Halsbeck and Preston Morrow. For a recent musical program to raise money for the school, the Community was invited to provide some numbers and did so. (CCI Secretary to AEM, 3/11/52)

Much of the activity recounted here was required by salaried jobs and, by local standards, well-paid jobs at that. Had they been confronted with this observation, the Community members might have pointed to the lower salaries they received in comparison with what they could command elsewhere. Thus they saw their teaching jobs as unselfish efforts to improve local life.

The image of themselves as leaders of local people was, in one sense, a way of distinguishing Celo from the surrounding social world. They were clearly superior, not just in educational attainment but morally, and thus separated from the rank and file they hoped to lead. Just this point emerged in a member's letter of 1961: "I think we all tend to take each other for granted; sometimes seeing the other person in a situation outside the Community is enough to bring home the special qualities [we possess]—as seeing Tillie Brooks chair a PTA meeting or lead a church program" (Member to AEM, 6/10/61).

Religious ceremonies provided a forum for marking differences between themselves and local people. Although most of the Community's membership participated to some extent in the activities of the Quaker meeting, they drew clear lines between Quaker activity and the religious exercises in local churches. I was told, during 1965–67, a number of tales in Celo that pointed out the conformity and rigidity of locals: of the shocked local storekeeper who refused to sell gasoline to a group of Catholic nuns visiting Celo; of the "hypocritical" secret drunkenness of local men recently converted in church revivals; of the strongly expressed opinions of elderly locals that it is sinful for adults to wear short pants. One member insisted to me (1965) that she refused to read the Bible "on principle," primarily because biblical literalism was the mainstay of local religious belief. Moreover, she had politely rejected many invitations to local church services, she said, because "I absolutely refuse to go and have somebody yell at me!" The staple of local religious ritual, of course, was a fervent and loudly delivered sermon.

Other members sometimes attended local churches to share their musical talent. One member, for example, told me of her experience in 1963. She had agreed to play the piano for religious services in one of the valley's Baptist churches. She recounted the difference between this occasion and her previous experiences in small-town churches elsewhere. In those earlier instances, she said, "I could play the songs and then sit back and think my own thoughts while the preacher talked." But custom in the Toe River Valley seemed to require her full attention: "they expected me to contribute with my presence, not just with my playing." Still, she found the emotionalism of the service "oddly attractive" and "I had to come home and recuperate by re-reading James's *Varieties of Religious Experience!*"

For their part, local people regarded the Quaker gatherings as not fully religious. Local children who visited schoolmates in Celo came home to inquiries about the Quaker "church service." A local preacher, confused about Celo after many years of experience in the valley, asked me (1965) if the Quakers believed "in the new birth, in being saved."

Contrasting themselves with local people, obvious differences of education and urbanity magnified by the apparent intellectual impoverishment of the valley, Community members regularly affirmed the boundary separating Celo from locals. Ranking these differences, implicitly for the most part, as leader and follower, progressive and backward, experimental and conservative, insightful heterodoxy and unthinking conventionalism, boosted the sense of superiority of the Community. To see themselves as only "neighbors," as local people subtly urged them to do, would have placed them in a position of equality to locals and labeled their helpful gestures as somewhat selfish calls for reciprocity. They expected no return for their assistance. Being good neighbors, to be sure, was one of their prominent goals, but they aimed for more.

For Community members compelled to make their living outside Celo, teaching, of the few jobs available, combined the practical necessity of gainful employment with morally useful purposes higher than the merely economic. Yet teaching positions were prime targets for aspiring local youth. Teaching afforded a degree of economic security, relatively high income, and prestige that was unusual in local society. For those lacking sufficient financial resources or inclination to set up their own small businesses, teaching was especially inviting as an avenue to a comfortable and esteemed life. In addition, jobs under the control of school authorities—janitors, lunchroom workers, secretaries as well as teachers—were political rewards for the offspring of loyal Democratic party workers.[11]

Trying to secure local teaching jobs, the Community's members collided with one of the most tightly controlled and exclusive groups in local society. Multiple linkages of kinship, political partisanship, and personal friendship securely bound together the county's school personnel. In 1966, for example, the valley school employed eight teachers, all of whom had kinship ties to local political leaders or were longtime friends of the school principal. The principal, a particularly high status position, was a nephew of a school board member. He took the job two years before acquiring the proper educational credentials.[12] Community members were unable to compete with more than infrequent success in this system. When positions opened for which no local person was qualified—in music instruction, for example—a Community member might be hired. Such jobs were only part time, however, and members usually looked for full-time employment in adjacent counties.

The hiring of the first Community member in the local school, in 1952, provoked a jubilant cry from the Community secretary: "We [have] even cracked the shell of the local schools. . . . a trial member . . . is teaching music at the new [valley] school to the apparent delight of all concerned" (Secretary to AEM, 10/11/52). It was, of course, a part-time position.

Only one Community member ever taught full time in the valley's consolidated public school, and suspicions of atheism and Communism made his tenure very insecure. He offended in another respect, by refusing to falsify daily attendance records. Since the allocation of teachers to each public school was based on "average daily attendance," and since the valley's population at that time was steadily decreasing, inflated reports of attendance were routinely submitted as a means of stabilizing the number of local teaching jobs. Never directly commanded to turn in phony reports, the Community member told me in 1966, he nevertheless was aware that other teachers falsified attendance records and felt their strong disapproval when he consistently made accurate reports. Even when granted a prized occupational slot, the utopians defied local interests; morality would not bend to expedience.[13]

Strange Lives, Stranger Deaths

The response to the Community's treatment of the dead, as played out over several decades, provides a series of specific events and assessments which should clarify the locals' conception of the strangers in their midst.

An early indication that Morgan and his Community were unusual was the strange burial of an infant in the Morgan family. Enroute to Celo in 1938, where he and members of his family planned to spend a few days on land that Morgan privately owned, an automobile accident occurred and an infant in the Morgan family was killed. It was nighttime when they arrived in the valley, but government permits had been obtained to bury the child on Morgan property. A local man overheard Morgan's declaration that he intended to inter the body forthwith. Borrowing a spade, Morgan dug two small graves, one for the body, the other for the bloody shroud. Later, shortly after midnight, about fifteen local men gathered outside the Morgan cabin, waking the family with their angry discussion of the event. Having no experience with the Humanist and Quaker custom of simplicity and dispatch in these matters, one of the men had fetched a deputy sheriff. Rumors had circulated during the evening that not only was a body illegally buried, but murder had been done. Only with the strenuous efforts of one of Morgan's local acquaintances was the threatening crowd dispersed.

In the years after, rumors continued, and there were fitful plans for exhumation. As Celo fell under suspicion of treason, the baby burial was transformed, in local gossip networks, into an urgent concealment of code books, short-wave radios, "German money," and other "spy equipment." The desire to open the grave seemed to Morgan so strong that he kept the location secret. As late as 1979 the tale of buried espionage apparatus still circulated in the less sophisticated neighborhoods of the region.

Later burials elicited calmer reactions, but the Community's scorn for the conventional left local people to ponder the vast differences they saw in funeral behavior. An older member of Celo died in 1965 and his funeral proceeded in what had become a standardized manner. A plywood coffin was built by several Community men and the body transported in a member's station wagon. Meanwhile, the grave had been dug in the Quaker burial ground on Community property by a member and several boys from the Morgan School. Branches of laurel and rhododendron covered the fresh dirt around the grave, and wreaths were fashioned from wildflowers and green branches gathered in the forest. The burial service was short and simple. The coffin was lowered into the grave with a bright yellow nylon rope borrowed from a member's garage, and several people stepped up to read selections from the deceased's favorite authors. Several minutes of silence followed, then volunteers filled the grave and covered it with greenery. Only one local person, a long-time acquaintance of the dead man, joined the entire Community at the ceremony.

The local reaction to this event, gathered from local people's remarks and questions put to me, was bafflement. Unsure of exactly what had happened, they firmly disliked how, they had heard, the dead man's body had been treated. The funeral was unnecessarily simple, the body should have been embalmed, there were no elaborate flower sprays, the ceremony had not been conducted in a church, no minister was present, a homemade coffin was inappropriate. "The last time anybody around here made their own box was thirty years ago," said one man. Stories circulated that, among other things, the body had stood for three days in a garage, wrapped only in a plastic bag. The entire affair, from the local perspective, had been mishandled and showed "no respect for the dead." "Why, I wouldn't treat an egg-sucking dog the way them people treat their dead," one outraged man told me. Others recollected the funeral of Arle Brooks, a Community member whose religious ardor was widely admired, in 1953. Local people who had tried to pay their respects felt rebuffed by the unfamiliar rites. Appearing at Brooks's home with sprays of flowers, they found that Community members had decorated only with green branches, and that, despite Brooks's acclaimed religiosity, no minister was present.

Conversations about the most recent burial resurrected memories of the Community physician's behavior when his mother died in 1959. He had her body cremated, an extremely distasteful notion for local folk. Then, some charged, he refused to reclaim the ashes: "just let what was left of her rot on a shelf somewhere." Talk of this incident led to expressions of a belief that cremation was a general practice in Celo Community. One man declared, "They have a big furnace over in there they use to burn up their dead just like you'd burn trash." There were no accusations of foul play or illegality about burials since the Morgan baby in 1938, but the sense of separateness, of contrast, of confusion and bewilderment, remained.

Change and the Persistence of Boundary

It was axiomatic for Morgan that if Celo's members regularly associated with their local neighbors, the barriers of ignorance and distrust on both sides would wither and perhaps disappear altogether. As those on each side of the Community boundary gained specific knowledge of each other, details would complicate mutual stereotypes and finally supplant negative images with accurate information. To be sure, due allowance had to be made for local customs; innovations should be introduced gradually.

Morgan's insistence on caution came forth in his response to a brash campaign, launched by Celo in 1947, to improve local schools by annexing the Toe River township to an adjoining county. Community members, he paternalistically admonished them, "are guests in the county." It was therefore "unwise for Celo Community's members' names to head such a petition. The impression might be given that Celo Community is trying to run the affairs of the township" (AEM to CCI Secretary, 9/25/47).

Community members, thoroughly convinced that enlightened and friendly relations fed on closer association with locals, singled out for me the best examples in the mid-1960s: the local people employed within the Community, at the health center, and the Morgan School. In each case, however, the employee seemed to define his or her relationship as limited to the employer, either to the physician or the school headmistress, not to the Community or its members. For example, the local woman in charge of the school's kitchen told me in 1967: "I sure am thankful for this job. It's about the only way my children would've ever been able to go to school [college]. Without this help, I just don't see how we [my family] could've made it." Speaking to this woman's kin, I discovered a view of the Morgan School identical to that held by other locals: an institution for retarded children which made handsome profits. Engaging the school's local employees in singing peace anthems and discussing racial equality with the school's staff and pupils rendered little, if any, change in their perspective. One might suggest that the effect was the opposite: local employees obviously had access to Community activity and their reports of their experience were given greater credence. Yet their portrayal simply confirmed the general speculation about Celo, its school and health center.

Those on either side of the Community boundary defined those on the other in contrastive terms. Community members saw local people, in large part, as unwitting victims of exploitation by the competitive forces of the national economy. Locals exemplified backwardness and ignorance or served as concrete evidence of American social and cultural failure. They were characterized as irresponsible, materialistic, easily roused to violence. Community residents sadly pointed out for me the changes in local life, from equality to hierarchy, simplicity to complexity, from informal reciprocity to mutual aggrandizement, all patterns promoted by industrial, urban America. From the position in years past of self-sufficient yeoman farmers and cooperating households, they had succumbed to the blandishments of consumerism. Growing numbers of factory jobs provided them with the material trappings of modernity—television, frozen TV dinners, new mobile homes and flashy cars, tapes and records of the latest popular music, video recorders—while older values declined along with the sound adaptive practices of the simple life. Entranced by superficial consumer goods, they had rapidly fallen from a state of pioneering grace.

For their part, the locals continued to puzzle over the Community. For some, it was a conspiracy to undermine America; if not Communist or German spies, the members certainly exhibited a lack of patriotism. Whatever they were, and whatever had lured them to the Toe Valley, they were abnormal. For models of the good life, local people looked to the urban scenes they saw on television screens and reported to them by kin who had migrated to Detroit, Cincinnati, Baltimore, and Seattle.

The strong sense of separation between Community and local people was reflected in the interpretation of past events as well as in day-to-day gossip. In my conversations with local people during 1965–67, Community members figured as contrasts. Broad hints were made of sexual promiscuity in the Community, and Community women were objects, for some local men, of inappropriate sexual references. (Such remarks were never voiced about local women, except for the few with a reputation for ready availability, and no factual basis could be discovered for the ascriptions of erotic excess among Community members.)

Individuals in Celo were singled out for praise, but local approval was limited to comments on their personal honesty, promptness in paying debts, willingness to contribute time and money for such projects as construction of a school gymnasium. Most often, the mention of Community residents elicited either of two responses, and occasionally both responses from the same person: (1) they are fair and honest as individuals but collectively involved in obscure illegal or improper activity; and (2) "people around here treated them awful bad, when they could've done some good for this country [i.e., this area] if we'd just let them." Even so, Community members should not have "gone around here talking down what folks believed and telling them what to do." Seldom did I hear Community residents referred to by their given name; among themselves, locals used first names or nicknames. The difference was striking.

Their respective frames of contrast were filled out by seizing on specific events and embroidering them with imputed motives and speculative inference. For local folk, the community's public denunciation of the "war effort" in the 1940s was interpreted as evidence of subversive intent. A desire for teaching jobs indicated the existence of a conspiracy to twist the innocent minds of local children with Communist doctrine. On the part of Community members, the bumbled attempt to rid the Community of conscientious objectors was taken as evidence that overt hostility and violence lay just under the surface of daily civility. The interpretation of behavior considered normal and unremarkable by one side took on bizarre tones for the other. For Community members, life in the valley was marked by outbursts of violence—spiteful barn-burnings, fistfights and more serious assaults (which were actually quite rare)—that showed local people to be irrational and potentially dangerous to themselves and to the Community. But the attention of the Community was devoted far more to distant groups of the like-minded than to local people. For them, local people were easily classified, and they could highlight, romanticize, praise, or condemn this or that characteristic of local social life.

Locals, however, faced the problem of explaining the very existence of people whose lifestyles were, until well into the 1970s, almost completely alien. A local woman's comments in 1967 captured the ambivalence of local attitudes:

> We've sat by and let them step in where they wanted to. Well, they do and they don't. I just can't understand them. Sometimes they want to take part in what we're doing in the community—I mean *our* community—but they don't let us know what they're doing down there [in their Community]. They're real educated people but they don't go about it [carrying on social relationships with local folk] the right way; they just don't know how to talk to people where people can understand them. They just want to have their little heaven down there.

In the main, Celo Community rested lightly on the local scene. The simultaneous recognition of friendly acquaintanceship with some and the latent hostility of most local people demonstrated a view widely shared in Celo: the innocent neighborliness of these simple, pioneer-like mountain people did not obscure their materialistic greed, competitive attitude, and blind conformity to standards beamed to them on television. Ignorance of local attitudes and an inability to predict their reaction to Community actions continued.[14] The divergent perspectives and aspirations, known or unknown, of locals and utopians reflected their well-honed sense of themselves as existing in different cultural worlds.

Managing Change

Changes came from several directions in the two decades from 1960 to 1980. During the 1960s, as part of the federal government's War on Poverty, young urban middle-class people were assigned, through VISTA (Volunteers in Service to America, a domestic Peace Corps), to the Toe River Valley to assist in relieving the effects of poverty. They were joined in these efforts by students from liberal Catholic seminaries, youth groups of the Methodist Church, and other private organizations. Many of them found in Celo congenial people with cultural and educational backgrounds similar to their own, people with whom they could carry on satisfying discussions. Some later returned to buy land and build homes in the valley; others spread word of the natural beauty of the region and inspired their urban acquaintances to move to the valley.

In the same period, Celo Community's appeal for new members was widely advertised and attracted interest from communal groups in large cities of the Northeast and Midwest. Membership in Celo began to grow, and in the 1970s it reached a point at which a temporary moratorium was declared for new members. Houses were in short supply, and some trial members were, by exception to the usual policy, allowed to begin their probationary period in residence near but not within Celo.

Back to the Land in the Toe Valley

By far the most significant change for Celo Community was the arrival, in increasing numbers from the late 1960s through the decade of the 1970s, of back-to-the-landers, young people, largely "products of the social changes taking place in the 1960s on American college campuses and in the society as a whole," who sought "refuge from the structures of American mainstream society" (Beaver 1992, 120). Together with the continuing increase of those who, since the late 1950s, had built summer homes in the valley and surrounding areas, the new immigrants added to the valley's population growth, from 1,290 to 1,682 in the decade 1970-80. The "summer people"—or "Floridy people," as they were locally known—had little effect on local social life and were inconsequential as far as Celo was concerned. These new back-to-the-landers were different: they became permanent, year-round residents and their proposed lifestyles were compatible with those of the Community members. Beaver's description of the new immigrants to the mountains fits Celo's new neighbors very well:

> They . . . hoped to create something new, a new way of living and a new relationship to the physical environment. Some were artists and crafts people with products to sell in local shows and shops, others, with experience on the land, came from counterculture communities elsewhere to the lush, sparsely populated mountains where land was relatively inexpensive. But most were relatively fresh from academic and professional communities, having worked for a few years in the public sector to establish equity that enabled them to buy into the mountain environments. (Beaver 1992, 121)

Not all of them were able to purchase land and a few, seeing in Celo a chance to join with those of similar purpose, applied for membership in the Community. Among these were several families, and some unmarried individuals, who had skills as potters, sculptors, woodworkers, and glassblowers. They easily met the perennial challenge offered to Celo's members: to make a living in this isolated valley without engaging in the "wage slavery" of commuting to factory jobs. Many others bought land or old farmhouses near Celo and set about homesteading.

A commune moved into the valley in 1969, dissolved within two years, and four people from it petitioned for membership in Celo as a group. Several lengthy discussions led to a rejection of the petition. Together with other objections to the proposal, the members saw structural difficulties with the Holding Agreement, which was "premised on strong husband-wife teams and the conventional family" (CCI, 1/13/71). The rejected communards retorted that Celo Community would lose a great deal if it failed to maintain a connection with the commune by formalizing the friendly relationship that already existed between the two groups. Further, they rebuked Celo for having "disintegrated into a bunch of 'old liberals'" (ibid.). The Community offered to rent land and buildings to the communards for a handicraft workshop and sales area (CCI, 12/9/70 and 1/6/71), but the offer was refused. Some months later, two of the communards were taken in as individual trial members.

Utopia Redefined

Partly due to the interests of new recruits, partly as a result of the membership's relentless attempt to find common goals for the Community, a shift
in emphasis came about within Celo. Environmental issues assumed greater importance. Of course, a concern for protection of the environment, expressed by the practice of organic gardening, careful management of their
fields and forest land, and the adoption of innovations designed to conserve
water, heat and power, had long been a feature of life in the Community. But
this concern assumed new proportions as the causes of civil rights and the
movement against the Vietnam War demanded less attention. The new emphasis provided an ideological bridge to the back-to-the-landers, and a number of links with them were forged in the 1970s.

In a sense, Celo was renewed, not only in the attraction of more members
than they could manage to take in, but in a revival of enthusiasm for worthy
causes, causes that had taken on new significance as national movements.
Celo residents were no longer alone in the struggle for making new and more
satisfactory lives. Ideological allies had arrived on the Community's door-
step.

By the mid-1970s, the alliance of Community and what members called
"our sane fringe" had blossomed into tangible form. A new cooperative store
opened in 1971 and counted seventy-five member households by the end of
the decade. Of these, only one-third were members or residents of the Community; the majority were drawn from young back-to-the-landers and retired couples who shared an interest in homesteading. An organization of
craftspeople opened a highway shop on Community property in 1974; less
than half of them belonged to Celo Community. Each of these enterprises
was granted startup loans from the Community.

At some time in the late 1970s, Celo's members began to conceive of the
Community as a "land trust." In its promotional mailings and its entries in
the recurrent community directories, the "land trust community" label grew
more frequent. In this capacity, Celo offered a protective haven for experimentation, often granting loans for new projects, but as a community confining itself to care of its real estate. Stewardship of Community resources had
always been important for the members, but now, with empty houses filled
and new ones going up, the Community was steward only of common land.
Attention was given to reserving part of its land free of individual holdings,
and discussions in the 1970s frequently focused on land management plans.

Land trusts achieved wide recognition in the 1970s and 1980s as a means
of protecting the environment, and the idea was traced to the nineteenth-

century single-tax theory of Henry George.[15] A central feature of the land trust ideal is the elimination of speculative profit in land. Any increase in the value of land should benefit the entire trust group rather than individual members. This was a major issue in Celo's effort to deal fairly with defectors in the 1950s, when the value of land in the Toe Valley underwent significant increases.

But a change of label required more than mere redefinition; a plausible history had to be constructed. Celo's members claimed to be the oldest land trust in the country, claims that took root in the publications of national associations of intentional communities.[16] Even deeper historical origins were conferred on Celo Community by outside commentators, tracing it back to Henry George's single-tax proposals (Questenberry 1992). In this historical transformation, George and his "Georgist principles" have fancifully supplanted that other nineteenth-century utopian, Edward Bellamy, for whom Arthur Morgan held such spirited admiration.

Along with other communities from the 1930s and 1940s, including Bryn Gweled and Tanguy, Celo is claimed as an early example of the land trust movement. The uniqueness of the Holding Agreement as "neither a deed nor a lease" is now forgotten outside the Community, and the members, it is now (erroneously) reported, "lease their homesteads on a lifetime basis with secure land tenure"; they are "tenured land stewards rather than owners." The system "discourages individual speculation in lease transfers" (Questenberry 1992, 119).

Adjusting its history to serve a new focus required less addition of past events than overlooking some of the Community's earlier characteristics. The utopian goal of constructing a model of a new society, proudly proclaimed in the 1940s and 1950s, now slid into silent obscurity. The example, if one were offered, was of a much narrower scale. The sense of retreat now outweighed the sense of mission, and escapism seemed less damning than before. Few of the newer members, who now made up a majority, had much interest in Community history; only those who joined during 1945–60 freely acknowledged that the Community's purpose had changed quite dramatically.

As its organizational focus narrowed to land management, the Community's activities more and more combined members with nonmember residents (mostly the school's staff and pupils), neighbors from the "sane fringe," and visitors. The Quaker meeting had always brought in a variety of people to attend Sunday meetings, discussion groups, and potluck dinners, and by 1980 the membership list was 80 percent non-Community people. Even official Community meetings were thrown open to anyone interested, and the meeting room was usually filled. It was a far cry from the mid-1960s, when a

monthly gathering drew only four or five people. The Community boundaries that had once enclosed not only common land but people who had
worldviews quite different from those of local neighbors, a separate social
system in many ways, now was reduced to the boundaries of commonly
owned land.

There were two important consequences of the changes, both justified by
the Community's new self-definition and its refurbished history: the impo-
sition of more restrictions on how members might use the land, and the di-
lution of the Community's stance as an outpost of experimentation. Con-
trols on the use of pesticides tightened, and many products were banned. Use
of chemical fertilizers came under closer scrutiny. To get Community approval for new construction, the simple sketches that satisfied in previous years
gave way to a demand for more elaborate plans and elevations. Mobile homes
(or house trailers, in local parlance), banned as unsuitable dwellings in the
Community, were tolerated only as temporary shelter while members built
permanent houses. In earlier days, about 1950, at least one member lived in
a hillside cave, another in a makeshift shelter-tent. Meanwhile, among the
local folk there was a noticeable increase in the number of mobile homes,
particularly as affordable housing for young families.

Conventional expectations of members' behavior replaced the broad tolerance of eccentricity that had marked them, to the astonishment and amuse-
ment of local people, in the past. The unique, the experimental, the mystical
lost place as important in themselves; a search for better ways no longer necessarily meant mere pursuit of the different. No more could one observe the
kind of agricultural experiment tried by one eccentric resident in the late
1940s, when he planted a field of sunflowers in a single, carefully calculated
spiral furrow. This would, he assured the skeptical, make for an especially
bountiful harvest. The episodes of mixed nude bathing in the river, an occasional event in the early period, would have been unthinkable in the 1970s.
The communards' charge of a Celo metamorphosis into a "bunch of 'old
liberals'" had some foundation.

The vision of the Community as a lonely but vital frontier of social and
cultural exploration was less persuasive when its paramount concern was
land management. Too, the presence in the valley of homesteaders celebrat-
ing the pleasures and validity of the simple life dimmed the light of the Community as a solitary guidepost for disentanglement from capitalist competitiveness and greed. It was no longer an easy conclusion that Celo possessed
a rare alternative for lives of ethical compromise and unprincipled competition. The back-to-the-landers shared many perspectives that formerly, on
the local scene at least, could be found only in the Community.

The change did not go unnoticed by Community members, particularly those who had known the situation of the early period. One of Celo's most dedicated and perceptive members offered her resignation in 1976 with an explanation of how the Community had changed since she joined in 1949. After five years on leave of absence to complete graduate degrees in social work, she returned in 1971 and "felt encouraged by the freshness I felt the new [members] brought to the Community." She went on, however, to describe a situation she found disturbing:

> What has struck me since I've been back—and that feeling has not gone away as I hoped it would—is that being a member involves considerable loss of control over one's personal affairs. . . . I do remember that in my early years here, I had a great sense of freedom, that I felt it was possible to attempt, here, things that couldn't be attempted elsewhere, and that Community restrictions seemed minimal—only those really necessary to maintain the basic welfare of the Community. People did try many different things, and some good things were, and still are being accomplished. The Community's backing of the Craft Shop is an important example of some of the positive things the Community still does. . . . But I did notice a difference when I came back that dismayed me— more attempts to regulate matters of individual taste and private concerns, more attempts to impose a given lifestyle, more demands for conformity, and ever more regulations. It seemed there was less freedom within the Community than outside it, while outside the Community, more and more people seemed to be sharing the kinds of concerns for a simple lifestyle and caring human relationships which once had seemed to be the exclusive hallmark of the Community. . . . Where I felt there was reasonable flexibility before, I see a movement toward rigidity. Where I felt there was enough tolerance for differences to ease the strain of those differences, I see, regretfully, quite a bit of intolerance. (Memo to CCI members, 8/3/76)

There was no doubt that Celo had undergone far-reaching change since the halcyon days of the early 1950s. After the discouraging loss of members, followed by a pervasive sense of failure reflected in the contingency plans for the Community's demise, a period of revitalization set in. The Arthur Morgan School opened in 1962 and, with the summer camps as a feeder system of potential students, quickly assumed a prominent place in the Community. Vacant houses were filled by the school's staff and a stream of new members. The cooperative store was revived in 1971, and the new craft shop opened to immediate success in 1974. Measured by the calendar, little more than a decade separated the birth of the school from the opening of the craft shop. But these few years marked a dramatic shift in the Community. From the fitful, often argumentative attempts to engage the entire membership in greater communalism and to define itself in radical cultural terms, attempts led most ardently by the defectors to the Society of Brothers, the Community had narrowed its self-defined role to land management.

Still, the redefinition and its historical accompaniment did not eliminate Celo's appetite for innovation nor the members' thirst for leadership roles. The Community's secretary boasted in 1988 that this "group of innovative people" originated different kinds of "social projects" which "promptly attract a much broader circle of participants," almost all of them "outsiders," while continuing to take on the burden of "active leadership" among local folk (CCI Secretary, 1/11/88).

Although Celo Community fell short of creating a model of a new society and culture, it persisted as a haven for those who felt themselves outcasts and misfits. Members came and went, worthy causes altered from one era to another, opposition to the direction of American life took new forms, and Celo did offer a beacon of hope for some Americans. In the end, however, Morgan's dream of its destiny as a "master community," a model to be emulated far and wide, remained just that: a dream.

Notes

1. A letter from the Morgan School headmistress to the State Selective Service (7/15/64) requested that a conscientious objector be provided to fill the position of counselor or maintenance man at the school. "We are interested in getting the services of a young man from Selective Service, both because we are on a slender budget and because it has been our observation that conscientious objectors are often thoughtful and idealistic young men with searching minds, well adapted to taking part in our education project.

"With rare exceptions, the young men who have worked with us have been enthusiastic about their experience, and this leads us to feel that we are doing a significant educational job in two directions."

2. On the *Catholic Worker*, see *Fellowship Magazine* 31, no. 9 (September 1965), and Coy 1988. For Dorothy Day, see Roberts 1984. Some of her writings are collected in Day 1983. A summary of events at Koinonia is in Berry 1992, 209–13.

3. Morgan wrote in 1936, just as he was making initial plans for Celo: "When I speak of the possibility of communities of like-minded and like-spirited people, it is not in the attitude of proposing retreat from the currents of the times. But since most of life today is not so much individual as social, in our economic activities we tend to be compelled to the type of conduct that is characteristic of the group. It is difficult under such circumstances for strikingly new and different types of action to emerge fully and to survive, and so under some conditions the grouping together of people of unique purposes may be wise" (Morgan 1936, 115).

4. They still had a community in England—by 1942, a group of twenty remained in England—and this grew to two hundred by 1952 (see Society of Brothers 1952; Zablocki 1971).

5. Links to the North American Hutterite colonies have been an on-again, off-again affair. Eberhard Arnold visited them in the 1930s to establish cooperative ties; the connection was broken in 1952, resumed in 1974, and now is under great strain, perhaps doomed to be broken again (Durnbaugh 1991).

6. By 1991 the Brothers had six colonies in the United States, one in England, and one in Germany (Durnbaugh 1991, 76).

7. The last year the Society of Brothers allowed a population census by an outsider was 1956 (Tillson 1958; Zablocki 1971, 95).

8. AEM to WHR, 4/13/40: "The old habits of a self-sustained community are dying out before present government policies and the industrial tendencies." According to correspondence from WHR to AEM, 4/20/40, government work programs "serve no purpose other than to make the acceptor thereof a permanent dependent on public funds" and the programs attract only those with little concern for their "self-respect."

9. It was never religious property nor exempt from taxation. The umbrella corporations of both community and health center were nonprofit, and thus not subject to corporate tax, but locals seemed unaware of these details.

10. The Vietnam War was another high time for unpatriotic suspicion, perhaps, but the distrust persisted long after the war ended. An example is found in a letter to the editor published in the county weekly newspaper in 1980. A local attorney, known for his intemperate and colorful speeches, addressed a proposal that young men not obey the federal requirement to register for Selective Service. His suggestions were more draconian than might be found among most local people, but his outrage was not unusual. The letter said, in part:

"I read with disgust the rotten article from the venomous pen of the so-called 'American Friends Service Committee' . . . urging our youth to be draft dodgers in open defiance of the Law. They are friends alright—of Russia and East Germany.

"Our Registration law, and in particular, the provisions of it dealing with violation of the same, is far from perfect. It should be amended. It is not fair to the murderers, thiefs and bank robbers who are now serving time in our Federal prisons to degrade them further by forcing them to serve time with such persons as these friends of Russia and East Germany. The Law should give such rotten characters as these so-called friends and the ones they have led astray by their rotten and treasonable advice the option of migrating immediately to Russia or East Germany or being castrated. Both the ones who gave the advice . . . and the traitors who heeded it, are lower in the scale of civilization than a crawling cockroach on the dirt floor of a Mexican whorehouse. Since biologically there is a tendency of like to beget like, we should stop such traitors from further breeding.

"The patriotic people of [this] county should lose no time or means of showing these people what we think of them. We should refuse to have any commercial or social intercourse whatever with such salamanders."

The response came in the next issue, a one-line letter: "I didn't know Tom Wilkins [pseudonym] had ever been in Mexico" (quoted, Hicks 1992, 110).

11. By state law, local school boards were appointed by the state legislature. The party in control of the state government controlled the local school system. Despite the presence of a strong local Republican Party minority, this meant that the county school board

was usually dominated by Democrats. Elective county offices, notably those of sheriff and county commission member, were sometimes occupied by Republicans.

12. To illustrate how intertwined were kinship, school teaching, and politics: two of the principal's brothers, his sister-in-law (a daughter of the county school superintendent), and his sister taught in the county's schools. His wife was working, in 1965, for a college degree with the expectation of getting a position in the Toe Valley school upon graduation.

13. As Celo's population decreased in the 1950s, a corresponding decrease occurred in the search for teaching jobs. With the arrival of the Morgan School, opening in 1962, the long-awaited and planned-for Celo boarding school was come at last, and teaching jobs there were held for Celo's members, residents, and conscientious objectors.

14. Ignorance of local attitude is reflected in discussions, for example, of posting of Community property against hunting or how to deal with motorcycle riding on roads through the Community (CCI, 3/1/72 and 5/2/73; see also 3/6/74 and 6/1/77).

15. A number of single-tax communities were founded in the nineteenth century (see Fogarty 1980 for summary descriptions). A historical account of one of the best known of these groups, located at Fairhope, Alabama, is Alyea and Alyea 1956. Paul M. Gaston, a historian and a descendant of Fairhope's founder, provides detailed biographical information on three early members of the community (Gaston 1984).

16. By 1988 the Community publically described itself as "the oldest land trust community in America, and one of the most successful," in which "group ownership and control" was "designed to exercise wise stewardship of the land." Part of their common land "by agreement of the members" was "set aside as a wildlife preserve." With thirty "family units," Celo was accepting no new members, and had a two-year "waiting list" (reprinted in Fellowship for Intentional Community 1992, 176).

PART 4

Variations of
Utopian America

10. Utopian Outcomes: Development and Change

THIS ACCOUNT of Celo Community—moving outward from the Community as "a separate, distinct entity" and attending to its "much wider historical and sociological context" (Pitzer 1989, 72)—is quite compatible with Pitzer's "developmental communalism" approach. Still, an investigation which primarily concentrates on a single community must fall short of Pitzer's ambitious stipulation that "developmental communalism examines whole movements and how they change over time, from their idealistic origins to their communal stages, and beyond" (1997a, 12).

Celo's course from experimental utopia, with aspirations of becoming a model of social and cultural forms for the entire nation or, alternatively, a master community to lead communities of similar organization, was not the only one possible. Celo could have simply disbanded, disposing of jointly owned property in various ways. There was indeed, in the aftermath of the dramatic reduction of population in the 1950s, the anticipation of this end to the Community. With the growth of population in the succeeding decades, the plan for dissolution receded farther and farther into the background. The Community might have undertaken to give greater emphasis to communalism by increasing joint economic efforts, or it might have underwritten its moral position with a religious ideology. Those members and residents who attended the Friends meeting, most of whom were involved in a summer camp and, later, the Arthur Morgan School, might have led this kind of change. A division of the Community into two parts, a proposal advanced by Evanson's wife in the tumult of their protracted departure, was also possible. As she suggested, those who wanted a more cohesive, more communally oriented community should separate from those, among whom the

physician Leonard Mann was most prominent, who pressed for limited communalism and fiscal conservatism. But this alternative was also not chosen.

These alternatives—dissolution, increased communalism, division into
two communities—are not mere logical possibilities. For other communities similar to Celo, they became actual modes of action. In the wake of the
Society of Brothers' missionary tour, Kingwood Cooperative Community in
New Jersey disintegrated as five of its resident families became members of
the Brothers. Another response to the Brothers' whirlwind was found in
Macedonia Cooperative Community, where defection to the Brothers led the
remaining members along the path of imitation. The diminished Macedonians copied the Brothers' practices until, three years after the missionary visit, the complete merger of the two communities occurred.

A comparison of Celo with Macedonia Cooperative Community, a remarkably similar enterprise, can supply a partial corrective to what might
otherwise be taken as an unnecessarily narrow study. A review of the two
groups can reveal crucial parallels and differences which resulted in very
different historical trajectories. Moreover, comparative analysis should establish firmer ground for a critical appraisal of the developmental approach itself. Finally, the measure of success and failure cannot be ignored; so this
chapter ends with a discussion of this vexatious analytical orphan.

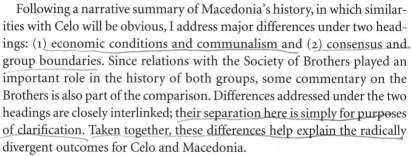

Following a narrative summary of Macedonia's history, in which similarities with Celo will be obvious, I address major differences under two headings: (1) economic conditions and communalism and (2) consensus and
group boundaries. Since relations with the Society of Brothers played an
important role in the history of both groups, some commentary on the
Brothers is also part of the comparison. Differences addressed under the two
headings are closely interlinked; their separation here is simply for purposes
of clarification. Taken together, these differences help explain the radically
divergent outcomes for Celo and Macedonia.

Macedonia in Brief

Started in the same year as Celo (1937), Macedonia occupied one thousand
acres of cut-over pine forest adjacent to the Macedonia Baptist Church in the
Appalachian foothills of northeastern Georgia. Macedonia's founder, Morris Mitchell, at that time instructor of community-based education in Columbia University's experimental New College, hired a local man as community manager, told him to recruit suitable local families as settlers, and

returned to New College. With only one exception, these first recruits were the manager's kin.

Mitchell's primary purpose was to build a community where local farm families would learn the benefits of cooperative life. He intended Macedonia to become a privately funded version of the federal community resettlement program. The frequently voiced criticism of the federal communities—that residents were not allowed to own land and must be content with long-term leases (Eaton 1950)—was countered in Macedonia by an agreement signed in 1939 between Mitchell and nine settlers, organizing themselves as the Macedonia Cooperative Association. Members became shareholders and had equal voice in making decisions for the community. New members would be paid for any capital they contributed and could recover their contribution if they left. Mitchell was insistent that the project not be fully communal (Orser 1981, 43).[1]

The founder was also an educational consultant to the federal Resettlement Administration and appeared to share the well-meaning but paternalistic self-satisfaction of many government reformers. About one resettlement project, he wrote: "What a challenge in community organization—to go there and with firmness and tact put order and beauty in the lives of those people—then spread that influence to the countryside about" (quoted, Orser 1981, 29).

Local suspicion of the Macedonia project arose almost immediately. Summer work-campers of 1939–41, college students and liberal strangers in a region of social and cultural conservatism, bewildered local residents who were not associated with the cooperative. "Behind short shorts and coed living lurked the specter of the radicalism of these outsiders" (Orser 1981, 64). By 1942 Mitchell's unusual notions about cooperation and his pacifist views had become common knowledge, and rumors abounded that Macedonia was undergoing investigation by the FBI for possible seditious activity.

Antagonism deepened with news, this time based on fact, of similar investigations into Mitchell's academic life. After New College closed in 1939, Mitchell had taken a position at Florence State Teachers College in Alabama. Many of his students at this small college registered for the military draft as conscientious objectors, and FBI agents arrived to examine a suspected conspiracy. Morris resigned and returned to Macedonia.

Meanwhile, membership in Macedonia shrank. Community men, all from the local area, found well-paying jobs in defense industries, and by the summer of 1943 none remained and none returned to Macedonia. For the duration of the war, Macedonia languished. In the eyes of local folk, it was an outpost of religious and social radicalism, Mitchell an eccentric and perhaps dangerous free-thinker of dubious patriotism. Men on leave from Civilian Public Service camps, college students, and visitors sympathetic to Mitchell's aims only served to confirm local mistrust. No violence broke out, however, and a postwar member boasted in 1948 that they had "successfully survived accusations of harboring 'nigger-lovers,' Communists, nudists, free love advocates, atheists, conscientious objectors and Yankees (which latter two we are)" (Newton 1948, 30).

Men who worked in the summer work camps went on to Civilian Public Service internment and spread the word about Macedonia. Mitchell himself gave lectures in CPS camps and in 1943 directed the School of Cooperative Living at the Walhalla, Michigan, camp. A number of his most zealous students visited Macedonia and anticipated living there after the war. They continued "seriously studying community building . . . seeking a sounder, simpler, more social way of living than they have known," and regarded themselves part of a lengthy utopian tradition: "The small community," they wrote, "has appealed throughout the ages to men desiring a more ideal life than the world has offered. Particularly in times of chaos groups have gone forth with the conscious intention of building a new world" (Trenton Community Group 1944, 316).

Mitchell responded with a spirited invitation: "Nothing could make more certain the success of Macedonia in demonstrating community organization, democratic in nature and appropriate in our times, than for a number of the co-op community group to make this their home following the war" (quoted, Orser 1981, 96). An advantage of Macedonia, he said, was that it already included local people and thus could eliminate efforts at "establishing an artificial community to which you might later on welcome the native born." Macedonia's mission of long-term improvement of local society conveyed the likelihood of constructing a new moral order without incurring the charge of escapism.

Of the many potential members attracted to Macedonia, few stayed and high turnover was the rule for the late 1940s. Early in 1947, for example, the population totaled twenty: six married couples with five children and three single men (Infield 1955b, 230). A year later, the group had dropped to thirteen: three married couples with six children and one single man. This, however, was the beginning of a large increase and by 1952, Macedonia's size had swelled to its peak of twenty-nine adults and eighteen children.

Mitchell disavowed any "choosey [sic] selection of membership" for Macedonia and thought it best "to let the community grow freely, naturally" (quoted, Infield 1955b, 230). He retained ownership of the property but left community government to the members, a position welcomed by the postwar membership. Beyond involvement in common economic effort, the Macedonians had "an intuition," according to Orser, "that common purpose, however necessary, ought somehow to grow organically out of the soil of the community experience rather than be imposed out of whole cloth from outside" (Orser 1981, 173).

They were trying, wrote a member in 1950, "to create a way of living in which there is no foundation for war or coercion, in which an individual may live creatively, in harmony with nature and in fellowship with others" (Wiser 1950, 13). Life in modern America, Wiser declared, was painfully fragmented; one's activities were parceled out into unrelated segments. To develop an alternative to the divisiveness that characterized daily life for individuals and poisoned group relations, Macedonians sought harmony and wholeness. Indeed, the preservation of mental health itself was at stake. He continued: "To preserve our own sense of individual responsibility, our sanity, and our creative capacity, we in Macedonia feel we must recreate an integrated way of living. All the circumstances, materials and relations attending our living must be patterned, insofar as we are able, into an integrated whole" (ibid.).

Eating together was emblematic of the wholeness they desired. From necessity in the penniless and difficult winter of 1946–47, the members cooked and ate all their meals together. Growing more prosperous in their manufacture of wooden blocks and furniture for children, they continued to dine communally, but only at midday when lunch was served on long wooden tables in the largest community building (Orser 1981, 119, 160; Wiser 1950, 17).

Much more significant in their pursuit of harmony and integration was the choice of consensus as the means of making decisions. There was no ambiguity about their purpose: at community meetings held every two weeks, "the consent of each individual is necessary in reaching decisions" (Wiser 1950, 18). One member recalled an extended discussion in the late 1940s regarding whether a community horse should be sold or eaten. The fate of the horse was not the only instance "where consensus was difficult" (Orser 1981, 156). Many similar situations arose in their struggle for unanimity (Newton 1948). Certainly the discussions were lively, but sheer boredom was frequent. Community meetings, one Macedonian remembered, took up tiny problems and wrung them out to excruciating lengths. As she put it,

> whether a cow should be bred, whether one truck should be fixed and another not fixed, whether the shop should produce so many or not so many blocks, or whether they should sell to somebody who perhaps had a shady past, or something—this was all brought up in the meeting and discussed for hours. The meetings seemed to be interminable. At the beginning I enjoyed them—it seemed to be democracy at work. But then when you get the total group con-

cerned with the littlest minutiae, it got to be wearying. I would usually take some
handwork with me, as most of the women did, some sewing . . . one of the men
was usually doing some carving . . . because the meeting was so long and bor-
ing. (Grace Foster, quoted, Orser 1981, 186)

The pitfalls of making decisions consensually included not just tedium but
the risk that a minority, even of one member, could exercise unjustifiably
great power or the danger that the disagreement of those who would check
the will of a majority would be muffled. Nevertheless, consensus held for
Macedonians much the same charm as it did for members of many other
experimental groups. Like common effort in economic enterprises, consensus gave strong evidence that community members faced each other on a
basis of equality. It was, as well, another ingredient in Macedonia's recipe for
an integrated and harmonious life.

By about 1952 "a distinctive communal life-style" had taken hold in Macedonia, and "life burned with intensity" (Orser 1981, 176). Mitchell had turned
over ownership of land and buildings to an unincorporated partnership of
community members. In return they owed him almost forty thousand dollars (in 1948). Combined with other debts, this continued to threaten Macedonia's stability; periodic pleas to prospective donors and lenders continued.
After the lean years of the late 1940s, however, it appeared that financial success might be at hand.

Just as Macedonia appeared to have attained a measure of prosperity and
a "full and, in many respects, satisfying" life for the members, a series of disasters struck (Orser 1981, 176). The community's central building, the Dairy
House—with its dining room, kitchen, nursery school, canning center, and
an apartment—burned to the ground in late 1952. In the same month, most
residents fell ill with flu and jaundice, and one member accidentally killed
his two-year-old child. To end the calendar of misfortunes, one family's cabin
burned while they were away visiting their parents for Christmas. Added to
these disasters, it was a very poor year for community businesses.

Came the spring of 1953 and several families decided to leave. One went
to resume a career in forestry, but several others disagreed with the majority's increasing demand for religious and social conformity. From the experiences of the previous year, the remaining members sought "to make the
suffering and difficulties redemptive" by urging more unity, "homogeneity
rather than diversity, and . . . mutual commitment to a common center of
values, something akin to a religious commitment" (Orser 1981, 194). The
departure of those opposed to basing community on religion wrought dramatic change. Religious meetings grew more frequent. Instead of a weekly

Quaker gathering of half the members, the entire community added daily worship sessions to the routine Sunday services.

Macedonia was caught up in the excitement that touched many American experimental communities upon the arrival of the Society of Brothers emissaries. Representatives from the Brothers visited Macedonia in the summer of 1953, and their message, coming after the calamities of the previous year and the ensuing atmosphere of uncertainty and doubt, made a powerful and enduring impression. Shortly afterward, Macedonia issued a new statement of purpose, incorporating much of what they had learned from the Brothers. They called for shared religious belief (although not specifically Christianity) as the basis for community life, and stressed group demands over individual desire: "We must give up self pride, self centeredness, and live our lives for all. Our constant thought must be doing, living, sharing, for others. We must be willing to do or go whatever or wherever the group asks" (quoted, Orser 1981, 198). The community's Christmas letter of 1953 announced their arrival at "a common inner purpose and meaning to our life that provides a religious center of belief in which we have found unity and strength together." They had undergone "a dying to the self and rebirth to a new way of life" (quoted, Orser 1981, 194).[2]

A meeting with five Brothers and members from Kingwood, Koinonia, and Celo communities convened at Macedonia in February 1954; some members of each group decided to join the Brothers. Half of Macedonia's population left, half stayed behind. As noted above, of Kingwood's six families, only one decided against joining the Society of Brothers.

The surviving population of three couples and five children at Macedonia set up cooperative arrangements with the Brothers to operate Community Playthings, the children's toy and furniture business. Part of the shop equipment went to the Brothers' new colony at Rifton, New York, and manufacture and sales were to be conducted jointly. Why were the assets not simply divided between those who left and those who stayed? Art Wiser, one of Macedonia's most articulate spokesmen, explained in a letter to Mitchell: "Divide the group, and the assets must be divided; divide the assets and the relations among them are destroyed and their value is diminished. Yet our liabilities remain constant." But an economic argument was only part of it. Wiser, a religious agnostic, went on to reveal how profoundly he and others had been affected:

> One can't simply say, "it [the Brothers' life] isn't for me," and go on living. One is forced into a concern to search out a way that might bear as good fruit. Each of us has been very deeply shaken in facing this challenge. . . . It is because they

are such fine people and because it is so obviously right for those to join who can that there is no resentment. They [members of the Brothers] are a fine, loving people, with a high sense of justice and integrity, and it is clear that the way of life and conviction which they follow helps all of them to be that way. (Wiser to Mitchell, 3/25/54, quoted, Orser 1981, 206, 202, 200)

Step by measured step, Macedonia took on the contours of a Society of Brothers colony. New members turned over all possessions to the community, without promise of future compensation. Communal meals increased, daily lunching together augmented with shared evening meals five days a week. The gap between members and visitors, including "helpers" (long-term visitors under consideration for membership), widened; only members could participate in making decisions. Shifts from job to job became more frequent, signaling a renewed emphasis on the absolute equality of each position. Already drawn out, community meetings grew longer and more numerous as the Macedonians instituted group sessions of "direct-speaking," a form of mutual criticism practiced in many communal societies. Members were enjoined to speak openly and critically of the shortcomings of others. Those being criticized were expected to remain "humble and free enough of self to accept [critical comments] . . . as constructive and loving, rather than responding defensively, that is, with self" (Orser 1981, 225).

Coupled with direct-speaking as a means of submission of the self to group demands—of reaching harmony by submerging individual differences—a significant change occurred in the use of consensus. Discussions now pointed toward disclosure of the correct decision that was assumed to exist for each situation. Rather than encourage individual proposals for alternative courses of action and calculate the relative advantages and disadvantages of each, Macedonians leaned more and more toward the position "that there was a truth to be discovered, an impersonal position that only could be arrived at once personal prejudices and disturbances had been dealt with in an atmosphere of complete openness and sharing" (Orser 1981, 225).

Turnover in Macedonia's membership continued. New people arrived, but some established members found the pressure for submersion of self an intolerable burden. Years later, two ex-members, explaining their decision to leave, noted the Macedonian "belief in the special wisdom arising from the committed group mind [which] led to the group dictating how each individual should live, in his family life, his work, his use of his free time, etc. . . . We left because we felt the dominance of the group over the individual was as bad as the jungle of competitive society outside, or worse, because it was more complete" (Dan and Betty Jackson to Orser, 1976, quoted, Orser 1981, 232). Another couple left because they felt "choked . . . controlled" by the insistent effort to erase individuality, declaring that "freedom to think and act as individuals was for us a necessity" (Norman Moody and wife to Orser, 1975, quoted, Orser 1981, 233).

Yet the community population climbed and, by early 1957, almost reached a new high point. Difficulty in operating the woodworking business jointly with the Society of Brothers brought on plans to divide the business. Then, within a few months, following meetings with Society of Brothers' leaders, the Macedonians distributed a letter to "Friends of Macedonia" declaring that the community was joining the Brothers. At a meeting attended only by community members, they wrote, each one "said what he felt he must do. To our wonder, we all felt the same thing: that a new community should be formed based on Jesus, and that the Society of Brothers should constitute that community. . . . therefore, Macedonia has become a community of the Society of Brothers" (quoted, Orser 1981, 234). Excluded from the members' deliberations, the helpers and visitors were shocked by the announcement.

In May of the following year, Macedonia's land and assets were sold at auction, the community's debts paid, and the balance of the proceeds paid to the Society of Brothers.

Parallels in Celo and Macedonia

So striking are the similarities between these two groups that informants familiar with both occasionally described them as "sister communities." There are other shared features, in addition to those implied in the summary above, which deserve mention. Among these are characteristics and avowed purposes of the founders and a few small but revealing details of community life.

Parallels: The Founding Fathers

Arthur Morgan and Morris Mitchell saw themselves primarily as educators; both offered a vision of education as an inseparable part of life. Each man sought to correct the major ill of American education: the artificial and unhealthy separation between formal education and the practical affairs of life. To be sure, Mitchell's modest efforts in this regard—as a rural school teacher and as instructor in Columbia University's experimental New College— were overshadowed by Morgan's national renown for his Antioch work-study curriculum. But both relied firmly on John Dewey's view that education must not be sealed off from other aspects of society. Living in appropriately designed communities, from their point of view, was the best education. Morgan's efforts to make Antioch College only one component of an integrated community, his assertion that the TVA charter mandated planned communities, and his hopes for Celo were all expressions of this idea that community life was the highest form of education. Like Morgan, Mitchell enthusiastically championed education as a "lifelong process" and thus "a potentially revolutionary tool for achieving social transformation" (Orser 1981, 26).

They were charismatic and somewhat dogmatically self-assured men, unusual in their ability to attract followers. Morgan amply demonstrated these traits at Antioch and in his initial years as chief of the TVA. Supremely confident of the moral correctness and usefulness of their views, neither seemed able to bear criticism of his ideas, a rigidity fully revealed by Morgan's biographer (Talbert 1987). Mitchell, too, did not easily tolerate dissent. Orser notes that Mitchell, "forceful and fascinating" in public appearances, who "clearly had the capacity to excite and stir the imagination" (1981, 131), considered his own "ideas . . . both simple and practical, and he apparently could not understand it when others criticized them for being naive, impractical, or vague. . . . [He] could be impatient with those who did not trust their instincts to lead them to the same vision of a better world" (26).

Neither endorsed extensive communalism in their respective communities. Morgan called on historical evidence to support his position: with the exception of a few religious groups, all fully communal undertakings in America had failed. "Americans," he wrote to a student in 1946, "crave a considerable range of independence of action. . . . In the [communal] . . . group, I am sorry to say, you will find many maladjusted, impractical, temperamental persons" (AEM to H. Dyer, quoted, Orser 1981, 105, 111; see also Morgan 1936, 1942b). Mitchell was dismayed to find Macedonia moving "in a communal direction as regards . . . the nearly complete subjection of the individual to the will of the group" (Mitchell to Charles Davis, 9/10/47, quoted, Orser 1981, 133). It was the "practical idealist," a term favored by both, whom they sought to populate Celo and Macedonia.

Parallels: Home, Children, and Others

Children played a central role in each community. Orser's comment about children in Macedonia fits Celo equally well: they were "a tangible expression of the desire for an integration of 'family, work, and social relationships,' a value which united the Macedonians as perhaps none other" (Orser 1981, 158). Both groups set up nursery schools, and their dissatisfaction with the quality of local schools led them to start community elementary schools as well.

A settlement pattern of scattered households evolved in both communities. Celo's house sites were in most cases not visible to each other. The ten houses at Macedonia, says Orser, "were scattered throughout the Macedonia tract in what appeared to be a rather haphazard fashion . . . [and] seemed to be one point at which the Macedonians chose to emphasize their individuality and separateness" (Orser 1981, 151).

Diverse relationships tied members of the two communities to other utopians. A mail-order pharmacy in Celo, for example, sold products at cost to people in Macedonia and to other communities like Koinonia. Financial assistance passed back and forth from one community to another. Members were sometimes exchanged in long-term visits and by permanent movement of families. To a minor extent, these links also included ties of kinship; of two brothers, for instance, both worked at Macedonia on leave from CPS camp and after the war, one joined Celo, the other Macedonia.

The peak of utopian enthusiasm came to each group at about the same time, in the early 1950s. After that, with the loss of significant numbers, each community plunged into doubt and painful reconsideration of its goals. Each took different paths, Celo on a course of redefinition, Macedonia headed toward fusion with the Society of Brothers.

Differences in Celo and Macedonia

Though justifiably seen as siblings, Celo and Macedonia were not identical; economically and organizationally, they were easily distinguished.

Differences: Economic Conditions and Communalism

From the beginning, a substantial difference existed in the financial condition of the two communities. An indication of the meager resources at Macedonia's command turned up at its very birth: Mitchell needed two years to complete the purchase of the land. Recruits brought little money to Macedonia, and each member assumed a portion of the group's heavy debt. To varying degrees over the years, the Community relied on financial contributions from outside supporters. Until the day Macedonia's property fell to the auctioneer's mallet, the shackle of debt remained a constant vexation, a goad to further commercial effort, and a source of anxiety.

Quite unlike Macedonia's collective poverty, Celo's solvency, underwritten by its wealthy benefactor, W. H. Regnery, provided firm financial stability. Individuals and families came to Celo with few assets, but the Community itself did not lack for funds. Members were frequently granted loans for building houses, starting businesses, and for other purposes, including education of their children. While Macedonians might face the question, Is there any way we can make a loan to a member?, the question at Celo was more likely, What interest, if any, should be levied on loans to members?

These dissimilar circumstances furnished the background for the communities' variation in communal ownership and activity. Strongly influenced by Arthur Morgan's dislike of extensive communalism, Celo's postwar membership quickly sold off most of the community-owned farm equipment and each household took responsibility for its own livelihood. An early decision not to undertake communal construction and ownership of a small factory set a precedent. Henceforth, common ownership would be limited to land and whatever houses were repurchased from landholders who left the Community. Although much shared property and jointly owned ventures existed, and their number increased over the years, such arrangements were made by individual members. As a community, Celo provided a locus for communal activity, but officially maintained little communalism (Brooks 1994 gives details of interfamily sharing).

In contrast, Macedonia's pacifists immediately embraced communalism. Like groups in nineteenth-century America—the early Shakers, George Rapp's Harmony, the Ebenezer Society (later Amana), and others—communalism at Macedonia began as an economic tactic and was only afterward enveloped in ideology. The Macedonians engaged in dairying and later, making and marketing wooden toys, as a community. Jobs were rotated among members; labor and whatever profits might accrue were shared. Communal meals were a feature of daily life, and the community maintained ownership of some residential apartments. Founder Mitchell's lamentations about the acceleration of communalism, and his plan that benefits reflect economic commitment, even if in principle only, went unheeded.

Driven by ideology, Macedonians themselves collaborated in restricting their economic prosperity. They "stubbornly insisted that the profit system was wrong and . . . they should charge no more [for their products] than was required to maintain themselves" (Orser 1981, 221), a stance affirmed in 1956. Business, they declared, must not be carried on for "pecuniary gain or profit," but only to support community members' "simple and frugal standard of living" (quoted, Orser 1981, 221). Twenty years later, one of them remarked: "The way we conducted ourselves as a business had to be completely consistent with the way we felt about our relationships with one another—open, nonexploitative, communicative" (Alice Lynd to Orser, 1976, quoted, Orser 1981, 168). Macedonians preferred to sell toys to individual buyers, rather than ship off large lots to department stores or public school districts, since "we should come to know the people with whom we deal and how they plan to use our products" (Wiser 1949, 7). Such direct sales allowed for personal, one-to-one contact with nonmember customers. It also, of course, eliminated an indifferent and profit-seeking middleman.[3]

Differences: Group Boundaries and Consensus

Part of the population in both Celo and Macedonia yearned to base community life firmly on religious principles. They wanted closer ties among members, greater sharing on a spiritual as well as a social level, and community acknowledgment that religious faith, whether Christian or other, was the foundation of their project. It was these members who responded most fervently to the message of the Society of Brothers. In Macedonia the religiously oriented segment of the membership was more numerous and more influential than in Celo. When members made decisions to leave for the Brothers, it was Macedonia who lost more. Partly to avoid a disastrous division of community assets, and partly from profound emotional turmoil, the remaining members of Macedonia chose to operate their toy business jointly with the Brothers. Those who stayed behind held the Brothers in high regard, and within a few years they had moved to a position from which the only option appeared to be a union of the two communities.

Celo's encounter with the Society of Brothers brought another result. The defectors, a minority of the membership, were most insistent in their call for increased communal activity and for closer spiritual bonds. They were frustrated not only with the apparent failure of Celo to achieve unanimity and harmony, but with what they perceived as a future direction of dissension and endless argument between members and former members. The Brothers siphoned off Celo's discontented, leaving the religiously oriented members even less influential than before.

The aftermath of their confrontation with the Society of Brothers was difficult for both communities. Both moved toward a weakening of their commitment to equality as hierarchical tendencies emerged. To fill houses left vacant by defectors, to the Brothers or to other pursuits, Celo began to accept residents who were not members, some of whom did not intend to become members. It became a matter of sheer survival. At Macedonia, as the surviving members drew closer and discussed their growing conviction that the Society of Brothers alternative was the best for them, a distinction appeared between full members and long-term visitors. Nonmember residents, formerly involved in all community meetings, found themselves excluded from some gatherings. When the full members deliberated and approached religious conversion, more and more decisions were taken without the knowledge of nonmembers. Finally, the announcement of a merger of Macedonia with the Brothers took other residents by surprise.

The redefinition and change in course undergone by Macedonia and Celo led to differences in the boundaries of the communities. As Macedonians drew nearer their consolidation with the Brothers, and the bonds of membership more and more assumed a spiritual and religious temper, their conception of Macedonia Community's relationship with the world beyond its borders changed. In the years following 1945, they had affirmed their link with radical pacifists, with large numbers of those who like themselves sought world brotherhood in a peaceful world. The means varied, from joint participation in conferences, communication through magazine articles, and personal correspondence, to the welcoming of visitors of like principles and goals. Economic activity also linked them with this larger population. Their sense of solidarity with their customers derived in part from an insistence on insulation from the market economy. This was a major point of contention in the initial stages of their association with the Society of Brothers. The Brothers held out for prices set by market factors, taking a position quite like that of other producers in a capitalist economy.

Macedonia's previous efforts at maintaining relationships with radical groups outside was reduced to a willingness to take in members who would accept the demands of religious service. In this respect, they became very like the Society of Brothers. Just as religious groups often have done, a major barrier was built between member and nonmember. The Society of Brothers—and, in the end, Macedonia in emulation of the Brothers—considered its "outreach" and lack of escapism to consist of an "open door" policy. Outsiders who wished to join were welcome, so long as they were willing to invest everything, material goods plus a loss of self in the totality of community.[4]

Consensus also assumed a different pattern in the two groups. Celo's members sought consensus only on large issues; that is, about matters framed as ethically significant. Decisions on questions tacitly categorized as routine or relatively minor were left to committees or to the discretion of individual members. For Macedonians, topics great and small came before the community and required consensual judgment. From the admission of members to the repair of farm equipment, from job assignments to selection of timber for the sawmill; all were topics of discussion by the entire membership. Meetings often went on for hours and exhausted participants' interest. Boredom must occasionally have worn down the objections of even the most tenacious, with fatigued acquiescence substituted for eager discussion. What were crucial matters demanding the attention of all members at Macedonia—for example, questions of direct and immediate economic impact—were for Celo's members less consequential. Many aspects of life in Celo, particularly those having to do with household economy, did not fall within the realm of Community authority.

In Macedonia, when their new course was taken—when, as they announced in early 1957, all full members had independently come to the same decision—they reached a new conception of decision making. With a new view of themselves as a body of believers, each existed as part of a single, indivisible unit. It was no longer a matter of coming to a consensual choice among alternatives. Now they had to find the single, true decision in every case. This understanding transformed decision making into a process of arriving at the *truth;* a single *right* decision awaits detection; members simply work their way toward it.

Given this perspective, the assertion in the Society of Brothers' literature that "we dare not experiment with community" takes on new meaning. Community—that is, the social and cultural order of the band of believers—has been ordained by God. All a believer must do is prayerfully submit to God and await His voice to provide the right way. A divine directive, community is not something that can be formed by the application of human intelligence and reason.

Members of the brotherhood promise "to die rather than knowingly sin," and to admonish other members about their wrongdoing, according to a former member. He explains the steps by which unity is achieved:

> The brotherhood . . . is therefore a group without sin. A brother or sister who sins . . . rends asunder the communal life, which at its deepest is the presence of the Holy Spirit among the members. Thus the united brotherhood speaks with divine authority, not just [as] a group of people. Non-believers or sinners in the brotherhood create a non-united brotherhood to which the Holy Spirit cannot be expected to descend. . . . [M]embers who realized that they were sinning asked to be excluded. Exclusion means that a member is put outside the brotherhood until he or she has properly repented and been forgiven. (Peck 1987, 118–19)

Troubled with doubt, a member had only to seek clarification from other members and spiritual leaders—the Servants of the Word. The rule that members should observe and judge the behavior of their fellows was an incentive to careful conformity in behavior.[5]

The problem for Celo and similar communities is that possible *alternative* actions exist—consensus is then a matter of persuasion aimed toward harmonious unanimity. There is no preexisting *correct* decision—but a number of possibilities. Hence, just as it was in the early Macedonia, reaching consensus, defined as unanimity, can be a long and tortuous process.

Historical Contingencies

Certainly it would be unreasonable to expect accurate prediction of the different histories of these two communities following their apparent achievement of intensity and enthusiasm in the enjoyment of life in the early 1950s. The destiny of each lay in unforeseen circumstances: the missionary rounds of the Society of Brothers, the economic uncertainty of the defecting families at Celo and the entire community of Macedonia, the yearning of members in both communities for closer spiritual and psychological bonds, and the differing proportions of receptive potential converts in each group. Taken together, these and other factors brought about fresh disturbances in community practices which had become stable and satisfying. The outcome in each case was due to the contingencies and uncertainties of historical events, and the response to those contingencies.

If an occurrence is to have some effect, however, it must be noticed. That is, it must be interpreted and significance assigned to it. Following Marshall Sahlins's forceful argument for doing away with the specious opposition between "stability and change" (and "structure and event"), historical incidents are relevant, that is, they make a difference in our lives, only when they are noticed and understood as calling for action. In Sahlins's words, "an event is not just a happening in the world; it is a *relation* between a certain happening and a given symbolic system. And although as a happening, an event has its own 'objective' properties and reasons stemming from other worlds (systems), it is not these properties *as such* that give it effect but their significance as projected from some cultural scheme. The event is a happening interpreted—and interpretations vary" (1985, 153).

So Celo's remaining members interpreted the defection of several families in the mid-1950s as a portent of ruin. In response, they were provoked to action, to establish rules for the disposal of property should the population reach a particular low point in the future. Their interpretation also led them to change policy and rent holdings to nonmembers, thereby inadvertently inviting hierarchy into an egalitarian situation. Confronted with the departure of half their number, Macedonians paid attention, transmuting a happening into an event, and set about shifting emphasis to the group and away from individual residents. Hierarchy appeared here too but could be justified by reference to a "band of believers" (and owner-debtors). Relying on Max Weber for inspiration, Sahlins writes: "Events . . . cannot be understood apart from the values attributed to them: the significance that transforms a mere happening into a fateful conjuncture. What is for some people a radical event may appear to others as a date for lunch" (1985, 154).

Repercussions of the absorption of Macedonia for the Society of Brothers also went well beyond the gathering-in of new believers; for the first time in their existence, the Brothers realized economic self-sufficiency. Until the fusion with Macedonia and the acquisition of Community Playthings, the Brothers had always relied on the financial resources of new members and contributions from outside. In their Paraguayan seclusion they had engaged in woodworking, but with little economic reward. Long before their removal to North America, they were in regular correspondence and visitation with Macedonians and other utopian groups, and one might speculate that the Brothers hoped to improve their condition by some sort of relationship with Macedonia. But unexpected and utterly unforeseen incidents on the national political scene spun their profitable woodworking business into a bonanza. At first, the business faltered for lack of experience in marketing, but soon things turned around. Only a few years after Macedonia brought along its machinery and expertise, the requirements of new federal law opened a vast new market. Tom Potts, the long-term manager of the Brothers' toy factory, recounted the effects:

> The sixties saw the enactment of a federal law in the United States which obliged primary schools to open kindergartens or a kind of pre-school. It was called "Head-Start" and its objective was to give educational motivation to the children of the poorer communities. The federal government injected a great deal of money into this project and all at once an almost unlimited market opened for our products, which apart from toys also included school furniture. The possibility of expanding our production coincided with the beginnings of the Bruderhof movement's expansion in the United States and this provided us with solid economic foundations for our activities. (quoted, Oved 1996, 181–82)

This historical "happening," to use Sahlins's term, was taken to be a divine blessing instead of an unanticipated and historically contingent dividend. Speaking for the Brothers, Potts stressed that "we view our success as a gift from God and believe that He guided, and will continue to guide us along the right road" (quoted, Oved 1996, 182). The less pious might translate this happening into an event by reference to "good luck" or "good fortune," but, then, as Sahlins insists, turning happenings into events demands interpretation in line with existing symbolic systems, and interpretations do vary.

Success and Failure Revisited

Students of American utopias nowadays generally agree that the research design put forth by Kanter in 1972 is too rigid in its equation of longevity with success and severely restricts consideration of the numerous linkages among communities, thereby excluding recognition of secular groups like Owen's influential New Harmony and the widespread reformist flurry of the Fourierist movement (Pitzer 1997b; Guarneri 1991, 1997).

Several years before Pitzer unveiled his approach, a vigorous objection to the longevity-as-success standard appeared in Robert Fogarty's exploration of the House of David (popularly known for its bearded baseball exhibition team). Although the community met Kanter's tests of endurance for twenty-five years (1903–30) and included all six of her commitment mechanisms, the success or failure of the House of David "cannot be measured solely in survival years nor solely in terms of member satisfaction" (Fogarty 1981, 134). After deciding that "the debate about the success or failure of communal societies is, in the long run, a futile one, since it necessarily directs our attention away from communities and toward some set of general principles that determines the context of success or failure," Fogarty moved on to endorse a somewhat mystifying substitute: "The relevant question remains: what did the colony 'mean,' regardless of its duration, organizational structure, or goals. For it is the community that matters, rather than any moral or political principles that its history refutes or sustains" (135). At about the same time, a critical review of the seven criteria for success "most frequently expressed or implied in the existing literature" concluded that "an element of arbitrariness seems inherent in all discussions of success," and we do well "to eschew the term 'success' altogether in favor of more specific and informative substitutes" (Wagner 1985, 99, 100).

Pitzer, too, is firm in his intent to vanquish the "unfortunate 'success-failure' pattern of earlier studies" (Pitzer 1997a, 13). Yet the issue cannot be easily forsaken; the allure of judgment appears irresistible. Immediately after discarding the pattern of success-failure, Pitzer continues: "[R]egardless of their time in existence, we prefer to evaluate the success of communal utopias in terms of how well they achieve their own objectives, service the needs of their own members, and influence the general society" (1997a, 13; see also 1984, 227). Even his coauthors occasionally surrender: Amana is "one of the most successful communal societies in American history," begins the essay by Andelson, and it soon becomes apparent that the salient criterion is longevity (1997, 181).

The standard announced by Pitzer is certainly unclear. He invests his three terms of success—achievement of community goals, provision for members' needs, and influence outside the community—with no particular priority of significance, hence almost ensuring a confusion of comparative evaluation. More than this, the developmental approach provides no means by which we may calibrate success or failure along any of the three dimensions. To what extent must a group realize its objectives in order to be counted as successful? Does wide influence outside add up to more than satisfaction of members' needs in the final score of success or failure? How is influence (or serving needs of members) defined, and what are its measurable elements? The answers may be implicit or not but appear to be left solely to the ingenuity of the observer.

In the end, added to these confusions, we are left with no distinction between the perspective of the analyst and the participants. From which point of view, for instance, should one evaluate the extent to which communities "service the needs of their own members"—that of the members themselves or that of an outside observer?

Fogarty's harsh indictment of the House of David at least has the merit of clarity of viewpoint, even if it discloses Fogarty's notions more than the members'. The House of David organization, he claims,

> contributed little to enrich the members' lives beyond the sustenance of millennial hope; education was denied, individual choices were severly [*sic*] limited, and "worldly" ideas were systematically excluded. It was a parochial colony intent on its own aims, turned in on its own problems, and unconcerned about its fellow man except for the purposes of recruitment for the ingathering or when that fellow man threatened the colony. In fact, the House of David's major success was that it did last so long and seemed to satisfy so many with so little. (1981, 134–35)

But if the House of David offered only such thin gruel, why did members continue to sup? Surely they did not fully agree with Fogarty's negative view of their community. Efforts to understand communities like the House of David—and Jonestown in Guyana; the Branch Davidians in Waco, Texas; the Children of God; the followers of Reverend Sun Myung Moon and his Unification Church; and many others—must encompass the participants' perspectives if we are to avoid the simplistic consignment of them to categories like "mass hysteria" or "collective paranoia."

Back to Macedonia and Celo: significant questions are glossed over when a distinction between the two perspectives—analyst and participant—is ignored. Macedonians' determined aversion to involvement in a market econ-

omy by refusing profit for their products appears to have been quickly overcome when they joined the Brothers. Among the Brothers' newcomers from
Celo was the family known as the most extreme vegetarians: in addition to
the avoidance of meat and eggs, they used no leather or other animal products. As the father remarked, however, they very soon abandoned their ideals and accepted the dietary practices of the Brothers: "We were vegetarians
and ate at a separate table, but after a short while we felt that our vegetari-
anism was hindering the group's social consolidation and that it really wasn't
that important to us, so we had no hesitation in stopping" (quoted, Oved
1996, 181). Aside from his explanation in the uncertain terms of social analysis ("hindering . . . consolidation"), what is striking is the lack of importance
attributed to what had seemed a fundamental and constantly observed family
rule. This rapidity and ease of conversion on a central ideological point calls
out for explanation. And explanation goes but part-way when we rely only
on the viewpoint of either analyst or participant. To take this participant's
view at face value merely short-circuits an understanding of how, in groups
like the Brothers, one reaches the point of self-satisfaction in the process of
suppressing self in favor of group demands.[6]

The failure to make adequate distinction between the perspectives of analyst and participant, characteristic of both Fogarty's assessment of the House
of David and Pitzer's measures of success, can lead directly to what Herbert
Butterfield years ago labeled a "Whig interpretation of history" (1931), a reading of the past to buttress present-day political or moral positions.[7] In such
readings, the analyst need not acknowledge that he or she speaks from a
particular viewpoint, and may assume (with the reader) that the interpretation presented is unquestionable or is at least widely accepted.[8]

Before turning to the Conclusion, I should pose a question, made more
serious in light of the muddled tests of success-failure embraced by even the
most recent programs of investigation: If we eliminate longevity as a standard of success, which one, Celo or Macedonia, should we consider more
successful?

Notes

1. Far more than Celo, Macedonia received widespread national attention in the 1940s
and 1950s, gaining notice in Dwight McDonald's journal *Politics* and in publications by
Paul Goodman, Hendrik Infield, and others. W. Edward Orser's book-length study of
Macedonia (1981) is the source for much of the information presented here.

2. The divine injunction for loss of the self takes on various phrasings in the Society
of Brothers. It is above all a call "to leave all for the life and way of community . . . to turn
away from all loveless self-interest . . . to abandon one's own life for the way which em-
braces the life of all men" (Society of Brothers 1952, 40–41). Only by complete effacement

of one's self in the group of believers is it possible "truly to gain life." The statement of belief goes on to declare: "The giving up one's life, which is the unalterable condition of true community, is the giving in of all self-will to the will of the one true Spirit which, in its universal comprehension, wills the life and joy of the whole" (41).

3. Every intentional community faces the problem of "its economic role in the great society," usually the difficulty of securing enough money to buy necessary machinery. But Macedonia, in the opinion of Paul and Percival Goodman, provided "a touching example of a contrary problem. The Macedonia (pacifist) community made pedagogic toy-blocks for cash, and distributed them, at cost of production, to like-minded groups like progressive schools; but the blocks became popular and big commercial outfits wanted a large number. Macedonia was then faced with the following dilemma: these commercial jobbers would resell at a vast profit; yet if Macedonia itself charged them what the market would bear, the community would itself be contaminated by commercialism" (1947, 108).

4. Emerging from a severe organizational and leadership crisis of the 1960s, the Brothers spread their reform efforts to larger movements, including protests against the Vietnam War. Their commitment, however, to follow their interpretation of Christian tenets of communalism and salvation, continued as the primary goal. Even in 1986, a kibbutz member observed a significant distinction between the Israeli kibbutzim and the American Society of Brothers: "One difference between you and us is that you withdraw from American society. You isolate yourselves on beautiful islands. Your reaching out is actually reaching out without ever becoming a part. American society has no meaning for you" (quoted, Oved 1996, 272).

5. As Peck notes, there was difficulty when admonishment went beyond acts to attitudes: "[T]here were no problems with the system so long as the sins were straightforward, like adultery. But when sin was interpreted as a different attitude, or a minor difference of faith, or the wrong kind of prayer life, opportunities for abuse arose that cut the community in pieces" (Peck 1987, 120).

6. The strength of bonds formed in the attempt at self-abnegation is indicated in the organization of former Society of Brothers' members, K.I.T. (Keep In Touch), which publishes a newsletter and a series of books to reinterpret former members' experiences in the Brothers (Oved 1996, 281–87, 313–14). Further evidence of the difficulty of renouncing individual choice in the interest of group cohesion is found in the journal of a young man in nineteenth-century Oneida (Fogarty 1994).

7. Of course, analysts as well as participants transmute "happenings" into "events," and each generation must write its own history. Hence, Whiggish readings are to some extent unavoidable as succeeding generations seize hitherto unnoticed happenings and remake them into events. But it would seem incumbent upon scholarly analysts to demonstrate an awareness of perspective, of differences in historical milieux, and the predominance of different taken-for-granted realities in one era or another.

8. In his apparent eagerness to sustain an ironic tone and to forward novel understandings, Kern frequently displays a similar tendency to presentism by applying modern feminist criteria to the nineteenth-century status of women among the Mormons, Shakers, and Oneidans (Kern 1981).

Conclusion: Americans and Utopians

AN EXAMINATION of American utopian communities reveals with uncommon clarity the tension between equality and individualism, between the simultaneous appeal of conformity and freedom of choice. Beeman maintains that the tension can be phrased as opposed but reconcilable commands. It constitutes a "double message" for Americans: "1. Be independent: achieve, be unique! [and] 2. Be well integrated: conform! Because these two dicta are fused in American ideology, they are able to coexist with equal moral weight. One can easily support both, citing situations when one or the other should take precedence" (Beeman 1986, 58). The tension, however, is not so swiftly and easily resolved by situational selection of one dictum over the other. Individualism and equality, as Beeman asserts for the synonyms freedom and conformity, are indeed fused and remain inseparable. To justify action by reference to one does not eliminate, even temporarily, awareness of the other.

Tocqueville discerned an American disposition to understand equality as uniformity, a kind of moral and psychological sameness. His assessment rested on a sense of equality as "equality of condition" and should not be confused with the modern incantation of "equality of opportunity." Sennett NOT explicates:

> The equality of conditions Tocqueville envisions is an equal capacity to realize one's desires in action: one could have the same goods as other people, if one wanted them; one could have any job one wanted, if once one knows one wants it; one's traffic with others is based on the conviction that people could switch places, if they so desired. . . . The conditions of society so equalized have in turn little to do with the concept of equality of opportunity, for that implies mobility above others, it implies that the result of action will be the chance to occu-

py a new place in the social hierarchy. In Tocqueville's future world, hierarchy is gone, and all the possible routes of action in society are equivalent. (1979, 108)

Uniformity, taken as a tendency to similarity of inherent ability and shared belief, is a strong American elixir; Wills comments, for example, on the necessity to demonstrate constantly a belief in the *idea* of America (Wills 1978, xxii). In Greenhouse's ethnographic report (1985), it is only similarity—an indication of uniformity—that her informants see as bonding individuals together in social groups. The emphasis on uniformity, in Tocqueville's description of the American notion of equality, resonates in young Karl Marx's utopian vision of an ideal "communist society, where nobody has one exclusive sphere of activity but each can become accomplished in any branch he wishes, society regulates the general production and thus makes it possible for me to do one thing today and another tomorrow, to hunt in the morning, fish in the afternoon, rear cattle in the evening, criticise after dinner, just as I have a mind, without ever becoming hunter, fisherman, shepherd, or critic" (quoted, Tucker 1972, 124, from *The German Ideology*).[1]

The Weight of Responsibility

When it forms a significant part of one's taken-for-granted reality, individualism imposes heavy burdens. Free to make oneself, one must accept the responsibility for whatever consequences result from choices made. Americans, says Sennett, "in ordinary life . . . act as if the responsibility for their satisfaction in life is an entirely individual and private affair" (1979, 124).

This message of individualistic responsibility takes many shapes. In the Great Depression, for instance, it was a commonplace observation that workers tended to blame themselves for loss of jobs and looked upon the acceptance of public aid, no matter how necessary, as personal failure. That was exactly the understanding of M. L. Wilson, the first director of the federal homestead program (Wilson 1939). Similar reactions, less widespread perhaps, can be recognized today. One manifestation of it is the accusation that public policy based on the notion of a "culture of poverty" is actually a form of "blaming the victim." Another is the argument for the denial of civil rights to homosexual Americans because they "choose" to be homosexual. Such sentiments are rooted in the idea that individuals are ultimately responsible for their own plight.

Members of Celo and most other American utopian communities experience the society they try to abandon as a condition of individual powerlessness, a sense that one is pressured to live inauthentically and hypocritically, and an almost desperate feeling of isolation and fragmentation in social relationships. In their own descriptive terms, they were American "outcasts" and "misfits." They did not take part in the consensus they imagined to be shared by everyone else (see Gusfield 1979). Hence, they were forced to act in a manner contrary to their beliefs and to present false impressions of themselves. At the same time, the dictates of individualism required them to be self-reliant and devise their own moral codes as the basis of individual behavior. In their view, to behave falsely was to betray one's true self and thereby incur the penalty of guilt and loneliness.

Among Kindred Spirits

Experiencing one's life as a lonely misfit and outcast can reasonably lead to a search for others who share that experience. And so it did for recruits to Celo, Macedonia, and hundreds of other utopian communities. Once made aware of an alternative setting with the potential for finding the "meaning of living," for undergoing those "primary experiences" denied them in the conventional social and cultural order, utopians—Veysey's American "cultural radicals"—withdraw from an unsatisfactory milieu and attempt to construct a better one. In alternative communities, they set out to explore the possibilities of new lives among the like-minded. They endeavor to eliminate the isolating specialization and fragmentation they feel and, in organic unity with kindred spirits, make a social unit in which an authentic self is possible, where one can have greater control over one's private fate and not suffer a life of inevitable hypocrisy. They condemn the enervating conformity of conventional America yet attempt to robe themselves in an organic and willful unity of ideologically similar comrades.

Zablocki suggests why America generated large numbers of these groups in the latter half of the twentieth century: "During historical periods (such as the present) characterized by ideological proliferation and the multiplication of meaning systems, to find a group of people with whom one can agree about fundamental values and goals can . . . become an end in itself" (Zablocki 1980, 200).

Balancing Consensus and Self

The faith in consensus, so characteristic of utopian communities, can be understood as an effort to stitch community firmly together with individualism. In the broader sense of agreement on values and perceptions, and as a technique for arriving at decision, consensus attracts utopian communitarians as a means of healing their sense of fragmentation by making decisions as an "organic" whole and harmonious body. As a way to resolve issues, consensual rule assumes the unequivocal equality of every participant, in moral authority and expertise.[2] At the same time, if taken to mean unanimity—as it usually is, and certainly was in Celo and Macedonia—consensus as technique incorporates an extreme form of individualism, where each member has the power of veto. Generalizing from his survey of over a hundred communal groups, Zablocki concludes that: "Consensus itself is the most prominent goal among communitarians" (1980, 200).

Aside from a shaky agreement on a few key symbols, however, the expected relief from the cacophony of "ideological proliferation" and conflicting "meaning systems" proved to be frail indeed for Celo's members. To sustain the fusion of individual diversity with unanimity on major issues, they resorted to evasive strategies: veto by a minority of one voluntarily forestalled by troubled abstention; regular and ad hoc committees empowered to break deadlocks; and, fatefully, the question of membership answered with majority rule. The implicit assumption that like-minded people think alike should have led to amiable unanimity: uniformity of perspective blended with ease of decision making. But diversity of outlook and opinion, dear to Celo's membership, prevented such desirable outcomes; the attempt to balance individualism—diversity—with collective harmony fixed conditions of repeated dilemma.

On a personal level, the pursuit of the true self reflects another aspect of the desire to eliminate segmentation and achieve a sense of individual unity and harmony. This, too, is a quality of American individualism, lodged in axiom and literature: be your own true self; to thine own self be true; march to the sound of a different drummer; and so on. Beneath the flimsy superficiality of ordinary existence, there is assumed to lie the precious lode of true selfhood. To mine it, bring it forth, lay it open to the inspection of others, is the mark of honesty and personal integrity. American advertising has been especially skillful at the deployment of innumerable versions of this sentiment (Beeman 1986; Lears 1994).

A determination to avoid situations in which one must play different, and potentially conflicting, roles figures significantly in utopians' struggle to uncover the true, essential self. One Celo informant (quoted in chapter 8) emphasized that playing multiple roles causes personal confusion: "the next thing you know, you don't know who you are." Finding and displaying an essential self (not subject to situational variation) enables one to act from conviction and reject pressures for conventional, hypocritical behavior. Behavior must match belief. At the same time, however, a willingness to compromise, particularly on issues of moral and ethical gravity, is reduced. When brought to public arenas like community meetings, the necessity to insist on the application of principles and opinions (taken to be part of the essential self) can bring an agglomeration of separate selves to an impasse.

This attitude strongly implies the union of private and public realms, just as endorsed by Lasch and other intellectual communitarians (see chapter 1). If one's behavior must issue from and faithfully mirror one's moral code, then there is no separation of private and public selves. The injunction to speak to fellow members in a frank and straightforward manner, frequently encountered in utopian communities, is part of the encouragement to renounce deception and hypocrisy, that is, to express one's true self. Applied rigorously, there could be little space here for gentle fibs to soothe the self-regard of others by casual but false compliment. Social relationships could easily drift toward the perennially harsh and irritable.

After all, one *is* one's convictions and behavior; disagreement with others tends to be sensed as personal attack, as aggression against the self. (The formula seems to be: When I disagree with you, I'm just expressing my true self; when you disagree with me, you are engaging in a personal attack.) Most of Celo's members lacked a taste for argumentation; situations of starkly revealed differences among them brought tears of distress to some. Others often kept silent when they anticipated objections to their proposals. Their concern for finding and displaying their "true selves" led them to expect that, below the specious surface of role-playing and induced conformity, all would not only share attention to the same significant symbols, but would agree on the meanings of the symbols as well. Had this expectation been met, however, it would have obliterated the valued diversity of members.

Etiquette and Difference

Anthony Wallace, in a study first published in 1961, argues convincingly that it is our ability for mutual prediction of others' behavior that makes orderly social relationships possible. His conception of the relationship of individual and culture as the "organization of diversity" raises the idea of public symbols/private meanings to an inevitability. Not only is it unnecessary for the persistence of society that "its members . . . [be] threaded like beads on a string of common motives" (Wallace 1970, 24), but "human societies may characteristically *require* . . . nonsharing . . . among participants in a variety of institutional arrangements." This, he suggests, allows for "a more complex system to arise than most, or any, of its participants can comprehend" and it frees participants from the "heavy burden of learning and knowing each other's motivations and cognitions" (35). This conception of culture as organized diversity easily accommodates Gusfield's proposition that participants believe in a wide consensus that does not necessarily include themselves. One might indeed propose that diversity and the assumption of widespread agreement go hand in hand, making for continuity in expectation of others' behavior at the same time that it allows for diverse motives and interpretations.

What is required for the coordination of behavior is a knowledge and use of appropriate rules in social relations (or "social consensus"; see Fernandez 1965), which includes proper attention to symbols but not agreement on their meaning. Associated with this view of social life, contends Wallace, is a "sense of tragedy" quite unlike that flowing from the view of society as the "replication of uniformity" of its members, in which social relations are based on similarity of personnel and agreed-upon symbolic interpretations. "The unwanted inevitability [of society as organized diversity] is not sin, nor conflict, but loneliness: the only partly bridgeable chasms of mutual ignorance between whole peoples and the failures of understanding between individuals" (Wallace 1970, 24).

In Wallace's model of social order, relations with others closely resemble "categorical relationships," as defined by J. Clyde Mitchell. Such relationships "arise in situations where . . . contacts must be superficial and perfunctory." People assign others to categories, usually by reference to some "visible characteristic," ignore any "internal divisions within a category," and "organize their behavior accordingly" (Mitchell 1966, 52, 53). Relationships between residents of Celo Community and their local neighbors were in large part categorical. Labels for the social categories changed as the history of relationships between them went on. At the Community's inception, local people strained to find a suitable category for the utopian newcomers, settling on "the company" as a convenient label. This concisely indicated the utopians' main impact upon local neighborhoods: a source of jobs and economic assistance much like the logging companies in the region in the early 1900s. With the disappearance of this aspect of the Community, as it turned toward social experimentation and aroused the suspicions of locals, other labels were applied, including "spies," "Germans," and "communists." The most general term used until about 1965 was "quare" or "those queer people." After that time, local people grew more and more aware of the world outside southern Appalachia, and the category label became "the community people."

For Celo, their neighbors were most often referred to as "the local people," usually with connotations of backward, ill-educated, and old-fashioned.
There was an implicit contrast with those labeled "the like-minded," a category not in residence in the valley (except for visits and camp experiences)
but considered to include the wide-ranging supporters of Celo and similar
endeavors. When back-to-the-landers and homesteaders appeared in significant numbers in the 1970s, a new category was invented by Celo's members:
"our sane fringe," a name thick with allusions to superiority over "local people" and "mass society."

Other kinds of relationships between Celo residents and the local mountain folk—for example, those in which a great deal of personal knowledge
of each other comes to bear—were very few. Local people might praise one
or another of Celo's members for honesty in financial dealings, or for help-
fulness in locally organized projects, but the contrast between their knowledge of individual members and the intimate details they could recount for
other locals was striking. And the same was true of Celo in regard to locals.

From the point of view of Celo's membership, the Community's existence
was also dependent upon the goodwill of locals. When some local citizens
barged into a Community meeting in 1946 to demand the banishment of
conscientious objectors, they delivered a vivid message of local hostility. This
incident, and others less dramatic, fed the conception of the local milieu as
seething with dislike and barely controlled vengeance. The memoir of an ex-
member contains an anecdote—perhaps fictitious but nonetheless revealing—which shows in part the members' view of local sentiment: "On the
surface, the mountain people were usually friendly. At first it was only we
children who knew the intensity of their hatred for us. Once when we visited a local church with our parents, someone handed me a hymn book. In it
was a scrap of paper on which was scrawled, 'Wy dont yall go up noth war
yall come from?'" (Greenbough 1959, 15–16). These few sentences reveal several components of how local people were regarded by Celo's membership.
The presumption of intense dislike is obvious. Added to that is the assumed
lack of education, illustrated by the poor grammar and spelling of the note.
Further, the passage reflects the ignorance of local mores on the part of Community members: the plural form of "you" in this region is consistently
"you'ns," not "yall" (the latter colloquialism is characteristic of the lowland
South, not the mountains).

Categorical relations, civil but distant, might serve very well as an interactional style with those outside community boundaries, but another standard applied within the circle of members. Celo's membership understood
diversity among themselves quite differently from Wallace's idea of social

interaction carried on without knowledge of others' motivations. Among themselves, the residents of Celo Community strove to make their behavior accurately reflect their "true selves." This is not to suggest that such a state of affairs was ever reached, but there was a strong tendency in that direction. The difference in these interactional patterns was especially marked in the case of disgruntled defectors from Celo, when, on the part of both defectors and members, formal relationships rapidly replaced personal bonds. Members put defectors into a category which contrasted with themselves, and tried to act as a corporate body toward former members. Relations with ex-members, as revealed during the process of appraising and paying for improvements made on landholdings, became formal, conducted in the main by written correspondence. An explicit boundary between private and public appeared, and members discussed their concern to present a united front toward the defector. Secrecy and discretion, aspects of social life distinctly at odds with expectations within the group of members, stood out in their negotiations with ex-members. Members frequently justified this attitude of exclusion and secrecy by reference to their innovative landholding agreement. Many of them feared that courts would not look favorably upon an arrangement that was, in their terms, "neither a deed nor a lease." But part of their stance followed from the definition of defectors as enemies ready to dismantle the Community for selfish reasons.

Community: Contingent, Constructed, Contested

The uncertainty about the legal status of their landholding agreement remained a troublesome reminder of the extent to which Celo Community's continued existence rested on outside forces. Should their holding agreement undergo legal tests, an openly discussed possibility in cases of defector dissatisfaction, the outcome could not be firmly anticipated. But this was only one aspect of the veil of ambiguity hanging over Celo.

For the members of Celo, and other similar communities, the cultural postulates of individualism take quite serious forms. The notion that all associations (outside the family) are contingent upon the continued assent and reaffirmation of the members was for Celo Community far more than just an intellectual possibility, more than just a philosophical implication of the preeminence of the individual as moral arbiter. It was an ever-present potentiality. Celo struggled through the results of rapidly dwindling numbers in the 1950s, when a large proportion of the membership left for reasons of individual conscience or the expectation of improvement in individual fortunes. That period of empty houses and near-extinction was not forgotten, even in subsequent decades of abundant applications for membership and the growth of the "sane fringe." It could happen again, they seemed to agree, and this awareness underscored their self-definition as an "intentional community."

Never envisioned as a conventional village, fashioned by accidents of history and geography, Celo did not allow inheritance of landholdings or membership for those reared in the Community. Community documents explicitly noted that landholding and membership agreements "terminated" with the "death of the Holder[-Member]." The problem of the second and succeeding generations, faced by all utopian communities, was made more difficult by the insistence that even those reared in Celo must apply and be accepted if they were to continue to live on community land. That is, children of Celo held at their maturity precisely the same formal status as any new applicants. This demand could hardly have been ignored for children of existing members without compromising the very foundation of the community, its *intentionality*. In addition, the equality of members could be eroded by special provisions such as the inheritance of membership and rights to land. In one sense, they simply put into writing the customary American expectation that one's offspring seek their own places to live. This is, as Robert Bellah urges, one consequence of American individualism: "One of the strongest imperatives of our culture is that we must leave home. . . . However painful the process of leaving home, for parents or for children, the really frightening thing would be the prospect of the child never leaving home" (Bellah 1987, 370).

Since members of utopian communities have rejected the conventional reality into which they were born, and have seen that repudiated conventionality as constructed rather than "natural"—the product of wrong institutions, exploitation, greed, and so forth—then whatever they construct is subject to the same critique. Highly self-conscious of their position in making a new world, rather than working for change from within, they have only the internal demands of conscience to guide them to moral conduct. That is, there is no higher authority than individual morality—which, of course, is presumed to be shared by the like-minded.

Here we approach the difference between communities like Celo and those which rest on a foundation of transcendent and unquestioned truth, a distinction observers have usually designated as *secular* versus *sectarian*. Modern secular communities, given the usual wide latitude allowed for diversity of members, are established with some blend of the dual goals of retreat and mission. To an extent that varies from one group to another, they conceive their mission to be the construction of a model for a better world. Were members of such groups to concede that their main purpose for living in community was personal satisfaction, it would call forth, from their noncommunitarian allies and from themselves as well, the charge of "escapism." The specter of escapism haunts them; their withdrawal from conventional social life demands justification as mission. Hence the maintenance of relationships with sympathetic groups outside utopian communities is vital to their survival.

Besides ensuring awareness of the utopian community among potential recruits and promising sources of financial support, sustaining relationships with congenial outsiders accomplishes two indispensable objectives: (1) it substantiates and affirms insiders' perception of themselves as part of a larger movement, and (2) it ensures their public visibility and fortifies their claim to be a model for social and cultural reconstruction. Macedonians deemed outside allies the customers for their wooden products. Together with other activities—for example, traveling to participate in peace marches, publishing essays in pacifist journals, welcoming visitors—the trade in children's toys and furniture was a way for Macedonians to reaffirm the link of themselves with world brotherhood, radical pacifists, that is, something larger than an isolated group of hard-working, impoverished dairy farmers and woodworkers. For Celo, these outside relations, both personal and formal, allowed members "to dramatize their efforts and transform them from the ineffectual acts of a small band of dissidents into potentially momentous innovations in social education" (Hicks 1971, 148–49).

Macedonians fed their hunger for certainty by conversion to the Society of Brothers' variety of Christianity. In the months leading up to their fusion with the Brothers, most of Macedonia's members began to see themselves bound together by postulates that went far beyond the morality and behavior emanating from individual conscience. In the process of conversion to a religious basis for their activity, Macedonians—and others who joined the Brothers—found solutions for some of their most vexing problems: an irrefutable footing for their moral codes, a path toward a comforting unanimity, and relief from the accusation of escapism.

Certainty in Brotherhood

From circumstances in which each person had equal justification for his or her definitions of appropriate behavior, religious conversion brought Macedonians nearer to a situation of certainty.[3] The goals they set could no longer be doubted or contested—the road to those goals became clear when they accepted the tenets of the Society of Brothers' Christianity. The purpose of building community was no longer an experimental effort but the following of God's blueprint for society. As the Brothers' statement of belief put it very plainly: "we must live in community because it is God's will for men" (Society of Brothers 1952, 40). All that was required was a death of the self in complete absorption into the community of believers.

Finding in God's will an indisputable ground for their beliefs and efforts, the members of the Brothers also moved closer to unity of purpose and goals. In his intensive analysis of the Society of Brothers, Zablocki explains some of the consequences of this outlook. Noting the strong demand for conformity among the Brothers, he suggests that it springs from the

> decision-making system. The idea of the pre-existent decision makes it a serious matter to be caught on the wrong side of an issue. One is not merely expressing a minority opinion, but possibly showing that he is out of touch with the Holy Spirit. Furthermore, the need for absolute unanimity, far from giving power to the individual dissenter, places a great burden upon him not to dissent unless he is pretty sure that he's right. It is an interesting paradox that, at least in a highly cohesive group, making the power of dissent equivalent to the power of veto is a means of weakening rather than strengthening dissent. (Zablocki 1971, 157)

The pressure for conformity was constant and ranged from a "total lack of confidentiality of low-level [casual] conversations" to the swift rebuke that followed criticism of group leaders, the Servants of the Word (Zablocki 1971, 209).

Obviously the kind of open discussion of alternatives that marked group discussion in Celo and the early Macedonia was precluded. If a lack of shared meaning persisted—as our analytical framework would suggest—it was certainly not subject to open expression and debate. "The struggle to become one with the community is assumed," writes a former member, Robert Peck, "but not a subject for public speaking" (1987, 114). For those whose misgivings continued, various means were available for temporarily or permanently excluding them from the community of believers. Voluntarily leaving the Brothers was also an option that was frequently taken, although given the closed nature of the group, accurate information about defection is lacking (but see Oved 1996). Of those who left Celo for the Brothers, only two families became members for lengthy periods of time (see Zablocki 1971, 179–81, for an interview with one who rejected the demands of the Brothers' life).

The gnawing anxiety in many communities that experimentation in community-building was more retreat than mission, that it signaled disengagement from a society badly in need of reform, was greatly eased when members entered the Society of Brothers. Their obligation changed from creating a model for humanity to obeying the dictates of God, and their primary duty to those outside was to welcome them should they join the Brothers as fellow believers. A passive "open door" policy replaced the active relationships with non-community allies so carefully nurtured in the past. One very forceful indication of this feature of life in the Society of Brothers was their withdrawal from the Fellowship of Intentional Communities in 1959.

When the manufacture of wooden toys and children's furniture served as Macedonia's economic base, the preferred buyers were individuals; prices were maintained at cost of materials plus a small charge for community labor. This policy combined a distaste for capitalist profit-making with a desire to forge new links with outside allies. By selling to individuals at low (and, more important from their point of view, *fair*) prices, Macedonians could demonstrate their commitment to a mission of social reform. Moved to the Society of Brothers, the woodworking industry was transformed into a profitable business with prices set at market value. Further, the most desirable customers were institutional: schools, day-care centers, and municipal recreation departments. But only new and unexpected federal policies, in particular the Head Start program, brought stunning, long-term financial success.[4]

The substantial income generated by woodworking, however, did not result in luxury for community members. The Brothers' involvement with the market economy was insulated from the disciplined frugality and simplicity of daily life. The separation of day-to-day activity from the economic footing which made that life possible paralleled other religion-based communities, both historical and modern. Thus there appears a dual boundary in these communities: one to separate the entire group from outside and another to isolate social aspects of life from the economic. Economic activity is much more firmly tied to institutions of competitive capitalism.

A great deal of change can be absorbed by utopian communities; but change can also lead to a transformation, even disappearance, of the community. Pitzer sees the "developmental process posing a double jeopardy threat to communal longevity. The movements that make needed adjustments away from their communal stage abandon their communes. The movements that become locked into their communal discipline often stagnate, killing their movements and their communes" (1997a, 13). Both Macedonia and Celo underwent significant change: one completed a lengthy pro-

cess of merger with a more communal, religious community; the other shifted to new goals and a new history to fortify the goals.

Celo Transformed: The Secular Survivors

The sobering events of the 1950s in Celo Community—the loss of members,
the debilitating feuds with disillusioned ex-members, the near-extinction of
the community—left the community-building endeavor so weakened that
the surviving members foresaw their experiment ending with an inconclusive whimper at any time. With the opening of the Arthur Morgan School
in 1962, Celo embarked on a new era. The radical enthusiasm of new currents
of thought and activity in the nation, brought to the Community by a new
crowd of visitors and taken by members to national venues of protest meetings and demonstrations, encouraged the members in a renewal of their vision. Perhaps, after all, their efforts had not been wasted, they seemed to say
to themselves; maybe Celo still had a chance for significance.

A decade later, the influx of the back-to-the-landers combined with the
growing cosmopolitanism of local folk to render the social and cultural features of Celo Community less distinctive and less threatening than before.
Its local boundaries underwent transformation from an embattled perime-
ter to a porous and inviting threshold. The Community welcomed nonmembers to its business meetings; the Quaker group grew to a large majority of
non-Community people; the Community buyers' cooperative and the crafts
store operated with more nonmembers than members.

In these circumstances, as Celo gradually lost its marks of strangeness and
exclusiveness, the expansive promises of its earlier years fell away. The grand
reformist dreams faded, becoming something of an embarrassment to those
who joined in the 1970s and afterward. Careful stewardship of communally
owned land—always part of the members' definition of the Community—
took hold as the primary object of the enterprise. "Land trust community,"
a category more recognizably significant in the United States after about 1970,
appeared to sum up the minimal common interest of Celo's residents. Their
long-term efforts at maintaining a safe and unwasteful environment, and
their strong sense that the Community land was theirs for wise use only, not
outright ownership and speculation, were accurately reflected in their new
label for themselves. Smaller projects involving fewer than the entire Community continued, much as they had in the past, but whatever carried the
sponsorship of the entire group—of Celo Community Incorporated—narrowed to matters directly related to its land and its cautious management.

Contingency and Explanation

Whatever the measure of success—mere longevity, satisfaction of members, or influence outside—indeterminacy of outcome must take center stage. To propose an explanation of Celo's persistence, whether judged as success or not, one has to deal with historical contingencies. At various times in its history, only small differences in the size of factions, or sharper demarcation between the factions, could easily have brought a stalemate over crucial decisions and perhaps resulted in the Community's division or termination. With a few more seekers of certainty, and a greater number of defectors to the Society of Brothers, Celo might well have walked the same gangplank as Macedonia. Even afterward, as they struggled through the 1950s and early 1960s, the departure of one or two families would have triggered their plan for dissolution and private ownership of holdings.

Like the Society of Brothers' financial rejuvenation by federal blessing, Celo's rescue arrived with the sudden appearance of nationwide excitement and activity among thousands of young communards and back-to-the-landers. Facing the "double jeopardy" noted by Pitzer, the Community reacted with creativity, inventing a new history and purpose and forming close ties with local nonmembers of similar outlook. The members' interpretation of their enterprise as in the main unchanged from previous periods, made possible by the use of existing understandings set upon new circumstances, permitted a smooth glide into a post-utopian phase.

The Uses of Utopia

Utopian communities, their practices and beliefs, have been put to a number of purposes among both scholars and the general public. There is, first, the popular assimilation of utopian fragments. Furniture designed by Shakers, for example, is praised for its simplicity of line and functional lack of ornamentation. Not only are original items sold for enormous sums, but reproductions, in a variety of quality and price, are available in national and foreign markets. Little or no consideration, however, is given to the Shakers' religious rationale for the spartan features of their furniture. In modern usage, the divine command of simplicity is forgotten. "Community Silverplate" by Oneida records the name of an impressive communal experiment; air conditioners and refrigerators preserve the title of Amana, much as names of streets and towns in America echo linguistic fragments of Native Americans: all part of a jumbled catalog of American pasts.

The circumstances are similar for Habitat for Humanity, an organization devoted to building low-cost housing for the poor, that aroused national interest with the endorsement and participation of former president Jimmy Carter and his wife. The religious justification for Habitat is, unlike that of the Shakers, not lost—Christianity is invoked as purpose in all its appeals for contributions—but reports of the organization's activities in the news media rarely give attention to its religious underpinnings. Even rarer would be an account that credits Koinonia Community for developing low-cost housing, even though it was the major inspiration and source for Habitat for Humanity (Hedgepeth and Stock 1970, 176–77).

It has frequently been said that utopian communities constitute a "laboratory" for social science, a kind of experimental situation otherwise not available. Whether this metaphor is applied or not, utopian groups have served a number of scholarly applications. Utopian experiments, including the socialist states of the Soviet Union and China, formed the basis for a sweeping comparative study of "how men provision the common good" (Erasmus 1977), and the kibbutzim became a cache of evidence for a sociobiological explanation of the incest taboo (Fox 1983). The nonconformist sexual practices (and good historical records) of three groups—the Mormons, Oneida, and the Shakers—inspired fascinating and valuable works on gender relations (Foster 1981, 1991; Kern 1981). Twentieth-century groups, too, offer material for the examination of change in women's roles (Chmielewski et al. 1993; Wagner 1982). Historical and contemporary utopians have been the subject of a number of studies of social cohesion (e.g., Deets 1939; Infield 1955a, 1955b; Kanter 1968, 1972), together with investigations of the relations of utopians with capitalistic modes of production (e.g., Cooper 1987). There is growing provision for future investigations of these groups with the publication of research journals and the construction of archives for the preservation of communities' records.

Obviously, utopian communities cannot serve as microcosms of an American macrocosm, a refraction of the nation in miniature. Such a leap fails to convince even when the microcosm is non-utopian, as criticisms of Lloyd Warner's efforts in Yankee City and Jonesville justly demonstrate (Warner 1959; Warner with Bailey et al. 1964). Nor are utopian communities useful for providing a sort of distillation of the "national character." Any searcher for a uniquely American national character would do well to remember Mark Twain's decisive objection to the fancies of a French observer, Paul Bourget: "There isn't a single human ambition, or religious trend, or drift of thought, or peculiarity of education, or code of principles, or breed of folly, or style of conversation, or preference for a particular subject for discussion, or form of legs or trunk or head or face or expression or complexion, or gait, or dress, or manners, or disposition, or any other human detail, inside or outside, that can rationally be generalized as 'American'" (1897, 155). Yet even Twain's sassy assurance of robust American diversity—a matter of considerable anxious discussion in the final decades of the twentieth century as well—should not blind us to the limited range of permissible difference. Individualism, diversity, eccentricity are constrained by our inclination to render equality as uniformity. Jean Baudrillard, a latecomer in the transatlantic stream of captivated French observers, points out that although the limits of American conformity are quite narrow, within that range, small differences are exaggerated to enhance the appearance of diversity: "the more conformist the system as a whole becomes, the more millions of individuals there are who are set apart by some tiny peculiarity. The slightest vibration in a statistical model, the tiniest whim of a computer are enough to bathe some piece of abnormal behaviour, however banal, in a fleeting glow of fame" (1988, 58–59).

Rather than America writ small, or an essential distinctiveness of American character, what we can discern in the founding and history of American utopian groups is an encounter with tensions and contradictions in American cultural postulates which are better laid open to inspection than in conventional social and cultural life. In utopian communities choices seem sharper and the balance of individualism and equality more self-conscious and visible. Utopians are far less contrastive with other Americans than they claim in their efforts to persuade themselves and others of their uniqueness. Community as an aspiration, a bond voluntarily taken on, seems far more problematic for them than other Americans. The self-consciousness and contingency of community formation and maintenance is simultaneously a delight and an ominous threat.

The appearance of deviation is surely present in the novel sexual relationships of Oneida, Mormons, and Shakers, or in some communities' attempts to eliminate specialized technological skills, or in the goal of wiping out private property. Utopian groups' typical retreat into isolation, too, is often taken as a sign of an alien nature that is both inexplicable and dangerous. Not only reviled groups like Jonestown and the Branch Davidians but the Mormons and numerous other less notorious settlements have been regarded with vigilant apprehension by their non-utopian fellow citizens. But in each case, one can recognize in the groups' justification for existence references to individualism, equality, a committed mission—all central postulates of American culture. The interpretation of these postulates, how and in what circumstances they are applied, differs from time to time and group to group.

After all the caveats and carefully qualified remarks about the existence of something distinctively American, it must be said that, at least in my view, America *is* different. It is not unique in substance, as Mark Twain insists, but in a perspective, a sense of possibility that has marked it from the start. The emphasis on putting unpleasant experiences "behind us" and "moving forward," phrases so frequently heard nowadays from public speakers, a habit of looking always to the future, of forgetting or ignoring the past, of, in short, living in a society that is still experimental and unfinished—this outlook need not demand new substance as it reworks the available material into new shapes.

Perhaps the essayist Lewis Lapham states it most clearly (if a bit romantically) when he tells us that our main concern as Americans is the quest for self. As Lapham writes: "If America is about nothing else, it is about the invention of the self. Because we have little use for history, and because we refuse the comforts of a society established on the blueprint of class privilege, we find ourselves set adrift at birth in an existential void, inheriting nothing except the obligation to construct a plausible self, to build a raft of identity" (1992, 46). One route toward this goal has been, and remains, the deliberate building of utopian communities which, in the variety of their forms and the persistence of their reappearance, activate an American pursuit of self.

Notes

1. Similar attitudes often find expression in utopian communities, where rotation of tasks is an ideal (usually, however, only within gender boundaries) and labor specialization is scorned. Macedonians, in their last months as a separate community, vigorously renewed their dedication to job rotation. One of the most successful at switching from task to task is Twin Oaks, although even in this self-consciously feminist community, conventional division of labor along gender lines has not entirely disappeared (Goldenberg 1993; Wagner 1982, 1–44, discusses the issue in detail).

2. Note the important distinction between this notion of consensus and that advocated by Arthur Morgan: "Consensus of judgment may be arrived at by the deference of the many who do not know to the superior judgment of the few who do. The balance of competence to judge may shift endlessly as different subjects for judgment arise" (quoted, Talbert 1987, 150).

3. The quest for a transcendent basis for morality need not be confined to religious pilgrimages. Thus Spiro's somewhat puzzling assertion that "in the absence of traditional religion, ideology becomes religion" (1963, 194) for members of his kibbutz becomes understandable if Marxism is regarded as an explication of inevitable forces that will usher us into a world beyond history. As Nordhoff suggested in 1875, the requirement that a successful utopian community be founded on religious belief can be fulfilled by nonreligious ideology, provided that it is "so important as to take the place of a religion" (1961, 387). Similarly, Hall suggests that "all communal groups . . . bear a religious character. . . .

Whether rhetoric draws on religious or political images, the associational form is that of a band of true believers" (1978, 1).

4. Innovative labor-saving techniques and market profits characterized the manufacture of wooden toys in the Society of Brothers, just as the mechanical inventions and sales to outsiders marked the industries of the Shakers and Oneida a century earlier. But the closest parallel of the Brothers' insulation of its relationship with the world of business can be found among the Hutterites, whose ideological basis is very nearly the same. Quite willing to adopt technological changes which increase their agricultural productivity, the Hutterites take special care that such changes do not threaten the communal and conservative basis of their community life. "Technology serves the goal of healthy maintenance of the [Hutterite] colony, and so long as it does not introduce personal differentiation in property, it can be accepted" (Bennett 1967, 269, 270–73; see also Deets 1939, 50; Hostetler 1974, 297–99; Hostetler and Huntington 1980). Van den Berghe and Peter (1988) offer a different interpretation.

Appendix: Celo Community Documents

No. 44376
Filed 12/28/38

CERTIFICATE OF INCORPORATION (CHARTER)
CELO COMMUNITY, INC.

This is to certify that we, the undersigned, do hereby associate ourselves into a corporation, under and by virtue of the laws of the State of North Carolina as contained in Chapter 22 of the Consolidated Statutes of North Carolina, entitled "Corporations," and the several Amendments thereto, and to that end do hereby set forth:

1. The name of this corporation is CELO COMMUNITY, INC.

2. The location of the principal office of the corporation in this state is at Celo, Yancey County, North Carolina.

The name of the registered agent of the corporation at the above address is Mrs. Dorothy Barrus.

3. The objects for which this corporation is formed are as follows:

(a) To encourage and assist in the promotion of community organization and development, especially in the vicinity of Celo, North Carolina. To establish, promote and assist in the development of an educational institution for general education and for vocational guidance; to encourage and assist in the establishment of homes and small holdings; to assist in developing means for subsistence for persons, so located;

to carry on research, experiments and demonstrations in community organization and development, in the development of vocations and in establishing men and women in suitable vocations; to assist in studying and development of the resources and economic possibilities of Western North Carolina and adjacent regions with the view of helping families to become economically and socially established; and for carrying out these purposes to borrow money, to purchase, sell, lease, mortgage, or otherwise to obtain, use or dispose of real or personal property. To publish periodicals or reports of the work done, of studies and researches made, and to cooperate with public or private agencies, organizations or persons; to manufacture, purchase or otherwise acquire, to hold, own, mortgage, pledge, sell, assign and transfer, or otherwise dispose of, to invest, trade, deal in or with goods, wares, merchandise and real and personal property of every class and description.

(b) To carry on any other business (whether manufacturing or otherwise) which may seem to the organization capable of being carried on in connection with the above or calculated directly or indirectly to enhance the value of its property or rights and privileges.

(c) To acquire and undertake the whole or any part of the business, property, assets and liabilities of any person, firm or corporation.

(d) To acquire any good will, rights, property and assets of all kinds and to undertake the whole or any part of the liabilities of any person, firm or corporation or association and to pay for the same in cash, bonds, debentures, or other securities of the corporation or otherwise.

(e) To hold, purchase, or otherwise acquire, to sell, assign, transfer, mortgage, pledge, or otherwise dispose of any property, bonds, debentures, or other evidence of indebtedness, created by other corporation or corporations, and while the holder thereof, to exercise all the rights and privileges of ownership, including the right to vote thereon.

(f) To cause or allow the legal title, estate, and interest in any property acquired, established or carried on by the company to remain or be vested or registered in the name of, or carried on by any other company or companies, foreign or domestic, formed or to be formed, and either upon trusts for, or as agents or nominees of this company, or upon any other terms or conditions which the Board of Directors may consider for the benefit of this organization and to manage the affairs or take over and carry on the business of such company or companies so formed or to be formed, either by acquiring the shares of stock or other securities thereof or otherwise howsoever and to exercise all or any of the powers of owners of shares, stocks, or securities thereof, and to receive and use the dividends and interest on such shares, stocks, or securities.

(g) To borrow money, to make and issue promissory notes, bills of exchange, bonds, debentures and obligations, and evidences of indebtedness of all kinds, whether secured by mortgage, pledge or otherwise, without limit as to amount, and to secure same by mortgage, pledge or otherwise.

(h) To adopt, have and use a corporate seal.

(i) To make any and all such by-laws as the corporation may desire, not inconsistent with any Statute of North Carolina.

(j) The following named persons shall act as Directors until their successors, or additional directors are selected:

William H. Regnery	Hinsdale, Illinois
Clarence E. Pickett	Moylan, Pennsylvania
Arthur E. Morgan	Yellow Springs, Ohio

Any successor to Clarence E. Pickett as a director shall be appointed by American Friends Service Committee of 20 South Twelfth Street, Philadelphia, Pennsylvania. Any other directors shall be selected by the other members of the Board. There shall never be less than three directors; the number may be increased by motion of the Board of Directors.

(k) The names and post office addresses of the incorporators are as follows

Name	Post office address
William H. Regnery	Hinsdale, Illinois
Clarence E. Pickett	Moylan, Pennsylvania
Arthur E. Morgan	Yellow Springs, Ohio
E. F. Watson	Burnsville, N.C.

(l) This corporation shall have a right to do all and everything necessary, suitable, convenient or proper for the encouragement of any of the purposes or the attainment of any one or more of the objects herein enumerated, or consistent with the powers herein named, or which shall at any time appear conducive or expedient for the protection or benefit of the corporation, either as holders of or interests in any property or otherwise; with all the powers now or hereafter conferred by the laws of North Carolina, under the law as hereinbefore referred to, including the right to make any and all such bylaws as said corporation may deem wise and not inconsistent with the laws of the State of North Carolina.

4. The corporation is to exist for ninety-nine years.

5. The Board of Directors of this corporation shall have power by vote of the majority of all the directors, and without the assent of or vote of the members to make, alter, amend, and rescind the bylaws, of this corporation.

6. The corporation is to and shall be organized upon a nonstock basis and shall be a nonprofit earning corporation.

7. Members may be admitted after organization of this corporation upon the following terms, to wit: upon receiving a unanimous vote of the Board of Directors of the corporation and upon their written agreement to subscribe to all the provisions contained in the charter.

8. In case of dissolution, all the assets of the corporation, after all its liabilities and obligations have been discharged or adequate provision made therefor, shall be donated to a nonprofit institution qualifying for exemption from taxes, under the provisions of the Internal Revenue Code in effect at the time of such dissolution. This article shall not be limited or repealed by the Board of Directors or the membership of this corporation.

IN TESTITMONY WHEREOF, we have hereunto set our hands and seals this _____ day of December, 1938.

Arthur E. Morgan _____ (seal)

William H. Regnery _____ (seal)

Clarence E. Pickett _____ (seal)

E. F. Watson _____ (seal)

CODE OF REGULATIONS OF CELO COMMUNITY, INC.
(Corporation ByLaws)

Article 1. OFFICES
The principal office shall be near the town of Celo, County of Yancey, State of North Carolina.

The Corporation may also nave an office at 114 East Whiteman Street, Yellow Springs, Ohio, and other places as the Board of Directors may from time to time appoint, or the business of the corporation may require.

Article 2. SEAL
The corporate seal shall have inscribed thereon the name of the corporation, the year of its organization, and the words Corporate Seal—North Carolina.

Article 3. MEMBERS
The term member shall mean a person who is accepted as a participant in the affairs of Celo Community, as hereafter indicated in these bylaws.

After organization, any person upon receiving an affirmative vote, with no more than 15% dissenting, of the members present and voting at a regular meeting of the Community members; and also the unanimous vote of the Board of Directors, and upon his signing of the Membership Agreement, may become a member of Celo Community, Inc.

The Community, by action in a regular meeting, may, if not more than 15% of the members in residence and of the directors dissent, dismiss from membership any member who, in its opinion, has not acted in accordance with the purposes and objectives of the Community or who has acted against the best interest of the Community. Grounds for dismissal include; but are not limited to:

1) Absence from the Community for more than 180 days out of any 12 months without having obtained a leave of absence.
2) Failure, after notice, to honor written agreements with the Community or any of its members.

3) Conviction of any felony.
4) Having been declared insane or incompetent by due process of law.

The members may from their own local organization adopt their own constitution and bylaws, and may exercise such functions of management as are approved by the Board of Directors. Every member shall be entitled to one vote, and no member shall vote or act by proxy. Annual meetings of the members shall be held on September 15th of each year, unless it is a holiday, and in that case on the first secular day succeeding, at 8 P.M. At such meeting they shall elect Officers and shall nominate candidates for the membership to the Board of Directors of the Corporation. The candidates so nominated shall be selected by the Board of Directors of the Corporation as a director for the period three years, or until his successor is chosen and is qualified.

The members at the annual meeting shall transact such business as may properly be brought before them. Any action on receiving new members, on expelling members, on making agreements for holdings or for sale or lease of land, and on matters of Community policy, shall be subject to the approval of the Board of Directors. By agreement of two-thirds of the members, at any regular or regularly called meeting, the annual meeting may be held at some other time and place. Written notice of the annual meeting shall be mailed to each member, at such address as appears in the records of the Community, at least ten days prior to the meeting. Other meetings may be called by one tenth of the members or by the Chairman, or by the Board of Directors. Such a call shall state the purpose of the meeting.

Business transacted at all meetings shall be the objects stated in the call, except that by unanimous agreement other matters may be considered.

Article 4. DIRECTORS
The property and policies of the Corporation shall be under the general control and direction of its Board of Directors. There shall be no less than three Directors. The Directors shall elect the candidates nominated as directors by the members. Such directors shall serve for three years or until their successors are elected. They shall serve for not more than two three-year terms in direct succession. The other directors shall be chosen as directed in Section 3 of the articles of incorporation, and shall serve until their successors are selected. Half of the members of the Board shall constitute a quorum for transacting business.

The Directors shall hold their meetings at their principal office near Celo, North Carolina, or at such other places as they may from time to time determine.

In addition to the powers and authority by these regulations expressly conferred upon them, the Board of Directors may exercise all such powers of the corporation and do all such lawful acts and things as are not by statute or by the certificate of incorporation or by these regulations prohibited. They may delegate elements of direct management and administration to the members.

Article 5. EXECUTIVE COMMITTEE
There may be an executive committee of two or more directors designated by resolution passed by a majority of a quorum of the Board. Said committee may meet at stated times or on notice by anyone of their own number. During intervals between meetings of the Board, such committee shall advise with and aid the officers of the corporation in all matters concerning its interests and the management of its business, and generally perform such duties and exercise such powers as may be directed or delegated by the Board of Directors from time to time. The Board may delegate to such committee authority to exercise all the powers of the Board, excepting the power to amend these regulations, while the board is not in session.

The executive committee shall keep regular minutes of its proceedings and report the same to the Board when required.

Article 6. COMPENSATION OF DIRECTORS
Directors, as such, shall not receive any stated salary for their services, but the expenses of attendance, if any, may be allowed for attendance at regular or special meetings of the Board, and the Board member selected by the community members may be allowed a per diem while attending meetings away from Celo.

Article 7. MEETINGS OF THE BOARD
The newly elected Board may meet at such place and time as shall be fixed at the annual meeting, for the purpose of organization or otherwise, and no notice of such meeting shall be necessary to the newly elected directors in order legally to constitute the meeting, provided, a majority of the whole Board shall be present; or they may meet at such place and time as shall be fixed by the consent in writing of all the directors.

Regular meetings of the Board may be held without notice at such time and place as shall from time to time be determined by the Board. Special meetings of the Board may be called by the president on five days notice to each director, either personally or by mail or by telegram; special meetings shall be called by the president or secretary in like manner and on like notice on the written request of three directors. By agreement of all the directors meetings may be held without notice or with shorter notice.

At all meetings of the Board half of the directors shall be necessary and sufficient to constitute a quorum for the transaction of business, and the act of a majority of the directors present at any meeting at which there is a quorum shall be the act of the Board of directors, except as may be otherwise specifically provided by statute or by the certificate of incorporation, or by these regulations.

Article 8. OFFICERS

The officers of the corporation shall be chosen by the directors and shall be a president, vice-president, secretary, and treasurer. The secretary and treasurer may be the same person. The secretary may appoint an assistant secretary, and the treasurer may appoint an assistant treasurer, and each may delegate to such assistant such duties as in his judgement may be desirable.

The Board may appoint such other officers and agents as it shall deem necessary, who shall hold their offices for such terms and shall exercise such powers and perform such duties and be paid such compensation as shall be determined from time to time by the Board.

The officers of the corporation shall hold office until their successors are chosen and qualify in their stead. Any officer elected or appointed by the Board of Directors may be removed at any time by the affirmative vote of a majority of the whole Board of Directors.

Article 9. THE PRESIDENT

a) The president shall be the chief executive officer of the corporation; he shall preside at all meetings of the directors; he shall have general and active management of the business of the corporation, and shall see that all orders and resolutions of the Board are carried into effect.

b) He shall execute bonds, mortgages, and other contracts requiring a seal, under the seal of the corporation, when authorized by the Board.

c) He shall be ex-officio a member of all standing committees, and shall have the general powers and duties of supervision and management usually vested in the office of president of a corporation.

Article 10. THE VICE-PRESIDENT

The vice-president shall, in the absence or disability of the president, perform the duties and exercise the powers of the president, and shall perform such other duties as the Board of Directors shall prescribe.

Article 11. THE SECRETARY

The secretary shall, whenever feasible, attend sessions of the Board and the meetings of the members and record the votes and the minutes of all proceedings of the Board in a book to be kept for that purpose; and shall perform like duties for the standing committees when required. He shall give, or cause to be given, notice of meetings of the Board of Directors, and shall perform such other duties as may be prescribed by the Board of Directors or by the president.

Article 12. THE TREASURER

a) The treasurer shall have the custody of the corporate funds and securities and shall keep full and accurate accounts of receipts and disbursements in books belonging to the corporation, and shall deposit all moneys and other valuable effects in the name and to the credit of the corporation, in such depositories as may be designated by the Board of Directors, or in the absence of such designation, wherever in his judgement is to the best interests of the corporation.

b) He shall disburse the funds of the corporation as may be ordered by the Board, taking proper vouchers for such disbursements, and shall render to the president and the directors, at the regular meetings of the Board or whenever they may require it, an account of all his transactions as treasurer and of the financial condition of the corporation.

c) He shall give the corporation a bond, if required by the Board of Directors, in a sum and with one or more sureties satisfactory to the Board, for the faithful performance of the duties of his office, and for the restoration to the corporation, in case of his death, resignation, retirement or removal from office, of all books, papers, vouchers, money and other property of whatever kind in his possession or under his control belonging to the corporation.

Article 13. VACANCIES
If the office of any director, or of any officer or agent, one or more, becomes vacant by reason of death, resignation, retirement, disqualification, removal from office, or otherwise, the directors by a majority vote may choose a successor or successors, who shall hold office for the unexpired term in respect of which such vacancy occurred.

Article 14. DUTIES OF OFFICERS MAY BE DELEGATED
In case of the absence of any officer of the corporation, or for any other reason that the Board may deem sufficient, the Board may delegate, for the time being, the powers or duties, or any of them, of such officer to any other officer, or to any director.

Article 15. MEMBERS MEETINGS
The members, by action taken at meetings, shall constitute the local community government and shall exercise such functions as are approved by the Board of Directors. The members may adopt a constitution and bylaws for such local government, with the approval of the Board of Directors.

Article 16. AMENDMENTS
These regulations may be altered or amended by the affirmative vote of two thirds of the Board of Directors and of the members. If the alteration or amendment be proposed at a regular or special meeting of the Board and adopted by the Board at a subsequent regular meeting; however, provision for notice may be waived by unanimous agreement of the members of the Board, and of the members, and by such unanimous agreement the regulations may be amended at the meeting at which they are first presented.

Approved by Board of Directors of Celo Community, Inc., May 9, 1965.

CELO COMMUNITY CONSTITUTION

The aim of Celo Community is to provide an opportunity for its members to enjoy a life that includes personal expression, neighborly friendship and cooperation, and appreciative care of the natural environment. No person is excluded from membership because of national or racial origin or religious belief.

We encourage personal enterprise among members by making land and money available when needed for suitable productive use. Regarding ownership of land as a trust, we do not sell it, but assign it for short or long periods at as low an assessment as feasible to those who give promise of improving it while living harmoniously with their neighbors. From our revolving fund we occasionally lend money at low cost to a member for the purpose of improving his property.

In the relation of the Community to its members the legal is an instrument of the moral. The relation is not an external one between a soulless corporation and indepent [sic] individuals. It is the internal relation between one person of a friendly neighborhood group and all the persons including himself. Thus a member consulting in a Community meeting on a course of action is both a private user and (in consensus with others) a public controller of land. A Community member through participating in Community government tends to develop a stable and considerate character along with responsible personal expression.

SUMMARY OF CELO COMMUNITY PROCEDURES AND RULES,
as of May 1, 1975

Changes and additions are to be summarized yearly by the Codifier and appended.

I. Community Property

1. APPRAISALS generally are of two kinds: (a) yearly, for the purpose of taxation (generally the county appraisal figure will be used), and (b) for use in establishing the value of holdings when a Holding Agreement is ended, or when
a change of renter occurs.

Any value received by the Community for improvements when others take
property should be paid to the makers of the improvements.

2. BOUNDARIES: the Community boundaries are to be kept marked by volunteers who shall report to the Property Committee each January, or earlier if desired.

3. BUILDINGS: A caretaker shall be appointed for each Community building, and
a list of caretakers and rentals shall be posted.

Duties of caretaker:

(a) The caretaker is responsible for keeping the building in good repair. He is
to report any necessary repairs which he cannot do himself to the Property Committee or to the subcommittee in charge of buildings. He may rent
the building for short terms (less than a month) after approval by the Chairman of the Property Committee.
(b) Have keys in possession and available (except when renter has key).
(c) At end of renting season, turn off all utilities (gas, water, and electricity)
and thoroughly prepare for winter (drain water lines, anti-freeze in toilet
bowl, pack junction boxes, etc.)
(d) Before renting season, turn on utilities, check pump, refrigerator, hot water heater, faucets, lights, wiring, plugs and outlets, fuses, etc.

(e) During renting season, check with Property Committee regarding lawns, clearing brush, etc. Collect rentals in accordance with rental schedule.

(f) During entire year, check houses regularly (monthly) for possible vandalism, minor repairs, etc. Report major repairs to the Property Committee.

(g) Before each occupancy, check cleanliness, and, when indicated, arrange for cleaning; window washing, etc.

Rentals should cover all costs including insurance, taxes, depreciation, and management. All rentals are payable in advance. If the term exceeds one month, payable each 1st day of the following month.

(a) Longterm rentals, unfurnished (more than three months) are 7½% of assessed valuation. The renter is responsible for all repairs and maintenance including the prorated share of county taxes, insurance, and Community assessments as set each year. The renter shall make an initial payment of $100. This will be returned when he leaves after deductions to cover any damage done to the building. Members of the Community are exempt from this deposit. Upon rental, the renter will be responsible for filing a report on the condition of the house with the bookkeeper's financial record on that house.

(b) Shortterm rentals, or furnished, or both, are to be established yearly and posted. Prospective summer renters may be asked to make a deposit of 25% of the rent at the time a house is reserved. This deposit is not refundable.

4. FOREST PRODUCTS: No permits for cutting or digging forest products for commercial use shall be given to nonmembers.

Members may dig shrubs and other plants from unallocated Community property without special permission if they intend to transplant them to their holdings and not for sale. They may also cut dead and unmarketable timber for their own use as firewood. Plants may not be dug from roadsides.

Members may cut dead trees and trees under 6" in diameter (breast high) on their own holdings and for their own use without approval. For cutting in other areas, or for cutting trees over 6" on a member's own holding, approval of the Property Committee and Community Chairman is required.

Members who wish to dig or cut forest products for sale shall request permission from the Property Committee. Permission will be granted for specified items in specified locations for a definite period. A report shall be made when a project is completed and an accounting rendered. Rates shall be:

(a) <u>Timber</u>: either a definite stumpage fee or a percentage of the price paid by the mill, as decided in each case in advance.

(b) <u>Firewood</u>: $0.10 per cord from laps, cull trees, etc.
$0.50 per cord from sound trees such as hickory cut for the purpose.

(c) <u>Shrubs</u>: 15% of the sale price.

In any logging operation, trees to be cut should be marked by the Property Committee or its designee. All marked trees approved for cutting should be cut within a reasonable length of time, as part of the same cutting operation, and before another operation is undertaken. Marked trees of little value may be poisoned instead of cut. Wood not suitable for saw logs can be sold for pulpwood or charcoal. No stumps or tops should be left more than 3' high. Access road should be stabilized with grass.

5. <u>EQUIPMENT</u> in the care of assigned custodians:

(a) <u>Hacksaw</u>: if not moved—$0.25 minimum and $0.25 per hour after the first hour. If moved—$1.00 minimum and $1.00 daily after the first day. The Community will furnish the hacksaw blades.

(b) <u>Record player</u>: to be used for Community functions; not for private use.

(c) <u>Transit</u> (and engineer's level): the transit and other engineering equipment are available to Community members only and cannot be loaned outside of the Community. No deposit is required. The rent is $1.00 minimum and $1.00 for each day after the first day, or part of a day, during which the instrument is in the borrower's possession.

6. <u>HUNTING</u>: The Community has decided not to post all of its property. Each holder may post his holding and also as much of the adjoining Community property as may be necessary for protection from careless hunters.

7. <u>LAND</u>: Rentals to Community members are generally for 5 years, automatically renewed each year if not otherwise decided.

Yearly rental fee of 5% of appraised value plus $1.80 per cleared acre. The renter shall pay for seed, fertilizer, fences, etc. He is responsible for keeping the land in as good tilth as when he took it.

<u>Rentals to non-members</u> should be payable in advance, and renters should make at the same time a deposit of the amount required to maintain the land during the rental period. Maintenance by the renter could be paid from this deposit, the amount of which should be arrived at by the Community in consultation with the Soil Conservation Service.

The renting agreement may be ended by either party at the end of any season. If ended by the Community before 5 years have elapsed, the renter shall be reimbursed for any loss he may sustain because of the expense of improvements which could reasonably be expected to last 5 years. At the end of 5 years, if the rental is not renewed, the Community may, at its discretion, reimburse the renter for improvements then evident. Fences will not be considered improvements.

If land is rented during the growing season, the full year's rent will be charged.

8. MINING LEASES: Conditions for granting:

   (a) At least $500 bond.
   (b) No bulldozing allowed except to build an access road and to fill up the mine hole at the end of the operation.
   (c) No timber to be cut unless marked for the purpose by the Community.
   (d) Only such land to be used as that specified in advance.
   (e) After the operation is finished, the site is to be restored, as nearly as reasonable, to its original condition.
   (f) The lease is not transferable.
   (g) Leases to run for 1 year with option to renew.
   (h) The Community to be protected from any liability arising from mining.

9. NUISANCES: The Community has no set policy or procedure for coping with such nuisances as stray animals, trespassers, picnickers, etc. It is left to individual initiative and judgment to do what seems best.

10. ROADS: Maintenance is the responsibility of holders and renters. The Community is responsible for roads to unoccupied houses. The cost of road maintenance leading to both a holding and a Community house will be prorated. Any private road used by the public or necessary as an easement is legally a cartway to a width of 14' and users may keep it cleared to this width.

11. WATERSHEDS: The Community is not responsible for the maintenance of watersheds.

12. WORKDAYS: Members are expected to participate in workdays scheduled for the benefit of Community property or of individuals within the Community. There is no set policy as to the number of workdays which will be scheduled or their duration. No penalty attaches to non-participation and no provision has been made for alternative Community services.

13. ZONING General plan:

<u>West of the River</u>: between River and highway to be kept natural. A strip West of the highway to be reserved for business and small industry. The hilly land West of the River may be divided into small (generally one acre or less) holdings of a residential type.

<u>East of the River</u>: to be divided into larger holdings (size to be determined by need) for agriculture, camps, etc., except for a strip North of Shingle Pole Creek planned for small holdings. We intend eventual limits on the density of development in order to preserve the original expectations of present holders. The land in the fork of Hall's Chapel Road is reserved for a picnic area, and the area west of the road and at the mouth of Little White Oak Creek for a Community Center.

<u>Streams</u>: in general, a strip 20'–50' wide will be reserved by the Community for protection of the banks.

<u>Wilderness</u>: several areas have permanently been set aside as wilderness areas. See wilderness map.

II. <u>Community Finances</u>:

1. <u>GENERAL</u>: Community funds are legally the responsibility of the Board of Directors, and especially of the Treasurer of the Corporation. Whenever feasible, the Treasurer of the Corporation will also be the Chairman of the Finance Committee, and the Bookkeeper will be appointed Assistant Treasurer to the Board. The Chairman of the Finance Committee is responsible to the Treasurer of the Corporation for a yearly audit.

The <u>Bookkeeper</u> is in charge of the Community books and bank accounts, and the only member authorized to disburse Community funds. He will report twice yearly to the general meeting, and the books are open to inspection at all times. The Annual Report will be presented at the February meeting.

The Bookkeeper shall send out a <u>statement</u> to each member yearly, as soon as the assessments have been established, and shall notify anyone who is late in his payments. All <u>payments</u> to the Community are due on December 1, unless otherwise agreed upon. Whenever possible, members are requested to make payments, all or part, before December 1. If a member is unable to make all or part of his payments by December 1, he shall request a moratorium, specifying how soon he will be able to make the payment. Failure to request a moratorium may result in a penalty charge on the amount unpaid.

Payments will be credited to members' accounts in the following order:

(a) Community assessments.
(b) Rentals.
(c) Interest, unless otherwise agreed beforehand.
(d) Loans. (Principal payments)
(e) Principal on holding payments.

In addition to the annual assessment paid by Holders and renters to defray County taxes on allocated Community land, there is an annual assessment paid by all non-dependent adults over 18 years of age residing in the Community to defray (1) County taxes on unallocated Community land (land neither in rental or holding status), and (2) annual operating costs.

2. DESIGNATED FUNDS, not available for other purposes:

(a) Emergency Fund.
(b) Loans: for education and quick loans.
(c) Petty cash: up to $100 at the discretion of the Bookkeeper.
(d) Reserve: (1) Operating—$1,000 or total of budgeted expenses, whichever is larger. (2) For holding repayments—25% of the sum of all holders' equities as defined in the Holding Agreements.
(e) Allen Fund: Available for loans and grants for the purpose of study (or experiments) of industries suitable for Celo Community.

3. LOANS: Loans are available to members only. In general, the following types of loans may be made:

(a) Land and existing buildings (loan in the form of deferred payments): 25% down, balance in 15 equal yearly payments with concurrent payment of interest on the unpaid balance.
(b) Construction of new buildings: repayable in not more than 12 equal payments, beginning not later than the start of the 4th year after the loan is granted. Interest payments as in (a) above.
(c) Equipment purchases, etc.: maximum term 5 years, but never longer than the reasonable life expectancy of the item to be bought. Repayable in equal yearly installments, beginning at the start of the 2nd year. Interest may be concurrent, or payable after repayment of the principal if agreed on beforehand.
(d) Short loans, one year or less: repayable in a lump sun, with interest.

The sum of the above 4 types of loans outstanding shall not exceed the cash balance of the Community after subtracting the sum of the designated funds listed in No. 2 above.

(e) <u>Quick loans</u>: may be obtained on 24-hours notice if approved by the Chairman of the Finance Committee and the Bookkeeper. Maximum term: 6 months. Maximum amount of any loan: $100. Maximum of all loans outstanding: $500. Interest: 1% monthly on any unpaid balance.

(f) <u>Education</u>: loans to be made from the reserve fund. The fund may be enlarged by borrowing at 5% interest from general Community funds or other sources. Loans must be approved by the Finance Committee.

<u>Eligible</u>: children of members after promotion to the sophomore class of a college or the equivalent. In exceptional cases, younger children may be eligible. The applicant, if over 18, is responsible for repayment. If under 18, the parents are responsible, and in any event must endorse the note. Loans will be made in amounts determined by need and by availability of funds. <u>Interest</u> is 5% and interest payments start upon graduation. The principal is repayable in 5 equal installments, not more than one year apart, beginning one year after graduation. If the applicant consistently does superior work academically, interest will be reduced to $2\frac{1}{2}$%.

4. <u>PROCEDURE FOR OBTAINING A LOAN</u> (except where otherwise noted above):

(a) The applicant submits his request to the Finance Committee, specifying in reasonable detail:
  (1) The amount desired.
  (2) The purpose for which it is to be used.
  (3) The proposed terms of repayment.
  (4) All other obligations, indicating which have priority over the proposed loan.
  (5) Itemized plans for repayment and of existing and expected sources of income which will make this possible.

(b) The Finance Committee submits this information with its recommendation to the next general meeting.

(c) If the loan is approved, the applicant signs a note (his or her spouse should also sign) for the amount of the loan (the terms of repayment should also be included). In cases of loans repayable after 3 years or more, the note shall also include a statement to the effect that the applicant is aware that the Holding Agreement does not confer title on the holder, and that if ever a decision is required as to whether it is a form of lease or of deed it is to be considered the former. The note shall be witnessed by the Bookkeeper and filed with other Community papers. The applicant also submits proof that his buildings are adequately covered by insurance (as defined in No. 5 below). The Bookkeeper will thereupon issue a check.

(d) The borrower shall make a brief yearly report of progress of the project for which the loan was granted. He shall make no change in the use to which he puts any part of the loan without prior consent of the meeting.

(e) Interest shall be 5% unless otherwise specified in advance, and may be compounded yearly at the discretion of the Bookkeeper. Interest will be charged from the date on which the loan is approved by the meeting. If an obligation is not met as scheduled, an additional 2% will be charged until payments are caught up.

5. <u>INSURANCE</u>: Every holder shall carry fire and extended coverage on his house and other buildings in an amount at least equal to the Community's equity in the holding, plus the amount still due on any loans or other obligations. If a proposed loan brings the total indebtedness to more than the value of all insured buildings, this fact shall be considered before the loan is granted. The Community shall be designated beneficiary. The Bookkeeper shall pay the premia, keep the policies, and bill the holder.

III. <u>Community Organization</u>:

1. <u>GENERAL</u>: In 1965, the Community revised its documents to bring them into line with the Community's practice and trend. These revisions were accepted unanimously by the Board of Directors. The present set of documents includes (1) the Corporation Charter, (2) the Corporation By-Laws, (3) the Membership Agreement, (4) the Holding Agreement (confined to members), (5) the Residential Community Constitution, and (6) the Community Procedures and Rules.

Legally, authority is vested in a self-perpetuating Board of Directors. Actually, by formal action of the Board, the Community is autonomous, and the members of the Board are elected after nomination by the members.

Community decisions are reached at the general meetings (first Wednesday of each month) and at occasional special meetings of the Community. New business is first discussed by the appropriate committee. All meetings, both general and committee, are open to members, trial members, and anyone else who may wish to attend. Members and trial members are expected to attend as regularly as possible, but attendance is not compulsory.

2. <u>COMMITTEES</u>: Committee <u>Chairmen</u> are elected at the Annual Meeting of the Community. It is their duty to convene committee meetings, execute policies delegated by the meeting, submit their agendas to the Community Chairman before the general meeting, keep an up-to-date list of existing policies in their field of interest, keep minutes of committee meetings, and prepare a sum-

mary of activities in time for the Annual Meeting. Any or all of these duties may be delegated.

Committee <u>members</u> sign up voluntarily after the Annual Meeting. The Community Chairman may request others to participate in committee work.

Committee <u>meetings</u> will, in general, be held at regular times.

All matters of Community concern should be discussed first by the appropriate committee. In case of routine items, the committee will bring recommendation to the General Meeting, with details of execution. In case of controversial items, the committee will search out the pertinent facts and present these with the essentials of conflicting opinions to the general meeting. In case of items concerning Community property or finance, new business is submitted to the chairman of the appropriate committee. After discussion in the committee meeting, it is brought to the general meeting for discussion. Other new business is submitted to the Community Chairman for inclusion in the agenda of the next general meeting.

Unless specifically authorized, the committees take no action until approved by the general meeting. The latter's decisions become final, if not previously challenged, after the reading of the minutes at the next meeting.

(a) <u>Emergency Committee</u>: It may make grants in case of emergency up to the limit of the fund. Repayment of these grants is expected, but no effort is made to enforce repayment. Composed of one elected member and the Chairman of the Finance Committee. The fund receives yearly excess funds from assessments and when its level becomes too low, the committee may appeal for contributions.

(b) <u>Finance Committee</u>: Passes on all monetary transactions, such as the granting of loans, settlement of holdings, establishing of special funds, and the investment of reserves. The Chairman is charged with seeing that all Holding Agreements, leases, and notes of indebtedness are duly executed and filed. The Bookkeeper and the Treasurer of the Corporation are Ex-Officio members of this committee. The Chairman is responsible to the Treasurer of the Corporation for a yearly audit.

(c) <u>Property Committee</u>: It is charged with the real property of the Community, including boundaries, roads, water line, land, buildings, and equipment. It passes on requests for use of land, or plans for improvement, and makes appraisals.

(d) <u>Other Division Chairmen</u>: Membership, Workday, Corresponding Secretary, Social, Hostess, Library, Education, Publicity, and News Letter.

(e) <u>Special Committees</u>: From time to time, the general meeting delegates special tasks to selected committees formed for the purpose.

3. <u>BOARD OF DIRECTORS</u>: Although legally self-perpetuating, the Board has agreed to elect to membership nominees of the general Community meeting, and to function in an advisory capacity. Its members are elected for terms of 3 years, and, except for the founding members, for not more than 2 consecutive terms. New members are nominated at the Annual Meeting of the members and elected at the next meeting of the Board. <u>Membership</u> on the Board is restricted by law to persons who do not owe anything to the Corporation. The Board consists of at least three members of whom a majority shall be resident members of the Community. The minutes of the Board meetings are made available to the members of the Community who may also attend Board meetings.

<u>Functions</u> of the Board, especially of its non-resident members:

(a) <u>Meet</u> at least once yearly. Discuss problems, purposes, and direction of the Community. This will give the members the benefit of a dispassionate experienced point of view and of constructive criticism.
(b) Advise on the qualifications of <u>new members</u>, although the final decision on membership rests with the Community.
(c) Assume <u>control</u> of the Community if it is in serious threat of dissolution.
(d) Advise and <u>mediate</u> if irreconcilable differences arise between the members.
(e) Offer practical <u>advice</u> to individual members.

The following <u>officers</u> are elected yearly by the Board:

(a) The President (signs official Community documents, calls meetings of the Board and is chairman at such meetings).
(b) The Vice-President (takes the President's place in case of incapacity).
(c) The Secretary (charged with the general supervision of Community records and the performance of Community officers and committees).
(d) The Treasurer (an ex-officio member of the Finance Committee of the Community, if not its chairman, and responsible for seeing that a yearly audit is made).

4. <u>HOLDINGS</u>: A Holding Agreement is not only a legal agreement but a personal moral obligation. It is a special type of agreement, different from the usual type of lease as well as from a deed; however, if it must be defined as either lease or deed, it is considered a lease. Thus, any land occupied in Celo Community remains Community property. The Community has no set policy about land

which members may own outside of the Community, and the above principles are not retroactive to members who obtained deed to their holdings in the early days of the Community.

(a) Taking a Holding: membership in the Community is sufficient qualification.

   Procedure:
   (1) The member applies to the Property Committee, describing the boundaries of the proposed holding, and submitting plans for its use and development.
   (2) The Property Committee inspects the proposed holding with the applicant and makes an appraisal.
   (3) The Property Committee shall appoint a committee to work with the applicant on establishing the boundaries. CCI shall do the surveying or arrange for it if the applicant so desires. In that case, the costs shall be paid by the applicant. An applicant shall not erect buildings or make permanent improvements on his holding before the land is surveyed and the Holding Agreement is signed.
   (4) If agreeable, it is submitted to the general meeting and to the Board of Directors for approval.
   (5) If approved, and after payment of 25% of the appraisal figure, the member may take possession.
   (6) If the holding is not surveyed, the corners marked with permanent markers, and the agreement properly signed within a year after occupancy, the member automatically forfeits his rights to the holding.

(b) Guidelines for Land Values (established at general meeting of 1/7/70)

   (1) For unimproved, relatively inaccessible land: $100 per acre.
   (2) For land that is more accessible to water facilities and other utilities needed for building: between $100 and $300 per acre.
   (3) For land along route 80 and for cleared agricultural land: between $300 and $600 per acre.
   (4) For house site (one acre or less): $600.

(c) Leaving a Holding: Neither the Community nor the holder shall profit from a transfer of holdings.

   Procedure:
   (1) The holder gives the Community at last three months notice.
   (2) Before the end of this period, the appraisal of the holding will be re-

viewed by the Property Committee. The appraisal (or in case of disagreement, the appraisal by a Board of Arbitration) is validated at the next general meeting.

(3) The departing holder discharges all his obligations to the Community (assessments, rentals, loans, payments on the holding).

(4) Following this, the Community pays to the departing holder $1,500 or 60% of the appraised value of the holding, whichever is lower. The Community thereupon takes possession.

(5) After the former holder's departure, and until he has been paid in full according to the terms of the Holding Agreement, the Community may rent the holding if no new holder can be found, but only on a month-to-month basis, leaving the property available for a permanent holding. Rental income will go to the Community until its equity has been repaid. Community equity consists of the total of CCI's investment, i.e. CCI's payment to the holder, plus all maintenance costs. (Holders should expect to be penalized for faulty planning, construction, or failure to maintain their holdings.)

(6) If a holding has not been taken within 10 years, the Community shall make an accounting to the former holder. The Community equity shall be subtracted from the accumulated rentals, and any balance will be divided equally between CC I and the former holder, who will have no further claims on the Community.

(d) Subletting a Holding: A holding may be sublet for periods of less than one month with the approval of the Property Committee. Longer periods require approval of the general meeting.

5. MEETINGS:

(a) All meetings are open.

(b) The chief duty of the Chairman is to help the meeting reach consensus, but he/she may express his own opinions. If the debate becomes heated, repetitious, or too involved, he may employ the following techniques: (1) call for a period of silence, (2) require that each speaker be recognized, (3) rule remarks out of order.

(c) Decisions of the meeting, if not protested in the interval, become final after the minutes are approved at the next meeting.

(d) The Annual Meeting is held in September. There will be 20 days official notice. In August, a nominating committee is elected by the meeting, charged with nominating candidates for the several positions of responsibility and determining whether they are willing to serve. Nomination may also be made from the floor at the Annual Meeting. The following offices and special fields are represented:

Chairman	Membership	Publicity and News Letter
Bookkeeper	Property	Library
Secretary	Finance	
Corresponding	Workday	
Secretary	Social Events	
Codifier	Hostess	

(e) <u>Election</u> is preferably by consensus, but if consensus is not readily reached, it will be by secret ballot. Outgoing committee chairmen shall submit summaries of the year's activities and important decisions which will remain on file.

6. <u>MEMBERS</u>: Procedure for acquiring membership:

(a) The prospective member is in general expected to visit the Community for a long enough time to become acquainted.

(b) Next, he will submit an application (on the form provided) to the Membership Chairman who will make a recommendation to the next general meeting.

(c) The general meeting will approve him for <u>trial membership</u>. This lasts in general at least six months. Trial members are expected to participate in general and committee meetings as well as in other Community activities.

(d) During this time, all members are responsible for getting acquainted with the trial member. The Membership Chairman will appoint a special committee to discuss Community philosophy and structure with the prospective member. He shall be given a kit containing:

(1) The Corporation Charter and By-Laws.
(2) The Membership Agreement.
(3) The current Holding Agreement.
(4) The Residential Community Constitution.
(5) The Community Procedures and Rules.
(6) A Community folder.
(7) A brief history of the Community.

(e) At the end of the trial period, the Membership Chairman will poll all of the Community members and make a recommendation to the general meeting.

(f) If the trial member decides to apply for full membership, he will make his decision known to the Membership Chairman. If the trial member does not apply for full membership or for extension of the trial membership at the end of 6 months, his membership lapses automatically.

(g) The Membership Chairman will give the general meeting one month's notice of a proposed election to full membership. The new member will be accepted if not more than 15% of the members present and voting and none of the directors dissent. The meeting may vote to accept, reject, or to extend the trial membership for another 6 months.

(h) After the first 6 months, a trial member is expected to pay the regular Community assessments.

Leaves of absence for members will be granted only for the purpose or vacation, study, or work if the member indicates his intention to return to the Community at the end of the stated period. Each member on leave, and on his own initiative, will submit at the time of the Annual Meeting a formal statement about his leave of absence: why he must have it, how long it is expected to be, what progress he is making in carrying out his schedule, and what his plans for his Holding are. If an absentee member does not submit a statement along these lines in time for the Annual Meeting, he will be sent a reminder by the Membership Chairman. Leave of absence will be granted on a yearly basis only.

Members are expected to prepare a valid will and indicate in their record where it is filed.

Expulsion: The Community may terminate this agreement if the holder violates any of its terms, or

(1) Is absent from the Community for more than 180 days in any 12 month period without having obtained a leave of absence.

(2) Fails to honor after notice any written agreement with the Community or any of its members.

(3) Fails to abide by duly enacted community decisions.

(4) Is convicted of a felony or is legally declared insane or incompetent.

Procedure for expulsion: (May not be applicable in case of (4) above).

(a) Decision by the general meeting that adequate grounds exist.

(b) The meeting appoints a special committee to meet with the prospect within two weeks to attempt reconciliation.

(c) If this effort fails, the prospect shall be given the grounds for expulsion in writing and allowed one month to reply.

(d) After a full hearing of this reply, the meeting will vote, and the decision to expel becomes final if the directors are unanimous and not more than 15% of the members dissent.

(e) the expelled member must leave the Community within 6 months after the final decision, or at the end of the next crop season if engaged in agriculture.

7. OFFICERS: Their terms begin with the next meeting following the Annual Meeting, except for the Bookkeeper whose term shall be the same as the Community's fiscal year. His duties have been enumerated, as have those of the Chairman.

The Secretary keeps the minutes of all meetings. They should specify where any important documents or correspondence which may be discussed can be found. He is responsible for keeping the current files (minutes, correspondence, committee reports, etc.) in order. Copies of the minutes are distributed without charge to all members, directors, trial members, and, if requested, to former members for one year after their departure. Others may receive them on payment of $2.00 per year.

The Corresponding Secretary handles Community correspondence. Letters of inquiry, in addition to being read (or resumed) at meetings, should be left in a visible box in the library for perusal by all members, who are encouraged to respond personally to interesting correspondents in cooperation with the Corresponding Secretary.

The Codifier abstracts the minutes and keeps a permanent file of the policy or precedent-making decisions arranged by subject. At the end of each year, he shall prepare a list of all new policies and rules and distribute it to all members.

8. RESIDENTS: other than members or trial members must have a member sponsor, and are expected to pay community unit tax after six months in residence.

MEMBERSHIP AGREEMENT

PART I

Celo Community accepts into full membership with all its privileges
and Obligations _____
on the ___ day of _____ 19__.

WITNESS _____ Signed _____
                                   President, Celo Community, Inc.

                                   _____
                                   Secretary
        Seal of the Corporation _____

PART II

Article 1. I, _____, accept membership in
Celo Community, and am in sympathy with its purposes as stated in the following
documents:

  (a) Certificate of Incorporation
  (b) Code of Regulations of the Corporation
  (c) Constitution and By-Laws of the members
  (d) Community Holding Agreement
  (e) Community Membership Agreement

Article 2. I have read, understand, and will abide by the Celo Community documents
listed in Article 1. I have read the current descriptive material, the historical summary, and the most recent codification of the minutes of Community meetings.

Article 3. In order to ensure a stable community environment, members are expected to have their principal place of residence within the corporate limits of Celo Community.

Article 4. I accept the privilege and duty of participating in the Community meetings, of actively serving on committees for the management of Community affairs, and of sharing with the other members the responsibility for maintenance, growth, and preservation of all Community land and other property and interests. I also agree to assume my share of the yearly Community budget.

Article 5. It is understood that the making of decisions and policies governing the Community and its members is based on an effort to apply the technique of consensus, and that each resident member has an equal voice in determining such policies and decisions. A member is expected to abide by all duly enacted decisions of the regular Community meeting and to accept arbitration according to Community rules in case of disagreement with the Community or another member.

Article 6. Membership in Celo Community may be ended any time by the written request of the member, on thirty days notice.

The Community, by action in a regular meeting, may, if not more than 15% of the members in residence and of the directors dissent, dismiss from membership any member who, in its opinion, has not acted in accordance with the purposes and objectives of the Community or who has acted against the best interest of the Community.

Grounds for dismissal include but are not limited to:

(1) Absence from the Community for more than 180 days out of any year, without having obtained a leave of absence.
(2) Failure, after notice, to honor written agreements with the Community or any of its members.
(3) Conviction of a felony.
(4) Being declared insane or incompetent by due process of law.

Procedure for dismissal from membership: Following the meeting at which dismissal is approved, with no more than 15% of the members in residence and of the directors dissenting:

(1) A Community Committee must make every reasonable effort to meet with the member to reconcile the conflict.
(2) If reconciliation is impossible, the Community must give its reasons for dismissal and give the member one month in which to reply.
(3) The member must be given opportunity to appear in his own behalf before a regular or special meeting of the Community.
(4) If dismissal is finally decided upon, it becomes effective immediately.

(5) The dismissed member must vacate his holding within one year of the date of the decision. Settlement of the Holding will be made as in case of voluntary departure.

Witness _____ Signed _____

Date _____ 19 ___

Revision
April 1965

CELO COMMUNITY HOLDING AGREEMENT

This agreement as to a land holding, made and entered into this _____ day of _____ , A.D. 19____ by and between Celo Community, Inc., a nonprofit corporation organized under the laws of the State of North Carolina, hereinafter referred to as the Community, and _____ hereinafter referred to as the Holder, who is a member of Celo Community, Inc.

Article 1. That the Community operates for the mutual benefit of all holders of lands under agreements with the Community for land holdings, generally similar to this agreement. This agreement is not a deed, but is a cooperative agreement between parties which have mutual interest in the development and welfare of Celo Community, Inc. Because the Holders and other members of Celo Community, Inc. are mutually interested in maintaining the common welfare of the Community, and are agreed to forgo some elements of private control in order to promote their common welfare, and in order to develop the greatest and best use and value of the community resources, the holder accepts on his part the conditions of possession and use of his holding, as set forth in this agreement, as part of the general program of mutual benefit to all holders in said Community, both for his own protection against loss due to improper or undesirable use of Community property by other Holders, and in order that all holdings and other Community resources may be developed for the fullest use and benefit of all the Holders and of the neighborhood.

Article 2. The Community, being the possessor of the title to a tract of land acquired for community development, hereby agrees that the Holder shall have possession, occupancy, and use of the following described real estate, under the conditions described herein, free from all encumbrances, except taxes and assessments not yet due and payable, and subject to such zoning, standards, regulations and restrictions as may be adopted and prescribed by the resident members of the community, and subject to all liens and defects which appear in the Community's chain of title, easements, rights of way, roads and highways, restrictions, exceptions, reservations and excepting and reserving to the Community all the oil, gas, coal, stone, and other mineral rights, powers, and privileges. However, the Community agrees not to mine any such resources without the written consent of the Holder. Any damage or loss to surface rights caused thereby is to be determined by the mutual agreement, or in the case of disagreement by arbitration, as provided in Article 10, and to be paid or credited to the Holder, the holding being described as follows, to wit:

(The following page, containing Legal Description and Plat of the Holding, shall be considered Page 2 of this agreement.)

[sample page 2 of original, omitted]

Article 3. In consideration of the services of the Community to the Holder, and for the use of the property described herein, the Holder shall pay to the Community all of the Community's equity in his holding, the Community's equity being the appraised value of the holding as determined by the last appraisal by the Community; less the sum of any principal payments already made by the Holder. He shall assume the maintenance, taxes, and assessments, and assume his share of the yearly Community budget. He also agrees to take out a fire and extended coverage insurance policy covering at least the amount equal to the Community equity in the holding with the Community named beneficiary to the extent of its equity.

The local administration, after 30 days written notice to the Holders, may cause a vote of the Holders to be taken on a proposal for a specified increase of the rate of assessment for Community purposes. In case three quarters or more of the Holders voting are in favor of such increase, the increased assessment shall be an obligation under this agreement in the same manner as specified in Articles 3, 4, and 5 of this agreement. Assessments may be made for construction, maintenance, and improvements of Community water supplies, sanitation, fire protection, roads, boundaries, timber and land improvement, recreation, administration, publicity, and to establish a reserve; and for such other purposes as may be agreed to by at least ⅔ of the members and of the Board of Directors, provided that assessments may not be increased more than 25% in any one year.

The Community shall make a yearly appraisal of the holding, which shall form the basis for apportioning the assessments and taxes.

The following appraisal of value of this holding is accepted by the parties as being a fair valuation as the basis for this agreement _____. The Holder agrees to pay this sum to CCI in the following manner:

Article 4. The Holder may use dead and unmarketable timber on this holding, and any other timber on Community land not included in any holding and which is designated by the Community, for his own fuel, fence posts and other home use; but the Holder shall not cut any growing trees of value on his holding or on other Community land, without the written consent of the Community. The Community agrees not to cut any timber on this holding without the consent of the Holder.

<u>Article 5</u>. The Holder shall at all times, to the degree which represents good conservation, agricultural and civic standards, maintain the holding and the improvements thereon in a clean and healthful condition, keep the buildings and structures in good repair, keep the land free from noxious weeds and plants, prevent and control erosion of the soil, and spray, fumigate or otherwise treat trees, shrubs, and other plants on the land as necessary and reasonably feasible to prevent the growth and spread of agricultural pests.

<u>Article 6</u>. The Holder agrees that he will not assign, mortgage, sublet, or otherwise encumber his interest in this agreement or any part of it, or in the premises, without the written consent of the Community; and no assignment, mortagage [*sic*], subletting or encumbrance of the Holder's interest shall be valid or effective unless the written consent of the Community has been secured.

<u>Article 7</u>. The Holder may terminate this agreement at any time by giving the Community at least three months notice.

The Community may terminate this agreement if the holder violates any of its terms, or

1. Is absent from the Community for more than 180 days in any 12 month period without having obtained a leave of absence.
2. Fails to honor after notice any written agreement with the Community or any of its members.
3. Fails to abide by duly enacted community decisions.
4. Is convicted of a felony or is legally declared insane or incompetent.

<u>Article 8</u>. Upon termination of this agreement there shall be a determination of accounts between the Community and the Holder. The Holder should be aware that he does not obtain enough equity for any reimbursment on departure until he has paid 40% of the evaluation and in fact is obligated to the Community for the unpaid part of the 40%. For the purpose of settlement the yearly appraisals referred to in Article 3 shall be used. The value of the holding shall be the average appraisal of the immediately preceding 5 years, unless there has been a catastrophic loss of value, in which case the yearly appraisal following the event shall be averaged. However, for the purpose of settlement no appraisal shall exceed $15,000.00.

From this appraisal value shall be subtracted any sum still due under the terms of this agreement, plus any other sums owed by the Holder to the Community. The resulting amount is the Holder's equity, and the Community will make payments to the Holder as follows:

Immediately, as soon as the holder vacates this holding: $1,500.00, or 60% of the Holder's equity, whichever is less.

In the course of the next 6 years, in equal yearly installments, plus 5% annual interest on the unpaid balance: the balance, if any be due, of 60% of the Holder's equity.

The Community shall have no further obligation, unless another Holder takes the holding within ten years.

After offering payment of the first installment the Community shall take possession of the holding.

The Community will endeavor to find another holder, and agrees to appraise the holding as follows:

During the first year after it is vacated: any value set by the former holder.

During the next four years: the appraisal value established at the termination of this agreement, except that a lower figure may be established if the former holder consents to the change.

If another holder is found for this holding within 10 years after it is vacated the Community shall pay to the former holder any sum received in excess of one half the holder's equity, but not exceeding the total holder's equity, after deducting any expenses to the Community for maintenance, improvements, insurance, and taxes. After 10 years the Community has no further obligations under this agreement.

If the Community fails to make payments as agreed to above, the former holder shall receive a deed to the holding, provided he repays to the Community any amount already received, plus his accrued obligations to the Community.

Article 9. If the Community is dissolved, the Holder shall be given a deed to this holding, upon payment of all his obligations to the Community.

Article 10. The by-laws of the Community are by express reference made a part of this agreement and it is agreed that all amendments and supplements thereto shall become parts of this agreement. In the event of any controversy arising under the terms of this agreement between the Holder and the Community, the controversy shall be submitted to the Board of Arbitration for decision.

The Board of Arbitration shall consist of one person chosen by the Holder, one by the Community, and a third chosen by the first two.

Article 11. The Community reserves the right to zone the holdings and other lands of the Community and to set standards and make regulations concerning the use of land, the design and placing of buildings, the clearing of land and cutting of timber, or other matters affecting the welfare of the Community. The Holder agrees that he will not violate the terms of any provisions of such zoning standards, regulations and/or restrictions. The general restrictions by which this holding shall be governed shall be those adopted by regular action of the Community and recorded as zoning standards regulations and/or restrictions, and assembled in a record book of the Community.

Article 12. The Holder agrees to hold the Community harmless for any loss or damage for injuries to persons or property arising out of the Holder's use and occupancy of the premises, from and against all claims, demands or rights of persons, firms, or corporations performing labor or furnishing materials, equipment, machinery, fuel, or supplies for use on said premises.

Article 13. The Community shall have a first and best lien, paramount to all others, upon every right and interest of the Holder to and in the premises covered by this agreement and in and to this agreement, and in all buildings and improvements erected or to be placed thereon, as security for and payment of the entire amount of payments accruing under this agreement, and for the performance of all the singular covents [*sic*], conditions and obligations of this agreement to be performed by the Holder.

Article 14. It is made an express condition of this agreement that no lien, by virtue of any act of omission or commission on the part of the Holder or anyone claiming by, through or under him, shall attach to said premises, or the title or estate of the Community therein, and any and all persons or corporations dealing with the Holder shall be charged with notice of this condition.

Article 15. Every notice given or required under any provision or requirement of this agreement, unless otherwise provided, shall in each case be a notice in writing, addressed to the party to be notified, signed by the party giving the same, or his or its agent, and either delivered to the party addressed, or mailed to the party addressed by United States Mail, postage prepaid; such notice sent by mail to be addressed as follows: if notice to the Community, the same to be addressed to it at R. R. 5, Burnsville, N.C. 28714, and if notice to the Holder the same to be addressed to him at R. R. 5, Burnsville, N.C. 28714.

Article 16. The Holder, keeping the covenants and terms of this agreement, on his part to be kept and performed, shall have peaceable possession and quiet enjoyment of the said premises throughout the term thereof, without let, hindrance or molestation of any person whomsoever, except as provided by the covenants of this agreement.

Article 17. The failure of this Community in any one or more instances to insist upon strict performance of any of the covenants of this agreement, or any other such agreement, or to exercise any option herein conferred, shall not be construed as waiver or relinquishment of any such covenants, conditions or options, but the same shall continue in full force and effect.

Article 18. At death of the Holder this agreement is terminated, and settlement will be made with his estate as in the case of voluntary termination.

If, however, the Holder has designated in writing a person to whom he wishes the holding to pass, and if the Community, at the time of the Holder's death, accepts that person as a member, the Holder's equity in this holding shall pass without fee to said person, upon his signing the holding agreement in force at that time.

Article 19. It is understood and agreed that the Chairman of Celo Community, Inc., or his successor in office, is authorized to act in behalf of the Community in connection with transactions with the Holder.

Article 20. Any notices to be given or payments to be made by or to the Community shall be made by or to the Secretary of the Community or by or to the officer of the Community designated to receive them. The business office shall be considered as the office of the Community.

Article 21. This agreement shall be valid and effective, except as herein otherwise modified, during the term of the life of the Holder unless sooner terminated according to the provisions thereof.

IN TESTIMONY WHEREOF, the Holders have hereunto set their hands and seals in duplicate and Celo Community, Inc. has caused said instrument to he signed by its authorized officers and its Corporate Seal to be thereto attached by order of its Directors duly given, all as of the day and year first above written.

ATTEST: Celo Community, Inc.

_____   By _____
Secretary   President

STATE OF_____   _____
                                       Holder

CITY OF _____   _____
                                       Holder

On this the_____ day of _____ 19__ personally came before the undersigned
Notary Public _____ who, being by me duly
sworn (affirmed) says that he is President of Celo Community Inc., and that the seal
affixed to the foregoing instrument in writing is the Corporate Seal of said Corporation, and that said writing was signed and sealed by him in behalf of said Corporation by its authority duly given. And the said _____
acknowledged the said writing to be the act and deed of said Corporation.

Witness my hand and notarial seal this the ___ day of _____ 19__

_____
Notary Public

My commission expires the
_____ day of _____ 19__.

STATE OF NORTH CAROLINA
COUNTY OF YANCEY

Personally came before me the undersigned Notary Public _____
and _____, who duly acknowledged the foregoing instrument for the purposes stated therein.

Witness my hand and seal this _____ day of _____ 19__.

_____
Notary Public

My commission expires _____

References

Abrams, Philip, and Andrew McCulloch. 1976. *Communes, Sociology and Society.* Cambridge: Cambridge University Press.

Adams, Robert M., ed. and trans. 1975. *Utopia, by Sir Thomas More: A New Translation; Backgrounds; Criticism.* New York: Norton.

Albertson, Ralph. 1936. "A Survey of Mutualistic Communities in America." *Iowa Journal of History and Politics* 34:375–444.

Alyea, Paul E. and Blanche R. 1956. *Fairhope, 1894–1954: The Story of a Single Tax Colony.* University, Ala.: University of Alabama Press.

American Friends Service Committee. 1945. *The Experience of the American Friends Service Committee in Civilian Public Service.* Philadelphia: American Friends Service Committee.

Andelson, Jonathan G. 1997. "The Community of True Inspiration from Germany to the Amana Colonies." In *America's Communal Utopias,* edited by D. E. Pitzer, 181–203. Chapel Hill: University of North Carolina Press.

Anders, Jentri. 1990. *Beyond Counterculture: The Community of Mateel.* Pullman: Washington State University Press.

Anderson, Mary Siler. 1990. *Whatever Happened to the Hippies?* San Pedro, Calif.: R. and E. Miles.

Anderson, Nels. 1942. *Desert Saints: The Mormon Frontier in Utah.* Chicago: University of Chicago Press.

Apter, David E. 1964. "Introduction: Ideology and Discontent." In *Ideology and Discontent,* edited by D. E. Apter, 15–46. New York: Free Press.

Arnold, Emmy. 1964. *Torches Together: The Beginning and Early Years of the Bruderhof Communities.* Rifton, N.Y.: The Plough Publishing House.

Aronowitz, Stanley. 1993. *Roll Over Beethoven: The Return of Cultural Strife.* Hanover, N.H.: University Press of New England.

Arrington, Leonard J., and Davis Britton. 1979. *The Mormon Experience: A History of the Latter-Day Saints.* New York: Knopf.

Bach, Marcus. 1961. *Strange Sects and Curious Cults.* New York: Dodd, Mead.

Baer, Hans A. 1988. *Recreating Utopia in the Desert: A Sectarian Challenge to Modern Mormonism.* Albany: State University of New York Press.

Bailey, F. G. 1965. "Decisions by Consensus in Councils and Committees: With Special Reference to Village and Local Government in India." In *Political Systems and the Distribution of Power,* edited by M. Banton, 1–20. ASA Monographs 2. London: Tavistock Publications.

Bainbridge, William Sims. 1984. "The Decline of the Shakers: Evidence from the United States Census." *Communal Societies* 4:19–34.

Barkun, Michael. 1984. "Communal Societies as Cyclical Phenomena." *Communal Societies* 4:35–48.

Barrett, Stanley R. 1977. *The Rise and Fall of an African Utopia: A Wealthy Theocracy in Comparative Perspective.* Waterloo, Ontario: Wilfrid Laurier University Press.

Barthel, Diane L. 1984. *Amana: From Pietist Sect to American Community.* Lincoln: University of Nebraska Press.

Bassett, T. D. Seymour. 1952. "The Secular Utopian Socialists." In *Socialism and American Life,* vol. 1, edited by D. D. Egbert and S. Persons, 153–211. 2 vols. Princeton: Princeton University Press.

———. 1954. "The Quakers and Communitarians." *Bulletin of Friends' Historical Association* 43:84–99.

Batteau, Allen. 1990. *The Invention of Appalachia.* Tucson: University of Arizona Press.

Baudrillard, Jean. 1988. *America.* New York: Verso.

Beam, Maurice. 1964. *Cults of America.* New York: Macfadden-Bartell Corporation.

Beaver, Patricia D. 1992. *Rural Community in the Appalachian South.* Prospect Heights, Ill.: Waveland Press.

Beeman, William O. 1986. "Freedom to Choose: Symbols and Values in American Advertising." In *Symbolizing America,* edited by Herve Varenne, 52–65. Lincoln: University of Nebraska Press.

Bell, Daniel. 1960. *The End of Ideology.* Glencoe, Ill.: Free Press.

———. 1980. "The End of American Exceptionalism." In *The Winding Passage: Essays and Sociological Journeys, 1960–1980,* 245–71. New York: Basic Books.

Bellah, Robert N. 1987. "The Quest for the Self: Individualism, Morality, Politics." In *Interpretative Social Science: A Second Look,* edited by Paul Rabinow and William M. Sullivan, 365–83. Berkeley: University of California Press.

———. 1988. "The Idea of Practices in Habits: A Response." In *Community in America: The Challenge of Habits of the Heart,* edited by Charles H. Reynolds and Ralph V. Norman, 269–88. Berkeley: University of California Press.

Bellah, Robert N., Richard Madsen, William M. Sullivan, Ann Swidler, and Steven M. Tipton. 1985. *Habits of the Heart: Individualism and Commitment in American Life.* Berkeley: University of California Press.

Bennett, John W. 1967. *Hutterian Brethren: The Agricultural Economy and Social Organization of a Communal People.* Stanford, Calif.: Stanford University Press.

———. 1974. "Cultural Integrity and Personal Identity: The Communitarian Response." In *The Cultural Drama: Modern Identities and Social Ferment,* edited by Wilton S. Dillon, 196–235. Washington, D.C.: Smithsonian Institution Press.

————. 1975. "Communes and Communitarianism." *Theory and Society* 2:63–94.

Bentley, G. Carter. 1981. "Migration, Ethnic Identity, and State-Building in the Philippines: The Sulu Case." In *Ethnic Change,* edited by Charles F. Keyes, 117–53. Seattle: University of Washington Press.

Berger, Bennett M. 1981. *The Survival of a Counterculture: Ideological Work and Everyday Life among Rural Communards.* Berkeley: University of California Press.

————. 1995. *An Essay on Culture: Symbolic Structure and Social Structure.* Berkeley: University of California Press.

Berry, Brian J. L. 1992. *America's Utopian Experiments.* Hanover, N.H.: University Press of New England.

Bestor, Arthur. 1970. *Backwoods Utopias: The Sectarian Phase of Communitarian Socialism in America: 1663–1829.* 1950. 2d ed. Philadelphia: University of Pennsylvania Press.

————. 1953. "Patent-Office Models of the Good Society: Some Relationships between Social Reform and Westward Expansion." *American Historical Review* 58:505–26.

————. 1957. "The Transit of Communitarian Socialism to America." *Proceedings of the Second Conference of the European Association for American Studies,* 3–16.

Bittner, Egon. 1963. "Radicalism and the Organization of Radical Movements." *American Sociological Review* 28:928–40.

Blumer, Herbert. 1958. "Race Prejudice as a Sense of Group Position." *Pacific Sociological Review* 1:3–7.

Borsodi, Ralph. 1929. *This Ugly Civilization.* New York: Simon and Schuster.

————. 1933. *Flight from the City: the Story of a New Way to Family Security.* New York: Harper.

————. 1948. *Education and Living.* 2 vols. Suffern, N.Y.: School of Living. Reprint, Melbourne, Fla.: Melbourne University Press.

Brooks, Arle. 1946. *We the Offenders.* Philadelphia: American Friends Service Committee.

Brooks, Arthelia Hilleary. 1994. *The Backside of Yesterday: My Life and Work.* Burnsville, N.C.: Celo Valley Books.

Bryn Gweled Homesteads. 1956. *About Bryn Gweled Homesteads.* Bryn Gweled, Pa.: Bryn Gweled Homesteads.

Buber, Martin. 1958. *Paths in Utopia.* 1949. Reprint, Boston: Beacon.

Burridge, Kenelm. 1969. *New Heaven New Earth: A Study of Millenarian Activities.* Oxford: Basil Blackwell.

Bushee, Frederick A. 1905. "Communistic Societies in the United States." *Political Science Quarterly* 20:625–63.

Butterfield, Herbert. 1931. *The Whig Interpretation of History.* London: G. Bell.

Carden, Maren Lockwood. 1969. *Oneida: Utopian Community to Modern Corporation.* Baltimore: Johns Hopkins University Press.

Case, John and Rosemary, and C. R. Taylor, eds. 1979. *Co-ops, Communes and Collectives: Experiments in Social Change in the 1960s and 1970s.* New York: Pantheon.

Chidester, David. 1988. *Salvation and Suicide: An Interpretation of Jim Jones, the Peoples Temple, and Jonestown.* Bloomington: University of Indiana Press.

Chmielewski, Wendy, L. J. Kern, and M. Klee-Hartzell, eds. 1993. *Women in Spiritual and Communitarian Societies in the United States.* Syracuse, N.Y.: Syracuse University Press.

Cohen, Anthony P. 1994. *Self Consciousness: An Alternative Anthropology of Identity*. London: Routledge.

Cohn, Norman. 1961. *The Pursuit of the Millennium: Revolutionary Messianism in Medieval and Reformation Europe and Its Bearing on Modern Totalitarian Movements*. 2d ed. New York: Harper.

Colson, Elizabeth. 1974. *Tradition and Contract: The Problem of Order*. Chicago: Aldine.

Conkin, Paul K. 1959. *Tomorrow a New World: The New Deal Community Program*. Ithaca, N.Y.: Cornell University Press for the American Historical Association.

———. 1964. *Two Paths to Utopia: The Hutterites and the Llano Colony*. Lincoln: University of Nebraska Press.

Cooper, Matthew. 1987. "Relations of Modes of Production in Nineteenth Century America: The Shakers and Oneida." *Ethnology* 26:1–16.

Coser, Lewis A. 1956. *The Functions of Social Conflict*. New York: Free Press.

———. 1974. *Greedy Institutions: Patterns of Undivided Commitment*. New York: Free Press.

Coy, Patrick G., ed. 1988. *A Revolution of the Heart: Essays on the Catholic Worker*. Philadelphia: Temple University Press.

Creese, Walter L. 1990. *TVA's Public Planning: The Vision, the Reality*. Knoxville: University of Tennessee Press.

Davis, Allison, Burleigh B. Gardner, and Mary R. Gardner. 1965. *Deep South: A Social Anthropological Study of Caste and Class*. 1941. Abridged ed., Chicago: University of Chicago Press.

Day, Dorothy. 1983. *By Little and by Little: The Selected Writings of Dorothy Day*. Edited by Robert Ellsberg. New York: Knopf.

Deets, Lee Emerson. 1939. *The Hutterites; A Study in Social Cohesion*. Gettysburg, Pa.: Times and News Publishing Co.

Dellinger, David. 1993. *From Yale to Jail: The Life Story of a Moral Dissenter*. New York: Pantheon.

Demos, John. 1970. *A Little Commonwealth: Family Life in Plymouth Colony*. New York: Oxford University Press.

Duberman, Martin. 1972. *Black Mountain: An Exploration in Community*. New York: Dutton.

Dumont, Louis. 1961. "Caste, Racism, and 'Stratification': Reflections of a Social Anthropologist." *Contributions to Indian Sociology* 5:20–43.

———. 1970. *Homo Hierarchicus: The Caste System and Its Implications*. London: Weidenfeld and Nicolson.

———. 1977. *From Mandeville to Marx: The Genesis and Triumph of Economic Ideology*. Chicago: University of Chicago Press.

———. 1986. *Essays on Individualism: Modern Ideology in Anthropological Perspective*. Chicago: University of Chicago Press.

Durnbaugh, Donald F. 1991. "Relocation of the German Bruderhof to England, South America, and North America." *Communal Societies* 11:62–77.

Eaton, Joseph W. 1950. "FSA Cooperative Farms." In *Cooperative Group Living: An International Symposium on Group Farming and the Sociology of Cooperation*, edited by Henrik F. Infield and Joseph B. Maier, 5–12. New York: Henry Koosis.

Egbert, Donald Drew, and Stow Persons, eds. 1952. *Socialism and American Life*. 2 vol. Princeton: Princeton University Press.

Egerton, John. 1977. *Visions of Utopia: Nashoba, Rugby, Ruskin, and the "New Communities" in Tennessee's Past.* Knoxville: University of Tennessee Press.

Erasmus, Charles J. 1977. *In Search of the Common Good: Utopian Experiments Past and Future.* New York: Free Press.

Erikson, Erik H. 1960. "The Problem of Ego Identity." In *Identity and Anxiety: Survival of the Person in Mass Society,* edited by M. R. Stein, A. J. Vidich, and D. M. White. New York: Free Press.

Etzioni, Amitai. 1993. *The Spirit of Community: Rights, Responsibilities, and the Communitarian Agenda.* New York: Crown.

Fairfield, Richard. 1972. *Communes USA: A Personal Tour.* Baltimore: Penguin.

Fellman, Michael. 1973. *The Unbounded Frame: Freedom and Community in Nineteenth Century American Utopianism.* Westport, Conn.: Greenwood.

Fellowship for Intentional Community. 1990. *Directory of Intentional Communities.* Rutledge, Mo.: Communities Publications Cooperative.

———. 1992. *Directory of Intentional Communities.* Rutledge, Mo.: Communities Publications Cooperative.

———. 1995. *Communities Directory: A Guide to Cooperative Living.* Langley, Wash.: Fellowship for Intentional Community.

Fellowship of Intentional Communities. 1959. *1959 Yearbook.* Yellow Springs, Ohio: Fellowship of Intentional Communities.

Fernandez, James W. 1965. "Symbolic Consensus in a Fang Reformative Cult." *American Anthropologist* 67:902–29.

Filler, Louis. 1954. "Pilot Plants, Utopias, and Social Reform." *Community Service News* 12:45–49.

Fitzgerald, Frances. 1986. *Cities on a Hill: A Journey through Contemporary American Cultures.* New York: Simon and Schuster.

Flanders, Robert Bruce. 1965. *Nauvoo: Kingdom on the Mississippi.* Urbana: University of Illinois Press.

Fogarty, Robert S. 1975. "American Communes, 1865–1914." *American Studies* 9:145–62.

———. 1980. *Dictionary of American Communal and Utopian History.* Westport, Conn.: Greenwood.

———. 1981. *The Righteous Remnant: The House of David.* Kent, Ohio: Kent State University Press.

———. 1990. *All Things New: American Communes and Utopian Movements 1860–1914.* Chicago: University of Chicago Press.

———. 1993a. "Afterword." In Charles Nordhoff, *American Utopias,* 421–28. Originally *The Communistic Societies of the United States,* 1875. Reprint, Stockbridge, Mass.: Berkshire House.

———. 1993b. "'Cults,' Guns and the Kingdom." *The Nation,* April 12, 485–87.

———, ed. 1972. *American Utopianism.* Itasca, Ill: F. E. Peacock.

———. 1994. *Special Love/Special Sex: An Oneida Community Diary.* Syracuse, N.Y.: Syracuse University Press.

Foster, Lawrence. 1981. *Religion and Sexuality: Three American Communal Experiments of the Nineteenth Century.* New York: Oxford University Press.

———. 1991. *Women, Family, and Utopia: Communal Experiments of the Shakers, the Oneida Community, and the Mormons.* Syracuse, N.Y.: Syracuse University Press.

Foster, Stephen William. 1988. *The Past Is Another Country: Representation, Historical Consciousness, and Resistance in the Blue Ridge.* Berkeley: University of California Press.

Fox, Richard Wightman. 1988. "The Liberal Ethic and the Spirit of Protestantism." In *Community in America: The Challenge of Habits of the Heart,* edited by Charles H. Reynolds and Ralph V. Norman, 238–49. Berkeley: University of California Press.

Fox, Robin. 1983. *The Red Lamp of Incest: An Inquiry into the Origins of Mind and Society.* Notre Dame: University of Notre Dame Press.

Fromm, Erich. 1947. *Man for Himself: An Inquiry into the Psychology of Ethics.* New York: Rinehart.

Garrett, Clarke. 1987. *Spirit Possession and Popular Religion: From the Camisards to the Shakers.* Baltimore: Johns Hopkins University Press.

Gaston, Paul M. 1984. *Women of Fair Hope.* Athens: University of Georgia Press.

Gide, Charles. 1930. *Communist and Co-operative Colonies.* New York: Crowell.

Goldenberg, Zena. 1993. "The Power of Feminism at Twin Oaks Community." In *Women in Spiritual and Communitarian Societies in the United States,* edited by W. Chmielewski, L. J. Kern, and M. Kee-Hartzell, 256–66. Syracuse, N.Y.: Syracuse University Press.

Goodman, Paul and Percival. 1947. *Communitas: Means of Livelihood and Ways of Life.* New York: Knopf.

Gorman, Burton W. 1969. *Education for Learning to Live Together.* Dubuque, Iowa: Wm. C. Brown Book Co.

Graham, Keith. 1984. "Consensus in Social Decision-Making: Why Is It Utopian?" In *Utopias,* edited by Peter Alexander and Roger Gill, 49–60. London: Duckworth.

Gray, J. Patrick, and Linda D. Wolfe. 1982. "Sociobiology and Creationism: Two Ethnosociologies of American Culture." *American Anthropologist* 84:580–94.

Green, Harvey. 1992. *The Uncertainty of Everyday Life, 1915–1945.* New York: Harper Collins.

Greenbough, Anna (pseud.). 1959. "Childhood at Winterstar." *Liberation,* September, 13–16.

Greenhouse, Carol J. 1985. "Anthropology at Home: Whose Home?" *Human Organization* 44:261–64.

———. 1986. *Praying for Justice: Faith, Order and Community in an American Town.* Ithaca, N.Y.: Cornell University Press.

———. 1992. "Signs of Quality: Individualism and Hierarchy in American Culture." *American Ethnologist* 19:233–54.

Greven, Philip J. 1970. *Four Generations: Population, Land, and Family in Colonial Andover, Massachusetts.* Ithaca, N.Y.: Cornell University Press.

Guarneri, Carl J. 1991. *The Utopian Alternative: Fourierism in Nineteenth-Century America.* Ithaca, N.Y.: Cornell University Press.

———. 1997. "Brook Farm and the Fourierist Phalanxes: Immediatism, Gradualism, and American Utopian Socialism." In *America's Communal Utopias,* edited by D. E. Pitzer, 159–80. Chapel Hill: University of North Carolina Press.

Gusfield, Joseph R. 1979. "The Sociological Reality of America: An Essay on Mass Culture." In *On the Making of Americans: Essays in Honor of David Riesman,* edited by Herbert J. Gans, Nathan Glazer, Joseph R. Gusfield, and Christopher Jencks, 41–62. Philadelphia: University of Pennsylvania Press.

Hall, John R. 1978. *The Ways Out: Utopian Communal Groups in an Age of Babylon.* London: Routledge and Kegan Paul.

Hayden, Dolores. 1976. *Seven American Utopias: The Architecture of Communitarian Socialism, 1790–1975.* Cambridge, Mass.: MIT Press.

Hazelton, Philip. 1970. "Trailing the Founders: On Being a Second-Generation Bruder." Parts 1 and 2. *This Magazine Is About Schools* 4, no. 2 (Spring): 11–41; no. 3 (Summer): 55–78.

Hedgepeth, William, and Dennis Stock. 1970. *The Alternative: Communal Life in New America.* New York: Macmillan.

Henry, Jules. 1963. *Culture Against Man.* New York: Random House.

———. 1971. *Pathways to Madness.* New York: Random House.

Hertzler, Joyce Oramel. 1923. *The History of Utopian Thought.* New York: Macmillan.

Hicks, George L. 1971. "Utopian Communities and Social Networks." In *Aware of Utopia,* edited by D. W. Plath, 135–50. Urbana: University of Illinois Press.

———. 1978. "Informant Anonymity and Scientific Accuracy: The Problem of Pseudonyms." *Human Organization* 36:214–20.

———. 1992. *Appalachian Valley.* Prospect Heights, Ill.: Waveland Press.

Hinds, William Alfred. 1961. *American Communities.* 1878. Reprint, New York: Corinth Books.

Hine, Robert V. 1953. *California's Utopian Colonies.* San Marino, Calif.: Huntington Library.

———. 1981. *California Utopianism: Contemplations of Eden.* San Francisco: Boyd and Fraser.

Hoffer, Eric. 1951. *The True Believer: Thoughts on the Nature of Mass Movements.* New York: Harper.

———. 1963. *The Ordeal of Change.* New York: Harper and Row.

Holloway, Mark. 1966. *Heavens on Earth: Utopian Communities in America 1680–1880.* New York: Dover.

Hostetler, John A. 1974. *Hutterite Society.* Baltimore: Johns Hopkins University Press.

Hostetler, John A., and G. E. Huntington. 1980. *The Hutterites in North America.* New York: Holt, Rinehart.

Ineson, George. 1956. *Community Journey.* London: Sheed and Ward.

Infield, Henrik. 1955a. *The American Intentional Communities: Study in the Sociology of Cooperation.* Glen Gardner, N.J.: Glen Gardner Community Press.

———. 1955b. *Utopia and Experiment: Essays in the Sociology of Cooperation.* New York: Praeger.

Infield, Henrik F., and Joseph B. Maier, eds. 1950. *Cooperative Group Living: An International Symposium on Group Farming and the Sociology of Cooperation.* New York: Henry Koosis.

Issel, William H. 1967. "Ralph Borsodi and the Agrarian Response to Modern America." *Agricultural History* 41:155–66.

Jacobs, Paul, and Saul Landau. 1966. *The New Radicals: A Report with Documents.* New York: Vintage.

Johnson, Paul E., and Sean Wilentz. 1994. *The Kingdom of Matthias.* New York: Oxford University Press.

Kagan, Paul. 1975. *New World Utopias: A Photographic History of the Search for Community.* New York: Penguin.

Kahler, Erich. 1946. "The Reality of Utopia." *American Scholar* 15:167–79.

Kanter, Rosabeth Moss. 1968. "Commitment and Social Organization: A Study of Commitment Mechanisms in Utopian Communities." *American Sociological Review* 33:499–517.

———. 1972. *Commitment and Community: Communes and Utopias in Sociological Perspective.* Cambridge, Mass.: Harvard University Press.

Kateb, George. 1963. *Utopia and Its Enemies.* New York: Free Press of Glencoe.

Kephart, William M. 1987. *Extraordinary Groups: An Examination of Unconventional Life-Styles.* 3d ed. New York: St. Martin's.

Kern, Louis J. 1981. *An Ordered Love: Sex Roles and Sexuality in Victorian Utopias—the Shakers, the Mormons, and the Oneida Community.* Chapel Hill: University of North Carolina Press.

Kinkade, Kat. 1994. *Is It Utopia Yet? An Insider's View of Twin Oaks Community in Its Twenty-sixth Year.* Louisa, Va.: Twin Oaks Community.

Kinkade, Kathleen. 1973. *A Walden Two Experiment: The First Five Years of Twin Oaks Community.* New York: William Morrow.

Klaw, Spencer. 1993. *Without Sin: The Life and Death of the Oneida Community.* New York: Penguin.

Komar, Ingrid. 1989. *Living the Dream: A Documentary Study of Twin Oaks Community.* 1983. Reprint, Louisa, Va.: Twin Oaks Community.

Kornhauser, William. 1962. "Social Bases of Political Commitment: A Study of Liberals and Radicals." In *Human Behavior and Social Processes: An Interactionist Approach,* edited by A. M. Rose, 321–39. Boston: Houghton Mifflin.

Kramer, Wendell Barlow. 1955. "Criteria for the Intentional Community: A Study of the Factors Affecting Success and Failure in the Planned, Purposeful, Cooperative Community." Ph.D. diss., New York University.

Kumar, Krishan. 1987. *Utopia and Anti-Utopia in Modern Times.* New York: Basil Blackwell.

———. 1991. *Utopianism.* Minneapolis: University of Minnesota Press.

Lapham, Lewis H. 1992. "Who and What Is American?" *Harper's,* January, 43–49.

Lasch, Christopher. 1977. *Haven in a Heartless World: The Family Besieged.* New York: Basic Books.

———. 1979. *The Culture of Narcissism: American Life in an Age of Diminishing Expectations.* New York: Norton.

———. 1988. "The Communitarian Critique of Liberalism." In *Community in America: The Challenge of Habits of the Heart,* edited by Charles H. Reynolds and Ralph V. Norman, 173–84. Berkeley: University of California Press.

Latimore, James. 1991. "Natural Limits on the Size and Duration of Utopian Communities." *Communal Societies* 11:34–61.

Leach, Edmund R. 1958. "Magical Hair." *Journal of the Royal Anthropological Institute* 88:147–64.

Lears, Jackson. 1994. *Fables of Abundance: A Cultural History of Advertising in America.* New York: Basic Books.

Leone, Mark P. 1979. *Roots of Modern Mormonism.* Cambridge, Mass.: Harvard University Press.

Leuba, Clarence J. 1971. *A Road to Creativity: Arthur Morgan—Engineer, Educator, Administrator.* North Quincy, Mass.: Christopher Publishing House.

LeWarne, Charles Pierce. 1975. *Utopias on Puget Sound, 1885–1915.* Seattle: University of Washington Press.

Lipset, Seymour Martin. 1996. *American Exceptionalism: A Double-Edged Sword.* New York: Norton.

Lockridge, Kenneth A. 1970. *A New England Town: The First Hundred Years, Dedham, Massachusetts, 1636–1736.* New York: Norton.

Lockwood, Maren. 1965. "The Experimental Utopia in America." *Daedalus* (Proceedings of the American Academy of Arts and Sciences) 94, no. 2: 401–18.

Loomis, Mildred J. 1965. *Go Ahead and Live!* New York: Philosophical Library.

Lord, Russell, and Paul H. Johnstone, eds. 1942. *A Place on Earth: A Critical Appraisal of Subsistence Homesteads.* Washington, D.C.: Bureau of Agricultural Economics.

Macedonia Cooperative Community. 1948. *Report of 1948.* Clarkesville, Ga.: Macedonia Cooperative Community.

Mann, Leonard. 1957. Untitled history of Celo Community. Manuscript. Celo Community documents file.

Manuel, Frank E. and Fritzie P. 1979. *Utopian Thought in the Western World.* Cambridge, Mass.: Harvard University Press.

McCord, William. 1989. *Voyages to Utopia: From Monastery to Commune—The Search for the Perfect Society in Modern Times.* New York: Norton.

McCraw, Thomas K. 1970. *Morgan vs. Lilienthal: The Feud within the TVA.* Chicago: Loyola University Press.

Melbourne Village. 1950. *A Home in Melbourne Village.* Melbourne, Fla.: American Homesteading Foundation.

Melcher, Marguerite F. 1960. *The Shaker Adventure.* Cleveland: Western Reserve University Press.

Melville, Keith. 1972. *Communes in the Counter Culture: Origins, Theories, Styles of Life.* New York: William Morrow.

Merton, Robert K. 1968. *Social Theory and Social Structure.* Enl. ed. Glencoe, Ill.: Free Press.

Miller, Perry. 1956. *Errand into the Wilderness.* Cambridge, Mass.: Harvard University Press.

Miller, Timothy. 1993. "Cornelius Plockhoy and the Beginnings of the American Communal Tradition." In *Gone to Croatan: Origins of North American Dropout Culture,* edited by Ron Sakolsky and James Koehnline, 117–26. Brooklyn, N.Y.: Autonomedia.

———. 1990. *American Communes 1860–1960: A Bibliography.* New York: Garland.

Mills, Richard. 1973. *Young Outsiders: A Study of Alternative Communities.* New York: Pantheon.

Mitchell, J. Clyde. 1966. "Theoretical Orientations in African Urban Studies." In *The Social Anthropology of Complex Societies,* edited by M. Banton, 37–68. ASA Vol. 4. London: Tavistock.

Moffatt, Michael. 1989. *Coming of Age in New Jersey: College and American Culture.* New Brunswick, N.J.: Rutgers University Press.

Molnar, Thomas. 1967. *Utopia: The Perennial Heresy.* New York: Sheed and Ward.

Moment, Gairdner B., and Otto F. Kraushaar, eds. 1980. *Utopias: the American Experience.* Metuchen, N.J.: Scarecrow Press.

Morgan, Arthur E. 1918. "Education: The Mastery of the Arts of Life." *Atlantic Monthly,* April, 337–46.

———. 1936. *The Long Road.* The National Home Library Foundation. Reprint, Yellow Springs, Ohio: Community Service, 1962.

———. 1942a. "The Community: The Seed Bed of Society." *Atlantic Monthly,* February, 222–28.

———. 1942b. *The Small Community: Foundation of Democratic Life—What It Is and How to Achieve It.* New York: Harper.

———. 1944. *Edward Bellamy.* New York: Columbia University Press.

———. 1945. *The Philosophy of Edward Bellamy.* New York: King's Crown Press.

———. 1946. *Nowhere Was Somewhere: How History Makes Utopias and How Utopias Make History.* Chapel Hill: University of North Carolina Press.

———. 1955. "The Prospects for Communal Societies." *Community Service News,* 13:24–32.

———. 1957a. "Notes from Memory: Celo Community." Manuscript. Celo Community documents file.

———. 1957b. *Search for Purpose.* London: Watts.

———. 1957c. *The Community of the Future and The Future of Community.* Yellow Springs, Ohio: Community Service.

———. 1968. *Observations.* Compiled by Vivian H. Bresnehen. Yellow Springs, Ohio: Antioch Press.

———. 1974. *The Making of the TVA.* Buffalo, N.Y.: Prometheus Books.

Morgan, Ernest, ed. 1962. *A Manual of Simple Burial.* With the Assistance of the Continental Assocation of Funeral and Memorial Societies and Its Member Organizations; the Medical Schools of the U.S. and Canada; the Eye-Bank for Sight Restoration, Inc.; The Eye-Bank Association of America; and the Canadian National Institute for the Blind. Burnsville, N.C.: Celo Press.

Morgan, Lucy Griscom. 1928. *Finding His World: The Story of Arthur E. Morgan.* Yellow Springs, Ohio: Kahoe.

Mumford, Lewis. 1962. *The Story of Utopias.* 1922. Reprint, New York: Viking.

Muncy, Raymond Lee. 1973. *Sex and Marriage in Utopian Communities: Nineteenth-Century America.* Bloomington: Indiana University Press.

Myrdal, Gunnar. 1962. *An American Dilemma.* 2 vols. 1944. Reprint, New York: McGraw-Hill.

Nahirny, Vladimir C. 1962. "Some Observations on Ideological Groups." *American Journal of Sociology* 67:397–405.

Newton, David R. 1948. "The Macedonia Community." *Politics* (Winter): 27–30.

Nordhoff, Charles. 1961. *The Communistic Societies of the United States.* 1875. Reprint, New York: Hillary House Publishers.

Noyes, John Humphrey. 1961. *History of American Socialisms.* 1870. Reprint, New York: Hillary House Publishers.

Noyes, Pierrepont B. 1958. *Goodly Heritage.* New York: Rinehart.

O'Dea, Thomas F. 1957. *The Mormons.* Chicago: University of Chicago Press.

Okugawa, Otohiko. 1980. "Annotated List of Communal and Utopian Societies, 1787–1919." Appendix A in Robert S. Fogarty, *Dictionary of American and Communal History,* 173–234. Westport, Conn.: Greenwood.

———. 1983. "Intercommunal Relationships among Nineteenth-Century Communal Societies in America." *Communal Societies* 3:68–82.

Orrmont, Arthur. 1961. *Love Cults and Faith Healers: The Story of America's False Religious Prophets.* New York: Ballantine.

Orser, W. Edward. 1981. *Searching for a Viable Alternative: The Macedonia Cooperative Community, 1937–58.* New York: Burt Franklin.

Oved, Yaacov. 1983. "Communes and the Outside World: Seclusion and Involvement." *Communal Societies* 3:83–92.

———. 1988. *Two Hundred Years of American Communes.* New Brunswick, N.J.: Transaction Publishers.

———. 1996. *The Witness of the Brothers: A History of the Bruderhof.* New Brunswick, N.J.: Transaction Publishers.

Peacock, James L. 1988. "America as a Cultural System." In *Community in America: The Challenge of Habits of the Heart,* edited by Charles H. Reynolds and Ralph V. Norman, 37–46. Berkeley: University of California Press.

Pearsall, Marion. 1959. *Little Smoky Ridge: The Natural History of a Southern Appalachian Neighborhood.* University, Ala.: University of Alabama Press.

Peck, Robert N. 1987. "An Ex-Member's Eye View of the Bruderhof Communities from 1948–1961." In *Utopian Studies 1,* edited by Gorman Beauchamp, Kenneth Roemer, and Nicholas D. Smith, 111–22. New York: University Press of America.

Perin, Constance. 1988. *Belonging in America: Reading between the Lines.* Madison: University of Wisconsin Press.

Peters, Victor. 1965. *All Things Common: The Hutterian Way of Life.* Minneapolis: University of Minnesota Press.

Phillips, Derek L. 1993. *Looking Backward: A Critical Appraisal of Communitarian Thought.* Princeton: Princeton University Press.

Pickett, Clarence E. 1953. *For More Than Bread: An Autobiographical Account of Twenty-two Years' Work with the American Friends Service Committee.* Boston: Little, Brown.

Pitzer, Donald E. 1984. "The Uses of the American Communal Past." *Communal Societies* 4:215–42.

———. 1989. "Developmental Communalism: An Alternative Approach to Communal Studies." In *Utopian Thought and Communal Experience,* edited by Dennis Hardy and Lorna Davidson, 68–76. Enfield, Eng.: Middlesex Polytechnic.

———. 1997a. "Introduction." In *America's Communal Utopias,* edited by D. E. Pitzer, 3–13. Chapel Hill: University of North Carolina Press.

———. 1997b. "The New Moral World of Robert Owen and New Harmony." In *America's Communal Utopias,* edited by D. E. Pitzer, 88–134. Chapel Hill: University of North Carolina Press.

———, ed. 1997. *America's Communal Utopias.* Chapel Hill: University of North Carolina Press.

Plath, David W. 1966. "The Fate of Utopia: Adaptive Tactics in Four Japanese Groups." *American Anthropologist* 68:1152–62.

———, ed. 1971. *Aware of Utopia.* Urbana: University of Illinois Press.

Questenberry, Dan. 1992. "Residential Land Trust Organizing." In *Directory of Intentional Communities,* edited by Fellowship for Intentional Community, 116–21. Rutledge, Mo.: Communities Publications Cooperative.

Rayman, Paula. 1981. *The Kibbutz Community and Nation Building.* Princeton: Princeton University Press.

Reich, Charles A. 1970. *The Greening of America.* New York: Bantam.

Rexroth, Kenneth. 1972. *The Alternative Society: Essays from the Other World.* New York: Herder and Herder.

———. 1974. *Communalism: From Its Origins to the Twentieth Century.* New York: Seabury Press.

Riesman, David. 1950. *The Lonely Crowd: A Study of the Changing American Character.* New Haven: Yale University Press.

Roberts, Nancy L. 1984. *Dorothy Day and the Catholic Worker.* Albany: State University of New York Press.

Roberts, Ron E. 1971. *The New Communes: Coming Together in America.* Englewood Cliffs, N.J.: Prentice-Hall.

Robertson, Constance Noyes. 1977. *Oneida Community Profiles.* Syracuse, N.Y.: Syracuse University Press.

Rothenberg, Winifred Barr. 1993. *From Market Places to a Market Economy: The Transformation of Rural Massachusetts, 1750–1850.* Chicago: University of Chicago Press.

Sandel, Michael. 1982. *Liberalism and the Limits of Justice.* Cambridge: Cambridge University Press.

Sahlins, Marshall. 1985. *Islands of History.* Chicago: University of Chicago Press.

Schneider, David M. 1968. *American Kinship: A Cultural Account.* Englewood Cliffs, N.J.: Prentice-Hall.

———. 1976. "Notes toward a Theory of Culture." In *Meaning in Anthropology,* edited by Keith H. Basso and Henry A. Selby, 197–220. Albuquerque: University of New Mexico Press.

———. 1977. "Kinship, Nationality, and Religion in American Culture." In *Symbolic Anthropology,* edited by J. Dolgin, D. S. Kemnitzer, and D. M. Schneider, 63–77. New York: Columbia University Press.

———. 1980. *American Kinship: A Cultural Account.* 2d ed. Chicago: University of Chicago Press.

———. 1984. *A Critique of the Study of Kinship.* Ann Arbor: University of Michigan Press.

Segal, Howard P. 1985. *Technological Utopianism in American Culture.* Chicago: University of Chicago Press.

Selth, Jefferson P. 1984. "The Ashram of Graton Road: Morning Star Ranch, a California Commune in the 1960's." *Communal Societies* 4:204–11.

Sennett, Richard. 1979. "What Tocqueville Feared." In *On the Making of Americans: Essays in Honor of David Riesman,* edited by Herbert J. Gans, Nathan Glazer, Joseph R. Gusfield, and Christopher Jencks, 105–25. Philadelphia: University of Pennsylvania Press.

Shenker, Barry. 1986. *Intentional Communities: Ideology and Alienation in Communal Societies.* London: Routledge and Kegan Paul.

Shi, David E. 1985. *The Simple Life: Plain Living and High Thinking in American Culture.* New York: Oxford University Press.

Shils, Edward. 1958. "Ideology and Civility: On the Politics of the Intellectual." *The Sewanee Review* 66:450–80.

Shor, Francis. 1987. "The Utopian Project in a Communal Experiment of the 1930's: The Sunrise Colony in Historical and Comparative Perspective." *Communal Societies* 7:82–94.

Simmons, J. L., and Barry Winograd. 1966. *It's Happening: A Portrait of the Youth Scene Today.* Santa Barbara, Calif.: Marc-Laird Publications.

Skinner, B. F. 1948. *Walden Two.* New York: Macmillan.

Skinner, Charles M. 1901. *American Communes: Practical Socialism in the United States.* Brooklyn, N.Y.: Eagle Library.

Slater, Philip E. 1970. *The Pursuit of Loneliness: American Culture at the Breaking Point.* Boston: Beacon Press.

Society of Brothers. 1952. *Ten Years of Community Living: The Wheathill Bruderhof 1942–1952.* Bromdon, England: The Plough Publishing House.

Spiro, Melford. 1963. *Kibbutz: Venture in Utopia.* New York: Schocken Books.

Stephan, Karen H., and G. Edward Stephan. 1973. "Religion and the Survival of Utopian Communities." *Journal for the Scientific Study of Religion* 12:89–100.

Sugihara, Yoshie, and David W. Plath. 1969. *Sensei and His People: The Building of a Japanese Commune.* Berkeley: University of California Press.

Talbert, Roy, Jr. 1987. *FDR's Utopian: Arthur Morgan of the TVA.* Jackson: University Press of Mississippi.

———, ed. 1968. "Arthur E. Morgan's Ethical Code for the Tennessee Valley Authority." *East Tennessee Valley Historical Society's Publications* 40:119–27.

Thomas, John L. 1965. "Romantic Reform in America, 1815–1865." *American Quarterly* 17:656–81.

Thomson, Watson. 1949. *Pioneer in Community: Henri Lasserre's Contribution to the Fully Cooperative Society.* Toronto: Ryerson Press.

Tillson, David S. 1958. "A Pacifist Community in Peacetime: An Introductory Description of the Woodcrest Bruderhof at Rifton, New York." Ph.D. diss., Syracuse University.

Tocqueville, Alexis de. 1945. *Democracy in America.* 2 vols. 1835, 1840. Reprint, New York: Knopf.

Trenton Community Group. 1944. "Preparation for Community in CPS." *Friends Intelligencer,* May 13, 316–17.

Tucker, Robert C., ed. 1972. *The Marx-Engels Reader.* New York: Norton.

Twain, Mark [Samuel L. Clemens]. 1897. *Literary Essays.* Vol. 22, The Writings of Mark Twain. New York: Harper and Brothers.

van den Berghe, Pierre L., and Karl Peter. 1988. "Hutterites and Kibbutzniks: A Tale of Nepotistic Communism." *Man,* n.s., 23:522–39.

Varenne, Herve. 1977. *Americans Together: Structured Diversity in a Midwestern Town.* New York: Columbia University, Teachers College Press.

———. 1986a. "Creating America." In *Symbolizing America,* edited by H. Varenne, 15–33. Lincoln: University of Nebraska Press.

———. 1986b. "Doing the Anthropology of America." In *Symbolizing America,* edited by H. Varenne, 34–45. Lincoln: University of Nebraska Press.

———. 1986c. "Introduction." In *Symbolizing America,* edited by H. Varenne, 1–9. Lincoln: University of Nebraska Press.

———, ed. 1986. *Symbolizing America.* Lincoln: University of Nebraska Press.

Veysey, Laurence. 1973. *The Communal Experience: Anarchist and Mystical Counter-Cultures in America.* New York: Harper and Row.

Wagner, Jon. 1982. "Sex Roles in American Communal Utopias." In *Sex Roles in Contemporary American Communes,* edited by J. Wagner, 1–44. Bloomington: Indiana University Press.

———. 1985. "Success in Intentional Communities: The Problem of Evaluation." *Communal Societies* 5:89–100.

Wallace, Anthony F. C. 1956. "Revitalization Movements." *American Anthropologist* 58:264–81.

———. 1970. *Culture and Personality.* 2d ed. New York: Random House.

Walzer, Michael. 1983. *Spheres of Justice.* New York: Basic Books.

———. 1990. "The Communitarian Critique of Liberalism." *Political Theory* 18:6–23.

Warner, W. Lloyd. 1959. *The Living and the Dead: A Study of the Symbolic Life of Americans.* Yankee City Series, vol. 5. New Haven: Yale University Press.

Warner, W. Lloyd, with Wilfrid C. Bailey et al. 1964. *Democracy in Jonesville: A Study in Quality and Inequality.* 1949. New York: Harper and Row

Weisbord, Carol. 1980. *The Boundaries of Utopia.* New York: Pantheon.

Westbrook, Robert B. 1993. "Fighting for the American Family: Private Interests and political Obligation in World War II." In *The Power of Culture: Critical Essays in American History,* edited by Richard Wightman Fox and T. J. Jackson Lears, 195–221. Chicago: University of Chicago Press.

Whisenhunt, Donald W. 1983. "Utopians, Communalism and the Great Depression." *Communal Societies* 3:101–10.

Wills, Garry. 1978. *Inventing America: Jefferson's Declaration of Independence.* New York: Doubleday.

———. 1996. "The Would-Be Progressives." *New York Review of Books,* July 11, pp. 13–16.

Wilson, M. L. 1939. "The Problem of Surplus Agricultural Population." *International Journal of Agrarian Affairs* 1:37–48.

Wiser, Arthur. 1949. "Exploring Responsibility." *Fellowship,* September, 4–7.

———. 1950. "Macedonia Community." In *Cooperative Group Living: An International Symposium on Group Farming and the Sociology of Cooperation,* edited by Henrik F. Infield and Joseph B. Maier, 13–21. New York: Henry Koosis.

Wood, Gordon S. 1992. *The Radicalism of the American Revolution.* New York: Knopf.

———. 1994. "Inventing American Capitalism (Review Essay)." *New York Review of Books,* June 9, 44–49.

Wooster, Ernest S. 1924. *Communities of the Past and Present.* Newllano, La.: Llano Colonist. (Reprinted by AMS Press, New York, 1974.)

Wunderlich, Roger. 1992. *Low Living and High Thinking at Modern Times, New York.* Syracuse, N.Y.: Syracuse University Press.

Zablocki, Benjamin David. 1971. *The Joyful Community: An Account of the Bruderhof, a Communal Movement Now in Its Third Generation.* Baltimore: Penguin Books.

———. 1980. *Alienation and Charisma: A Study of Contemporary American Communes.* New York: Free Press.

Zicklin, Gilbert. 1983. *Countercultural Communes: A Sociological Perspective.* Westport, Conn.: Greenwood.

Index

Note: Celo Community documents in the appendix have not been indexed.

GEORGE L. HICKS was a professor of anthropology
and former chair of the Department of Anthropology at Brown
University. He was the author of *Appalachian Valley* and the
coeditor of *Ethnic Encounters*.

Composed in 10.5/13 Minion
with Minion display
by Barbara Evans
at the University of Illinois Press
Manufactured by Thomson-Shore, Inc.

University of Illinois Press
1325 South Oak Street
Champaign, IL 61820-6903
www.press.uillinois.edu